THE LEAST RESTRICTIVE ENVIRONMENT

Its Origins and Interpretations
in Special Education

The LEA Series on Special Education and Disability
John Wills Lloyd, Series Editor

Crockett/Kauffman • The Least Restrictive Environment: Its Origins and Interpretations in Special Education

Gallimore/Bernheimer/MacMillan/Speece/Vaughn (Eds.) • Developmental Perspectives on Children With High-Incidence Disabilities

Lloyd/Kameenui/Chard (Eds.) • Issues in Educating Students With Disabilities

Simmons/Kameenui (Eds.) • What Reading Research Tells Us About Children With Diverse Learning Needs: Bases and Basics

THE LEAST RESTRICTIVE ENVIRONMENT

Its Origins and Interpretations
in Special Education

Jean B. Crockett
Virginia Polytechnic Institute and State University

James M. Kauffman
University of Virginia

1999

LAWRENCE ERLBAUM ASSOCIATES, PUBLISHERS
Mahwah, New Jersey   London

The final camera copy for this work was prepared by the author, and therefore the publisher takes no responsibility for consistency or correctness of typographical style. However, this arrangement helps to make publication of this kind of scholarship possible.

Lawrence Erlbaum Associates, Inc., Publishers
10 Industrial Avenue
Mahwah, New Jersey 07430

Cover design by Kathryn Houghtaling Lacey

Library of Congress Cataloging-in-Publication Data

Crockett, Jean B.
    The least restrictive environment : its origins and
interpretations in special education / Jean B. Crockett, James M.
Kauffman.
        p. cm. -- (The LEA series on special education and
disability)
    Includes bibliographical references (p.   ) and indexes.
    ISBN 0-8058-3101-0 (cloth : alk. paper). -- ISBN 0-8058-3102-9
(pbk. : alk. paper)
    1. Inclusive education--United States. 2. Handicapped children-
-Education--United States. 3. Handicapped children--Education--Law
and legislation--United States. 4. Special education--United
States.   I. Kaufman, James M. II. Title. III. Series.
LC1201.C76 1999
371.9'046--dc21   99-12804
                                                              CIP

Books published by Lawrence Erlbaum Associates are printed on acid-free paper, and their bindings are chosen for strength and durability.

Printed in the United States of America
10   9   8   7   6   5   4   3   2

Contents

Preface   ix

1. **Placement: The Central Issue of Late 20th Century Special Education**   1

    The Nature of the Current Problem *4*
    The Purpose of this Volume *5*
        The Importance of Conceptual Foundations *6*
        The Importance of Legal, Educational, and
          Parental Perspectives *6*
        The Methodology of Historical Inquiry *7*
        Voices From the Field *10*

2. **The Politics of Placement in an Era of Reform**   12

    Anchoring the Issue: Instructional Settings
      for Exceptional Learners *12*
        Current Realities of Service Delivery *13*
        Placement Trends *14*
        Legal Foundations of the Least Restrictive
          Environment Requirement *17*
    Capturing the Controversy *19*
        LRE and Social Reform *20*
        LRE and Improved Student Performance *22*
        Conflicting Views *23*
    Dilemmas of Service Delivery *27*
        Terminology *27*
        Separating the Issues *29*
    A Pragmatic Conclusion *31*

3. The Viewpoint of History: Educational
    Environments and Social Context   34

    A Call to Service 34
        The Public Good 35
        Social Change and Exceptionality 37
        Personal Interests and Public Concerns 40
    Social Thought and Political Action 48
        Political Parables 48
        The Social Origins of the EAHCA 51
        Origins of the Term LRE 58
        Reflections on the Roots of LRE 61
    Educational Equity and Productive Learning 62
    Focus on the Purpose of Learning 64
        Dynamic Reciprocity 66
        Productive Learning 67

4. The Viewpoint of the Law:
    Environment and Liberty   68

    Legal Reasoning and Social Conflict 68
        The Language of Legal Reasoning 70
        The Power of the Particular 72
    Legal Reasoning and LRE for Exceptional Learners 73
        Federal Legislation: EAHCA/IDEA 74
        Constitutional Basis of the Least Restrictive
            Alternative (LRA) 82
        LRE and Values: Personal Liberty
            and Individual Needs 86
        Dimensions of the LRA Policy 93
        Rebutting the Presumption 95
    LRE Court Decisions and Federal Directives 98
        The Evolution of Special Education Law 100
    LRE Case Law Related to Inclusive Placements 102
        The 1980s 103
        The Early 1990s 106
        The Mid-1990s 108
        Analytic Frameworks 114
        Comparison of the Frameworks 116
        Trends in LRE Case Law and Federal Directives 118
    What Lies Ahead 120

5. The Viewpoint of Educators:
    Environment and Learning   123

    Environment and Learning   *124*
        The Meaning of Place   *125*
        Effective Educational Environments   *126*
        The Student and the Environment   *127*
        Education and Exceptionality   *129*
        The Interface of General and Special Education   *129*
        Service Delivery Goals   *132*
    Educational Foundations of LRE   *132*
        The Language of Educational Placement   *132*
        Definitions of LRE   *133*
        The Continuum of Alternative Placements   *137*
        Individual Students and Classroom Environments   *139*
    Contemporary Classroom Environments   *141*
        Students and Teachers   *141*
        Instructional Interventions for Exceptional Learners   *143*
        Curricular Organization and Management   *145*
        Management of Student Diversity in Inclusive Settings   *147*
        Research Issues and LRE   *148*
    Conceptual Themes and Historical Trends
        [in placement literature, 1966-1996]   *151*
        Method of Literature Search   *151*
        Coding the Abstracts   *153*
        Results of the Abstract Analysis   *154*
        Research Literature   *156*
        Themes in the Professional Literature   *156*
        Summary   *158*
    Commentary From Contemporary Theorists   *159*
        Maynard C. Reynolds   *159*
        Dorothy Kerzner Lipsky   *162*
        Laurence M. Lieberman   *163*
        Douglas Fuchs   *165*
    Principles for Educational Leaders   *168*

6. The Viewpoint of Parents: Environment
    and Full Participation   170

    Background   *170*
    Parental Concerns and Choices   *171*
        The Development of Parental Involvement   *172*
        Parental Projects   *178*
        Parents and Student Placement   *179*
        Parental Advocacy: A Case in Point   *182*
    Focus on Instruction & Assessment of Student Progress   *187*

7.   Implications and Future Directions   188

      Instructional Settings and Concerns for Equity   *190*
      Instructional Settings and Dynamic Systems   *194*
      Instructional Settings and Social Justice   *195*

Appendix   203

References   214

Author Index   228

Subject Index   233

Preface

Special education reform initiatives place educators in predicaments for which there are few blueprints and many alternative readings. In the flux of restructuring schools to produce higher student outcomes, teachers and administrators are challenged to provide, with confidence and integrity, a free appropriate public education (FAPE) in the least restrictive environment (LRE) as required by law for their students with disabilities. Without an understanding of the history of the plans for FAPE and LRE and alternative interpretations of the few existing blueprints, educators risk creating a structure that is illegal, untrustworthy, or both. This volume is intended to give educators insights into how FAPE and LRE emerged as guiding principles of special education and how these concepts have been interpreted in case law, in educational research and practice, and by advocates and parents.

The emphasis on site-based management in current school reform shifts the focus away from centralized accountability for special education services. As a result, building principals and their assistants frequently serve on committees that determine the type of instructional setting in which a special education student will be placed. These administrators participate in decision making in an era of interest in creating innovative educational environments and school choice. However, their decisions are undermined by vague definitions and disagreement about the terms used to describe special education placement options such as *mainstreaming, inclusion,* or the *continuum of alternative placements*. Often lost in the rhetoric is the explicit goal of the federal law—the Individuals with Disabilities Education Act (IDEA)—most recently reauthorized in 1997. IDEA requires that all students with disabilities be provided a full educational opportunity through FAPE in the LRE, and that promising practices, materials, and technology be employed. This trio of FAPE, LRE, and validated practices has been called by some "the holy trinity" of special education law. Nevertheless, the nature and very legitimacy of one member of the trinity—LRE—is questioned by some advocates of special education reform. Consequently, the discussion here is focused on questions of placement and the meanings attached to the term *least restrictive environment*.

The intent here is to provide greater clarity to issues of student placement by examining the concept of the LRE from a variety of perspectives. Our goal is a deeper understanding of the principles that undergird placement decisions, and our method is an examination of the relation over time between the legal requirement of an appropriate education for students with disabilities and the restrictiveness of the educational environments in which they are served. Our inquiry is prompted by the overall question of how integration became the central discourse in special education. The questions for which we have sought answers include the following: Has the regulatory relation between an appropriate education and the LRE changed since the passage of Public Law 94-142, the Education for All Handicapped Children Act (EAHCA), in 1975? Have the meanings of LRE shifted over time? Have the underlying assumptions of FAPE and LRE changed since the 1970s?

We examine these questions in seven chapters beginning with an overview in chapter 1 of why we studied LRE and why we opted for an approach that is grounded in history and elaborates special education's conceptual foundations. Chapter 2 anchors the contemporary issue of implementing the LRE and captures the debate surrounding its interpretation. It addresses perspectives and terminology to facilitate clear communication about service delivery and student placement. Chapter 3 describes the cultural conditions that led to contemporary special education. It analyzes through scholarly literature and personal interviews the history of U.S. social thought and schooling for students with disabilities before and after the passage of the EAHCA in 1975. Chapter 4 explains and interprets the concept of LRE from a legal perspective to determine whether underlying assumptions about LRE have changed, placing more emphasis on instructional integration, and if so, whether the cause resides within shifts in the legal interpretation of LRE, new understandings of the underlying principles of LRE, or imprecise implementation of legislation. To help in this effort, the thoughts of lawyers, legal scholars, and developers of legislation have been drawn from the texts of judicial decisions, federal directives, legal analyses, and personal conversations. The intent of chapter 5 is to explain and interpret the concept of LRE from an educational perspective to determine whether underlying assumptions about LRE have changed, and if so, whether the concept remains an ethical educational strategy. To further inform this chapter, interviews were conducted with contemporary educational theorists who represent contrasting perspectives on the concept of LRE. The power and inclination of parental politics is examined in chapter 6 to determine whether cultural values have redefined for parents the purpose of schooling, the status of exceptional individuals in schools and society, and the desirability of the LRE principles. In conclusion, chapter 7 focuses primarily on the interrelations between instructional settings, legal prescriptions, and social values in providing a full educational opportunity to students with disabilities. In doing so, conceptual and historical elements are drawn together to underscore the importance of providing equitable strategies, powerful instructional practices, and meaningful parental participation to ensure the best interests of exceptional learners.

We thank Betsy Balsdon, Jane DeWeerd, Donna Cattell-Gordon, Douglas Fuchs, James J. Gallagher, Thomas K. Gilhool, Laurence M. Lieberman,

Dorothy K. Lipsky, Edwin W. Martin, Maynard C. Reynolds, Karen Silver, Donald Stedman, and Frederick J. Weintraub for sharing with us their insights into the origins and interpretations of the LRE concept. In addition, we acknowledge our colleagues Nicholas Anastasiow, Margaret Grogan, Daniel Hallahan, and Jennings Wagoner for their helpful suggestions, Jeni Crockett for her editorial support and preparation of the manuscript, and Paula Burdette and Nina Rosalie for their research assistance. We are also grateful to John Lloyd, Special Education and Disability Series Editor for Lawrence Erlbaum Associates, for his encouragement. We are especially grateful to our respective spouses—Jay B. Crockett, and Patricia L. Pullen—for their loving support.

J. B. C.
J. M. K.

1

Placement: The Central Issue of Late 20th Century Special Education

The hottest issue in special education during the 1980s and 1990s was where, not how, students with disabilities should be taught—the schools and classrooms they should attend, not the instruction they should receive. No leader in special education, nor anyone else, to our knowledge, has suggested that all students with disabilities should be taught in special, separate classrooms and schools. However, advocates of full inclusion argue that all students, regardless of the nature of their disabilities, should go to the schools they would attend if they had no disabilities. Moreover, these advocates urge that all students with disabilities attend ordinary classrooms alongside nondisabled classmates for most or all of the school day (e.g., Lipsky & Gartner, 1997; Stainback & Stainback, 1991). Those opposing full inclusion argue that a full continuum of alternative placements ranging from regular classrooms to resource classes, special self-contained classes, and special day or residential schools and hospitals is necessary if every student with a disability is to receive an appropriate education (e.g., Bateman, 1996; Kauffman & Hallahan, 1993). The assumption underlying full inclusion is that the regular classroom in the neighborhood school is—always and for all students—the least restrictive alternative placement, if not the only place in which they can be given an appropriate education. In contrast, the assumption underlying a full continuum of alternative placements is that the least restrictive environment (LRE) for learning will vary from student to student and often from time to time for a particular student as well.

We begin our examination of how placement took center stage among special education issues in the last decades of the 20th century and of the varied meanings of LRE by recounting a personal experience of author Jean Crockett. In September 1986, the comments of a university student who was participating in a tour of the aquatic center at Henry Viscardi School on New York's Long Island led inadvertently to clarification of the LRE issue by one of the concept's progenitors. During the tour, the student remarked that although this regional school was impressive in some ways he did not see how it could be considered the LRE for students with physical disabilities, some of whom traveled as far as 60 miles from home to attend. With impeccable timing, Dr. Edwin W. Martin, the school's chief executive and a prominent figure among those who had helped congressional staff draft the Education for All Handicapped Children's

Act (EAHCA) of 1975 (Public Law [PL] 94-142), came down the hall and joined the tour group. He explained that Viscardi students had severe medical and physical needs that exceeded the capacities of local school districts to provide the supports required for their appropriate education. An appropriate education included the skilled services and sophisticated equipment, available only at schools like Viscardi, that were essential if these students with severe physical disabilities were to benefit from their schooling. Martin went on to clarify that when PL 94-142 was drafted, he and his colleagues in Washington intended to require school districts to provide a full range or continuum of alternative placements for students with disabilities. They did not envision just a single environment assumed to be appropriate for the academic and social learning of all students. These alternative environments were to be chosen on a case-by-case basis to fit each individual student's needs. The concept can be best understood, he suggested, by considering which environment least restricts an individual student's ability to derive educational benefit. A special day school was conceived as just one possible stop on a continuum for students whose physical needs interfere with their learning.

From 1986 through 1994, much of Crockett's professional responsibility as principal of the Viscardi school focused on defining and articulating this view of special education placement at well over 1,000 committee meetings in 70 different school districts. During these prime years of what was then known as the Regular Education Initiative, some parents became fearful that their district, in an effort to be more inclusive, would deny their child placement in a separate but appropriate setting. These parents realized that all school districts are not equal in what they can or will provide to children with disabilities. They wanted evidence that their children would continue to receive the same appropriate level of services in the local program—including access to resources, fullness of participation, successful academic outcomes, meaningful interaction with nondisabled peers, and regular association with peers who share similar physical and emotional disability issues. Only if these resources and opportunities were in place did the parents know that everyone could work closely to ensure a smooth transition from one program and place to another.

At Viscardi, many children with severe physical problems begin their schooling in a separate setting and make the transition to a more normalized program. Others make the transition in reverse; they move from an ordinary school to a separate place with extraordinary services. Annually the number of students entering Viscardi for whom the ordinary school has not been appropriate equals the number who are, by virtue of their special education at Viscardi, able to make the transition to a more typical school setting. Because of this two-way flow, parents and professionals at Viscardi can see first hand the need for the smooth, well-oiled continuum of alternative placements that Dr. Martin described. From the perspective of those who know Viscardi, the stance of those who advocate full inclusion, to which the university student alluded, remains incomprehensible. Full inclusion is unfathomable to them because it repudiates placement options and defines the LRE in all cases by geography, that is, the general education classroom in the neighborhood school. This radical redefinition of the least restrictive place of appropriate instruction for students with disabilities represents a departure from current federal law, enacted in 1975, and a significant reform initiative for which there are few blueprints and many controversies.

The term LRE is unusual, perhaps holding more meaning for lawyers and parents familiar with incarceration or institutionalization than for educators. Legal scholar Barbara Bateman (personal communication, 1996) asked how the term made its way from the back wards of institutions to the third-grade classroom, suggesting that there is more to this story than simple logic would explain. Why would the developers of special education law select a term referring to personal liberty and apply it to the schoolhouse, where the word environment conjures up conditions facilitative of instruction and learning, if not to appease the fears of parents whose children had for too long been in confinement? The promise of the 1975 federal law was to ensure access for each child with a disability to a free appropriate public education (FAPE) in the LRE. Two fields—law and education—were conjoined, and, together with parents of children with special educational needs, lawyers and educators forged an enterprise dependent upon their mutual understandings. These understandings of LRE have not always been clear.

Teachers who receive the endorsement of a state to teach exceptional learners are not required to complete coursework in special education law. Moreover, school administrators are often prepared inadequately for the legal task of implementing sound special education practices or understanding basic principles of special education. Hirth and Valesky (1990) surveyed 66 university programs in school administration to determine their requirements for special education law and for administrative certification in their states. Only 27% of all general administrator certifications required knowledge of special education law. Only 14% of universities responding required a special education law course. The most common method for obtaining such knowledge was enrollment in a general school law course where the exposure to the subject matter of special education is extremely low. Although 86% of the universities included special education legislation in their law syllabus, more than 74% of these devoted to it less than 10% of class content. Fourteen percent neither required such a course nor devoted any portion of their general school law course to special education legislation. And yet, educators and parents must work in partnership with ineluctable legal principles often complex and unfamiliar to both.

THE NATURE OF THE CURRENT PROBLEM

In the flux of restructuring schools toward greater excellence as well as equity, the challenge is tremendous for educational decision makers to provide, with confidence and integrity, an appropriate education for their students with disabilities in the LRE as required by law. There is deep confusion over what is meant by the term *least restrictive environment* in the federal regulations. For some, the word *restrictive* is synonymous with *segregated* so that the LRE becomes the least segregated environment, or the environment in which children with disabilities are least separated from their nondisabled peers (Villa & Thousand, 1995). For others, the term implies an ecobehavioral interaction among an individual student, a prescribed educational plan, and an instructional setting calculated to provide him or her with academic and social benefit that includes nondisabled peers to the maximum extent appropriate for that student (Gottlieb, Alter, & Gottlieb, 1991; Morsink & Lenk, 1992).

Recently, courts have challenged placement recommendations across the nation, at times putting pressure on local districts to include children with disabilities in general education classes and to provide a higher level of proof to justify another placement (Osborne & DiMattia, 1994). Some concerned individuals have noted that it is about time: From the enactment of the Education for All Handicapped Children Act of 1975 (EAHCA) until the early 1990s the proportion of children served in separate settings remained fairly constant (Lipsky, 1994). Others caution that approaching the education of students from a placement perspective at the outset clouds what the law says is the primary issue: appropriate individual programming geared toward improved student performance (Kauffman, 1995).

In the 1986 report entitled *Educating Students with Learning Problems: A Shared Responsibility*, Madeline Will, then Assistant Secretary for Special Education in the U.S. Department of Education, recommended that school principals be empowered to control all programs and resources at the building level (Will, 1986b). This call, along with the current emphasis on site-based management, shifts the focus from centralized to greater building-level accountability for special education services. In the current context of reform, building principals and their assistants frequently serve on committees that determine the type of instructional setting in which a special education student will be taught. These administrators do so in an era of interest in educational environments and school choice but vague definitions and little agreement about the terms used to guide special education placement decisions. These terms include *mainstreaming, inclusion, continuum of alternative placements*, or the phrase that guides their implementation: a *free, appropriate, public education* (FAPE) *in the least restrictive environment* (LRE). At the core of this quandary is the tension that exists in the law between offering an individually appropriate program and doing so in a setting that offers interaction with nondisabled peers to the appropriate degree for each exceptional learner. Can the LRE be identified as a specific place or only as a setting in relation to an individual child? Is LRE an end in itself or a means to an end? How educational leaders interpret LRE—with the emphasis on either place or unique educational needs— has a significant effect on how schools will be structured and classrooms designed to address the needs of all students.

The professional literatures of both law and education are confusing. Lawrence Siegel (1994), an attorney and advocate for special education, describes the IDEA as a placement law, and in fact the issue of student placement has emerged as a prime target of litigation since the enactment of the federal law in 1978. Cases determining LRE hold fifth place in frequency between 1978 and 1994, with the sister cases of FAPE ranking sixth (Maloney & Shenker, 1995). Yet case law relevant to LRE is confusing to many, who misinterpret the implications of federal appeals court decisions (cf. Bateman, 1996).

To educational decision makers seeking guidance on LRE from professional literature, however, the ERIC and PsychLit data bases from 1966 to 1996 reveal a confusing quantity of published material. Numerous books, articles, and reports focus on the implementation of the law's requirements but provide little insight into the legal reasoning supporting its prescriptions. Varying opinion pieces abound, yet empirical studies reviewing the educational effectiveness of varying service delivery models are scant in comparison. Diverse accounts of parental experiences, across the years and disability categories, reflect heart-wrenching testimony but reflect voices both supportive of and adverse to full inclusion.

A wide range of topics in professional literatures is subsumed under the headings of mainstreaming, inclusion, and LRE and reflects both an emphasis on the process of implementing an appropriate education in the LRE and, to a lesser degree, its outcomes. The usage of terms varies with years of publication, and confusion over terminology obfuscates searches. For example, the same citations are found under various headings, suggesting that the terms are synonymous and interchangeable. There is no evidence of an historical or conceptual organization of terms and topics that might guide placement decision makers through relevant literature and provide evidence of either the evolution of special education practice or the stability of principle.

THE PURPOSE OF THIS VOLUME

Our purpose in this volume is to provide greater clarity to issues of student placement by examining the concept of restrictive educational environments from a variety of perspectives. We hope to further the understanding of the principles that undergird placement decisions by examining the relation over time between the law's requirements for an appropriate education for exceptional learners and the restrictiveness of the educational environments in which they have been served. In doing so, the questions we address include the following: Has the regulatory relation between an appropriate education and the LRE changed since the enactment of PL 94-142? Have the meanings of key terms related to LRE shifted over time? If so, then has there been a change in the underlying assumptions of FAPE and LRE since the 1970s?

The Importance of Conceptual Foundations

As principal of a special school, Crockett was frequently asked to discuss issues of educational benefit and LRE. Having been trained as a general educator and administrator, she felt fortunate to have as tutors in rehabilitation, special education, and developmental disability such pioneers as Hank Viscardi, Ed Martin, and Nick Anastasiow. Crockett assumed that the practices in which she was primed were supported by a canon of principles that she had not had the opportunity to explore fully. She was surprised, therefore, and felt professionally out on a limb when she read Kauffman's (1994) observation that special education developed more out of pragmatic solutions to educational problems than from coherent propositions about educational exceptionality and public education: "Our philosophies have been more implicit than explicit and so loosely grounded in shifting, unstated assumptions that we are easy prey for anyone who challenges our purpose, offers a critique of basic assumptions, or states that special education fails in basic concept" (p. 614). Kauffman (1993) argued that the real hope for remedy resides in these strategies close to the field's conceptual core and "grounded in memory of the past: disaggregating special education populations, repairing and elaborating special education's conceptual foundations, and strengthening special education's empirical base" (p. 11). We have attempted to be mindful of all three in our preparation of this volume.

The Importance of Legal, Educational, and Parental Perspectives

Hallahan and Kauffman (1997) suggested that "Individuals and ideas have played crucial roles in the history of special education, but it is accurate to say that much of the progress made over the years has been achieved primarily by the collective efforts of professionals and parents" (p. 28). More than any other statute, the EAHCA of 1975 placed parents at the core of educational decision making on behalf of their children by mandating parental participation as a fundamental component of the law.

A cursory examination of legal history reveals a national trend of parental activism born in the 1940s and maturing in the civil rights era of the 1960s, with legislative victories securing access to educational opportunity for all students, regardless of disability (Winzer, 1993). The revolutionary federal legislation involving special education, PL 94-142, pulled together various components of local decisions and earlier legislation, resulting in the provision of a free, appropriate education in the LRE for all school-aged students with disabilities. In 1986, PL 99-457 extended these benefits to exceptional learners 3 to 5 years of age and encouraged states to implement early intervention programs for infants and toddlers with disabilities or at risk of incurring developmental delays. Reauthorization of the law in 1990 as the IDEA increased the scope of the law even further, embracing new students and services previously unaddressed. The IDEA amendments of 1997 are the fifth set of amendments to the EAHCA or PL 94-142 (which is often referenced more simply and broadly as the Education of the Handicapped Act [EHA]).

In the United States, 20 years after the passage of PL 94-142, FAPE in the LRE is available by law for every child with a disability from birth to age 21. This development and expansion of special education rose from the passion of parents, the compassion of professional educators, and the support of legislators. If assumptions underlying these terms have changed, it is through these three perspectives—that of the parent, educator, and legislator—that such an alteration can best be discerned.

In examining shifts in the meaning of an appropriate education in the LRE, we have sought evidence in legal, educational, and parental data to determine whether the causes of change in meaning are imprecise implementation of the law, greater readiness of general education to meet the needs of exceptional learners, or sociopolitical developments and changes in cultural values.

The Methodology of Historical Inquiry

An historical inquiry addresses the issue of altered meanings qualitatively. We heeded Edson's (1986) four exhortations: (a) *to honor past contexts and the complexity of the contextual issues* by explaining a variety of sociopolitical and cultural perspectives and interpreting multiple meanings; (b) *to broaden understanding by reflecting the natural setting* through analysis of primary documents, personal experiences, and historical trends in professional practice; (c) *to develop a sense of the whole experience through the interpretation of several individuals* by interviewing parental advocates, developers of federal legislation, and educational interpreters; and (d) *to enhance the meaning of past events by explaining and interpreting their significance* through a case study presentation and research summaries of classroom ecologies.

Why History is Important. "Hoisting the banner of the existentialist or the radical constructivist, one might profess that history may only serve to cloud or misguide an individual's thinking" (Alexander, Murphy, & Woods, 1996, p. 34). Although agreeing that historical reflection is no guarantee of thoughtful analysis, Alexander et al. exhort educators to heed Krathwohl's admonition:

> Read particularly the top minds in the field and not necessarily just the current ones, but go back in time—the most productive researchers do. Remember, we all got where we are by standing on someone else's shoulder: It helps if you start with tall persons. (p. 34)

The 1980s and 1990s have been boom years for the provision of educational services to exceptional learners. In that time, individuals and ideas have risen to prominence within the field of special education, providing tall shoulders upon which to stand and look back "to understand what is happening today, or what will happen in the future" (attributed to Oliver Wendell Holmes, Jr., 1841–1935).

Alexander et al. (1996) raised concerns, however, about educators' limited knowledge of the people, movements, and writings that underlie current innovations. They make a distinction between researchers and practitioners who do what they know and those who know about what they do. They argue that a lack of rich understanding contributes to superficial implementation of intended change "or results in the reinvention or recycling of old movements under new labels" (p. 31). In their view, "informed innovation that is in touch with its source or sources is preferable to innovation that springs solely from a sea of discontent and frustration" (p. 36).

Choice of History. Making the choice to view LRE through a historical lens raises issues of methodological perspective and the importance of not letting history become the extension of one's politics. In reflecting on American educational reform since the 1960s, Ravitch (1981) made a distinction between historical and sociological thought. She argued that educators and educational policy makers, in emphasizing the principles of equity or in responding to political demands, have succumbed to the habit of analyzing school issues in sociological and economic terms. She identified a persistent tendency "to neglect the role of schools as educational institutions, to treat them as sociological cookie cutters without regard to the content of their educational program . . . to view schooling as an instrument to achieve some other goal, only rarely as an end in itself" (p. 337). An understanding of history, however, elucidates shared values, distinguishing, as she suggested, democratic debate from chaos and pluralism from anarchy.

In his critique of recent revisionist thought, Lazerson (1973) described an inquiry critical of both America's past and its educational institutions:

> The portrait they draw assumes that our educational system is bad and that schools have been essentially harmful to children. The system's oppressiveness is neither accidental nor an unforeseen consequence of once noble reform, but rather reflects the values of a bureaucratic, inegalitarian, racist society.... The schools are thus primarily concerned with selecting out rather than educating in. (p. 281)

Much of what Lazerson described resembles those who castigate special education for its sins rather than respect it for its successes (cf. Kauffman, 1981).

Lazerson (1973) described the "radical" revisionist's view of educational reform as "a surrogate for social reform" and allowed that these arguments are persuasive, while standing good scholarship on its head. Substituting rhetoric for analysis, some revisionists have avoided asking questions key to understanding the choices of educational reformers such as who made the decisions? How were they implemented? What were their effects? Why was one value structure accepted rather than another? Said Lazerson:

> Few educational historians have asked Aileen Kraditor's questions about the reform movements: "What conditions at that time determined the organizational forms that the movement took as well as the changes in society that it worked for? What was the relation between the real possibilities and the reformer's perceptions of the possibilities and how may we account for the discrepancy, if any?" (p. 282)

In an effort to address these questions, our narrative acknowledges history not as a backdrop but as a lively art that helps us to better understand the human condition:

> Histories can only be of use if we put ourselves into the historical picture, allowing history to affect our lives and our lives to affect history. Doing history does involve reconstructing the past in its own terms, but this cannot be the end of it. Engagement with historical enquiry is bound to influence the resulting narrative, but this should not be seen as negatively contaminating.
>
> There are social and political contexts for historical, as for any other, enquiry or research. To acknowledge these contexts is, in this case, to recognise a relationship between historian, subjects, and audience and taking responsibility for this relationship requires an engagement with the contexts of research. This should not be confused with the methodological issue of allowing personal values

to influence enquiries unjustifiably, but should be seen as the basis
for a reflective and useful approach to history. (Potts, 1995, p. 410)

Voices From the Field

Gardner (1995) was concerned with the thoughts and mental images of leaders,
believing that through these ideations leaders manipulate symbols and captivate
followers through their storytelling. English (1997) suggested that in
considering issues of leadership we concentrate on context variance, "those
situational-cultural aspects of the human experience that enable leaders to lead
within specific situations. The principal sources will not be policy studies or
behavioral researches, but narratives from biography and history that illuminate
the interplay between action, character and context" (p. 2).

We are grateful to several educational leaders and dedicated parents who
permitted us to catch a glimpse of the issues surrounding LRE from their tall
shoulders and who, through their reflections, brought life and reality to our
exploration. The following chapters are filled with the words of dynamic
characters whose vision and energy influenced both the development and the
implementation of the concept of LRE. We have interjected their perspectives
where they seem most appropriately to illuminate historical events or provide
conceptual insight. Each person is introduced in context in the chapters to
come, but the following is a brief introduction and synopsis of the items
we discussed.

Developers of Legislation. Several of the professionals we interviewed played
key roles in the early development of federal legislation and continue to influence
the field of special education. In the course of this study, Crockett met with Donald
Stedman and James Gallagher at the University of North Carolina at Chapel Hill;
Edwin Martin, now retired from federal service and the presidency of the National
Center for Disability Services, in Florida; Frederick Weintraub, then Assistant
Executive Director of the Council for Exceptional Children, at the association's
headquarters in Reston, Virginia; and Thomas Gillhool at the Public Interest Law
Center in Philadelphia. We discussed the origins of the LRE concept and their
subsequent reflections on its usefulness in bringing about full educational
opportunity for exceptional learners. Our conversations included the following
issues: What educational, social, and political conditions at the time of the
development of PL 94-142 determined the choice of the term least restrictive
environment? Were other options considered? What educational, social, or
political changes did you hope to achieve at that time by including these
principles? What was the relationship between your perceptions and the real
possibilities for change at the time? Upon what did you think success would
hinge? How would you size up the effects of the LRE concept?

Educational Theorists. The following educational theorists, who have written significantly and influentially in the professional literature, contributed their perspective regarding the ethics of the LRE concept. Crockett met with Maynard Reynolds, professor emeritus of the University of Minnesota, at his home in St. Paul. She met with Laurence Lieberman in Boston, the home base of his national consultancy. Douglas Fuchs conveyed his thoughts in a telephone interview from Vanderbilt University in Nashville, Tennessee; and Dorothy Lipsky, of the National Center for Educational Restructuring and Inclusion at the City University of New York, shared her perspective in a letter. Each person responded to the following questions: Has your opinion of the usefulness or suitability of the LRE concept as an educational strategy changed over time? Upon what did you think its success would hinge? How would you size up the effects of the LRE concept? Would you suggest the LRE principles be refined or replaced?

Parents of Exceptional Learners. Several parents of exceptional learners discussed their experiences in providing an appropriate education for their children and their impressions reflect practices in student placement that span the years from 1958 to 1998. Crockett met with Betsy Balsdon in Roanoke, Virginia, about her experiences raising her daughter Holly on Long Island before the concept of LRE was put into law. Holly was born in 1958 with cerebral palsy and severe mental retardation and now lives in a group home in upstate New York. Crockett spoke by telephone with Karen Silver, also a Long Islander, who has worked as a committed advocate for her daughter, Alison, who has cerebral palsy, is visually impaired, and is academically able to address her grade-level curriculum. Donna Cattell-Gordon and Jean Crockett met at the Virginia Institute for Autism in Charlottesville, Virginia, a school started by parents in the fall, 1996, to provide early and intensive services to children like her 6-year-old son, Daniel. In addition, Crockett met with Jane DeWeerd, former coordinator for parent training and preschool dissemination projects with the U.S. Department of Education, in Arlington, Virginia. The issues discussed were similar to those in other interviews, but the conversations covered more personal ground as well. Each parent was asked how their child's education has been affected by the concept of LRE, whether this concept supported his or her education, and how they would size up the effect of the LRE concept for their own child.

By blending scholarly data, historical perspectives, and ethical dilemmas, our comprehensive examination of the notion of least restrictive environment is intended to fill in the rich details of the multiple complex contexts this dynamic concept represents.

2

The Politics of Placement
in an Era of Reform

> We seek the establishment of a democracy of individual participation
> governed by two central aims: that the individual should share in
> those social decisions determining the quality and direction of his
> life; that society should be organized to encourage independence in
> men and provide the media for their common participation.—Port
> Huron Statement, Students for a Democratic Society, 1962. Cited in
> Dionne, p.10

In this chapter we provide a practical framework for decision makers who need to understand the current controversies surrounding the least restrictive environment and educational placement. We anchor contemporary LRE issues in their political background and summarize the debate surrounding the interpretation of LRE. Subsequently, we sketch the perspectives and conditions that are essential to clear communication about service delivery and student placement, including the definition of terms. These terms include *integration, segregation, mainstreaming, inclusion,* and the *continuum of alternative placements.*

ANCHORING THE ISSUE:
INSTRUCTIONAL SETTINGS FOR EXCEPTIONAL LEARNERS

Providing service delivery to special education students has been fraught with controversy about which students should be served, which curricula and instructional methodologies should be used, and where instruction should be provided (Crockett & Kauffman, 1998; Kauffman & Trent, 1991). Consequently, many educators in elementary and secondary schools are facing predicaments with regard to special education reform initiatives for which there are few blueprints. Administrators' skills, knowledge, and understanding are challenged as they attempt to accommodate increasing numbers of students with disabilities into general education classrooms while they cope with their own and their faculty's lack of preparation for educating students with special needs (Bailey,1989; Kritsonis, 1992–1993; Sage & Burrello, 1994; Scruggs & Mastropieri, 1996).

The international school reform movement—including initiatives in Canadian provinces, European nations, and Australian states as well as the United States—reflects similar rearrangements. Information is being shared globally as educators attempt to make classrooms more accommodating for their students with disabilities ("Special Educators Worldwide," 1995). Recently, in an internet post to SpedTalk (an electronic forum for discussing special education), a South African special educator asked for help in finding research to support his school's move toward more inclusive services. His question echoed Garnett's (1996): "Can the general education classroom be reshaped to allow for these youngsters to learn more, not simply to find a social niche?" (p. 25).

The international call for competitive standards, accountability, equity, and excellence for all students occurs simultaneously with concerns about opportunities to learn for those least equipped to compete. Most educators, although embracing greater participation of students with disabilities in the mainstream, fear a loss of equity for exceptional learners unless they are provided with appropriate curriculum and instruction, supportive peer and teacher interactions, and suitable organization and management of their educational environments.

Current Realities of Service Delivery

American classrooms are currently experiencing rapid growth. At a time when government funding is scarce and public confidence in the nation's schools is declining, the student population is growing as fast as it did in the 1960s. Six million more children are attending school in the late 1990s than did in the late 1980s, and it is estimated that by 2025 the school population will increase from 49 million to 58 million children, a startling rise of 18% (Society, 1995). In addition to increased enrollments, recent data powerfully illustrate emerging student diversity:

> From 1980 to 1990, the number of children with limited English proficiency increased nationwide by 20%, the number of immigrant children by 24%, and the number of linguistically isolated children (those in households in which nobody older than 14 speaks English "very well") by 20%. The percentage of minority children in the schools has grown steadily from 21% in 1970 to 40% by 1992. Whites now account for 7 out of 10 school-age children; by the year 2020, the figure will change to 5 out of 10. By the same year, the proportion of Hispanics will increase from one in nine to one in four. During the same period, the proportion of poor children in the schools is expected to rise to 26%. (Carnegie Foundation, 1995)

Clearly, in addition to redesigning the schoolhouse, administrators must also adapt fiscally as well as instructionally to overcrowding, higher poverty rates, greater ethnic diversity, and increasing numbers of children with disabilities in regular classrooms.

According to the 19th Annual Report to Congress on the Implementation of the Individuals with Disabilities Education Act (U.S. Department of Education, 1997b), 5.6 million children with disabilities from the ages of 3 through 21years received special education services in the 1995-96 school year (U. S. Department of Education, 1997; see also U. S. Department of Education, 1996). About 95% of these students were served in regular schools. In 1994–1995, approximately 44.5% of school-age students with disabilities spent at least 80% of their day in regular classrooms. The pattern of such inclusion (i.e., 80% or more of the day in regular classrooms) varies by age and disability category. At the end of the 20th century, regular classrooms are the primary placement for approximately 55% of all students aged 6 to 11 years with disabilities, and 33% of those aged 12 to 17 years. The majority of students with speech impairments are served in the regular class. Students with learning disabilities, orthopedic impairments, emotional disturbance, and traumatic brain injury are generally placed in regular school buildings but tend to be served in a variety of instructional settings, ranging from regular classes to resource rooms, separate classes, and occasionally special schools. Among the categories just named, students with learning disabilities are most often placed in regular classrooms, and those with emotional disturbance are most likely to be placed in separate classes or schools. Students with mental retardation, autism, and multiple disabilities are more often placed in separate classes. Of the approximately 2.5 million students with learning disabilities receiving services in the United States in 1994–1995, about 40% were assigned to regular classes for at least 80% of their instructional time. Frequently, the performance of these students in the general education setting calls for a special instructional response.

Placement Trends

In its obligation to report to Congress the extent to which the LRE provision of IDEA is being met, the U.S. Department of Education's Office of Special Education Programs (OSEP) annually collects data on educational placements for all school-age children with disabilities served under IDEA and Chapter 1 of the Elementary and Secondary Education Act (ESEA). These data have been challenged for their inability to depict accurately the variance in state and local practices, resulting in OSEP's attempts to clarify its year-to-year data and provide technical assistance to states in applying instructions for data collection (Sawyer, McLaughlin, & Winglee, 1994).

In determining the status of placements nationwide, the Second Annual Report to the Congress on the Implementation of P. L. 94-142 (U. S. Department of Education, 1980) used only four broad categories to describe placement options: regular classes, separate classrooms, separate school facilities, and other environments (considered to be home or hospital settings). OSEP has since defined the following categories as representative of the law's requirement for the provision of a continuum of alternative instructional settings for exceptional learners (U. S. Department of Education, 1996):

- *Regular class* includes students who receive the majority of their instruction in a regular classroom and receive special education and related services outside the regular classroom for less than 21% of the school day.
- *Resource room* includes students who receive special education and related services outside the regular classroom for at least 21% but not more than 60% of the school day. This may include students placed in resource rooms with part-time instruction in a regular class.
- *Separate class* includes students who receive special education and related services outside the general classroom for more than 60% of the school day. Students may be placed in self-contained special classrooms with part-time instruction in general classes or placed in self-contained classes full-time on a general education school campus.
- *Separate school facility* includes students who receive special education and related services in separate day schools for students with disabilities for more than 50% of the school day.
- *Residential facility* includes students who receive education in a public or private residential facility, at public expense, for more than 50% of the school day.
- *Homebound/hospital* environment includes students placed in and receiving special education in hospital or homebound programs.

According to Danielson and Bellamy (1989), three factors should be considered in interpreting placement trends from nationally reported data. The first factor is a reminder that the law's LRE emphasis is on the process of determining a placement in which an appropriate education for a student can be provided:

> No particular pattern of placements is consistent with or contra-
> dictory to these requirements. However, the statute is clear in
> creating a presumption that services [will] be provided in the
> regular educational environment to the extent appropriate for each
> student. One must conclude from the data that some states have

> been more successful than others in providing services in regular
> settings that were seen as appropriate by local decision makers.
> (Danielson & Bellamy,1989, p. 452)

Second, although some states have higher rates of placement in regular settings, they do not necessarily have increased quality of special education and related services. In other words, "a low placement rate in segregated settings is not necessarily a testimony to effectiveness of services. To demonstrate such effectiveness, states would also have to show that students receive the services necessary and achieve successfully" (Danielson & Bellamy,1989, p. 453).

Finally, some variance in state data over time could reflect such problem areas as "(a) faulty exclusion/inclusion of particular types of students in various placement categories; (b) use of nonuniform definitions of placement categories; and (c) misinterpretations of OSEP instructions" (Sawyer et al., 1994, p. 206). Variance is also attributable to the less empirical and more contextual notion of a locality's cultural values: "The extent of variability does suggest that factors in addition to the characteristics of students are determinants of individual educational placements, and that the decision-making power vested in the IEP process has not been sufficient to overcome these factors" (Danielson & Bellamy, 1989, p. 453).

With these caveats in mind, Verstegen's (1996) analysis is illustrative of placement data for children, aged 3-21 years, served in different educational environments. Verstegen observed that for exceptional learners, the data show that the continuum of placements has been weighted more toward separate placements, with little variance over time:

> In 1991–1992, although 94% of children with disabilities attended
> public schools, only about one-third received their education in the
> general classroom setting full-time. Two-thirds were served in
> resource rooms (which may be located in the neighborhood public
> school) or in segregated, self-contained settings, including separate
> classes, schools, or residential facilities. Often more severe disability
> categories are linked to more restrictive settings; and patterns of
> overrepresentation and segregation in special education programs
> prevail, particularly for African-Americans, males, and linguistic
> minorities. (p. 488)

In considering the relation among federal, state, and local fiscal approaches and subsequent placement practices, Verstegen's (1996) analysis provides evidence that federal law is interpreted variously across localities with little agreement as to what degree of fiscal accountability is actually required by the IDEA or presumed to be mandated by overly strict interpretations of accountability. One respondent in Verstegen's study pointed out that "there is no need to amend the

IDEA to allow for greater integration among students. Nothing precludes special education students from being educated in the regular classroom [under current law]" (p. 484). Verstegen reported that, "overall, the sense of respondents was that fragmentation and segregation were 'implementation problems rather than statutory problems'" (p. 485). These views are supported by Martin's (1995b) observations on funding related to student placement:

> Nothing prevents programs designed to benefit children without disabilities along with disabilities from being funded by general education funds in combination with special education funds—in proportion to the children included and the services received by each population. But let's make sure that special education students receive the resources they are entitled to and need to achieve in our schools. (Martin, 1995, p. 14)

Legal Foundations of the Least Restrictive Environment Requirement

The legal parameters that guide service delivery for American students with disabilities are provided by Section 504 of the Rehabilitation Act (1973) and the Individuals with Disabilities Education Act (IDEA, enacted in 1990 and amended in 1997), the federal financing statute originally known as the Education for All Handicapped Children Act of 1975, Public Law 94-142 (EAHCA) (cf. Yell, 1998). Bateman (personal communication, January, 1996) described the IDEA as a funding act and a voluntary affirmative action law that sets out to reduce disadvantage; Section 504 provides no funds but mandates nondiscrimination on the premise that "the rocks and roses of life should be thrown equally to prevent lopsided rocks to some and roses to others." Bateman (1996) also noted that "a few students are eligible for services under Section 504, but not under IDEA. They may, but need not, be provided with an IEP. Typically these students do not need special education, but may need modifications or accommodations in the regular classroom" (p. 135). Both Section 504 and the American with Disabilities Act (ADA) contain a similar LRE requirement to that of the IDEA, providing further support to IDEA-eligible students and protections to students not eligible for funded services (Pitasky, 1996).

The IDEA provides to every child in America who has a disability and who needs specialized instruction and related services a free appropriate public education. The law and its regulations have distinct components to achieve this goal: evaluation and identification; individualized education program; placement; funding; and procedural protections (Bateman, 1996). Placement decisions, which Bateman noted should follow only after establishing a student's unique educational needs and the development of a specialized program to address them, have become "the center of an ideological storm in special education. While the storm has raged the law has stayed quiet and unchanged. More and more students with disabilities are being educated full-time in regular classes" (Bateman, 1996, p. 8).

FAPE: Free, Appropriate, Public Education. According IDEA, once a child has been found eligible to receive special education services, an individualized education program (IEP) must be developed based upon his or her unique educational needs. Only after programming has been agreed upon should consideration be given to the student's placement (Bateman, 1996). Simply put, for any child with a disability placements are to be individualized; based on availability of a full continuum of alternative placements ranging from the regular classroom to a residential school; consistent with the principles of the least restrictive environment; and "secondary to the primary purpose of special education that is the provision of an appropriate program" (Bateman & Chard, 1995, p. 286).

In writing the decision for the well-known *Hendrick Hudson District Board of Education v. Rowley* (1982) case, Supreme Court Justice Rehnquist declared that education is "appropriate" when it is a program that has been developed in a procedurally correct manner, is individualized, and is reasonably calculated to provide the student with educational benefit. The degree of benefit is to be determined on a case-by-case basis—except in one instance. When a student is placed in the regular classroom, all necessary aids and services are to be provided to enable him or her to earn passing marks and legitimate passage from grade to grade. Bateman (1992) remarked that, realistically, districts mainstream perhaps millions of children with disabilities with no expectation of grade level performance or anything near the support needed to approach it: "The discrepancy between what the U.S. Supreme Court believes mainstreaming practice to be and what it actually is, is a mile wide and equally deep" (p. 30).

Least Restrictive Environment. The term *least restrictive environment* appears only twice in the original text of the EAHCA/IDEA regulations, once as a column heading and once in the following requirement: "In selecting the LRE, consideration is given to any potential harmful effect on the child or on the quality of services that he or she needs" (34 CFR 300.552(d)). Bateman and Chard (1995) remarked that other than general requirements for an appropriate education, this is the only original regulation referring to quality of services. Critical to the issue of service delivery is wording under this heading that calls for children with disabilities to be educated with their nondisabled peers "to the maximum extent appropriate" (34 CFR 300.550 (b)(1)). Those who argue for cautious movement toward fuller inclusion take issue with others who substitute this precise reference with the phrase *to the greatest degree possible.* Such conceptual distinctions between *maximum extent appropriate* and *greatest degree possible* represent more than semantic quibbles. They imply a vastly different regard for the law's intent and for its provision of a continuum of alternative placements beyond the regular classroom.

CAPTURING THE CONTROVERSY

For more than 20 years, in close to 15,000 school districts across the United States, the continuum and cascade of services model has driven the provision of education and related services. Fuchs, Fuchs, and Fernstrom (1993) raised a contemporary question and offered a strategy for finding an answer: "Should special education abolish or maintain the cascade?... We believe its credibility depends on a rediscovery of its original meaning and intent" (pp. 152–153).

In analyzing the controversial positions related to LRE, Fuchs and Fuchs (1991) described those who call for the preservation of the continuum of alternative placements (CAP) or cascade model *conservationists*, because they believe in retaining an array of instructional settings for exceptional learners. Help for those students whose degree of disability might exceed in severity the range of variability appropriate for the regular class could be provided more readily, conservationists hold, in separate settings. Failure of students to move along the continuum toward instruction in the regular class is seen not as a fault of the model but of professionals who use it incorrectly. Conservationists are depicted as being either mildly or strongly supportive of the preservation of the CAP. *Abolitionists*, who favor the abandonment of the model, span a range of three degrees of support for their position. According to the Fuchs and Fuchs (1991) analysis, those occupying a mild spot favor inclusion but acknowledge separate settings for some students whose severe needs require specific intervention. Others who argue for a modified cascade without recourse to separate or residential schools fall between this mild position and the most extreme represented by Gartner and Lipsky (1989):

> The concepts of Least Restrictive Environment, a continuum of placements, and a cascade of services, were progressive when developed but do not today promote the full inclusion of all persons with disabilities in all aspects of societal life nor do they serve as guiding principles for the education that is the necessary means toward that goal's achievement. (p. 52)

The controversy surrounding LRE can be viewed from a sociological perspective that champions integration and societal reform. This viewpoint is favored by abolitionists, many of whom represent students with severe cognitive disabilities who traditionally have been denied access to school programs. Conservationists are most often aligned with an educational perspective that sees LRE as secondary to the goal of providing improved academic and social outcomes for students who are considered mildly or moderately disabled and who often have been functionally excluded from regular classes. Fuchs and Fuchs (1991) described the essence of the conflict between those who would abolish and those who would conserve the continuum of placements as residing within their experiences with the public schools:

> Abolitionist and Conservationist viewpoints clash because, in an important sense, they and the students for whom they tend to speak have very different histories with regular education: For many Abolitionists, their orientation reflects a literal lack of history; for Conservationists, their pragmatism reveals a cautiousness based on past frustrations and disappointments. (p. 252)

LRE and Social Reform

Much of the concern about placement in the LRE follows from the data found in the U.S. Department of Education's annual reports to Congress on the implementation of IDEA. In reacting to these data, some professionals and parents have expressed concern that the inclusion of exceptional learners into regular class settings is moving too slowly. They have made impassioned appeals to facilitate greater instructional inclusion to eliminate what they term segregation and violation of a student's civil rights (Lipsky & Gartner, 1997; Stainback & Stainback, 1988). Others raise the question of whether equating special education with racial segregation is appropriate or unfitting (Kauffman & Lloyd, 1995; Shanker, 1994). Not only might students have learning differences that are relevant to various individualized interventions, but these disabilities—unlike characteristics of race or ethnic origin—often are malleable: "Handicapped individuals may therefore pass from one classification to another during the course of their development and education, requiring a more carefully weighted approach to legal rights involving separation (Kauffman, 1989, p. 261).

Another issue of societal equity and civil rights was addressed on July 26, 1990, when the ADA was signed into law. This legislation prohibits discrimination on the basis of disability and

> establishes the basis for a national policy that focuses on the inclusion, independence, and empowerment of individuals with disabilities.... Under the ADA, disability is recognized as a natural

> part of the human experience and in no way diminishes the right of
> individuals to live independently, enjoy self-determination, make
> choices, contribute to society, pursue meaningful careers, and
> enjoy full inclusion and integration in all aspects of American
> society (Harkin, 1993, p. 25).

Some theorists have taken this spirit of societal inclusion as a moral imperative and applied it directly to the schools, seeing such inclusion as "the right thing to do" (Johnson & Bauer, 1992, p. 1). In the fall, 1993, Judith Heumann, Assistant Secretary of Education for Special Education and Rehabilitative Services, fueled the fire by comparing the IDEA mandate with *Brown v. The Board of Education* (1954). Her remark at a public hearing that schooling children with disabilities in segregated settings was immoral drew strong reaction from the education community (cf. Heumann, 1993). Confusing the issue were conflicting statements by Thomas Hehir, Heumann's federal colleague and Director of the Office of Special Education Programs, that the inclusion of all children with disabilities in the regular classroom will not work for all special needs children (personal communication, November 17, 1993, to S. L. Kolbe, National Association of Private Schools for Exceptional Children). An unclear message emanated from Washington and clearly reflected the debate surrounding the urgency for social change and the requirement for individually appropriate programming.

The Ethics of Social Reform. In summarizing the arguments of abolitionists who champion inclusive schools as linchpins of a new social order, it can be said that inclusive classrooms should help to develop and eventually reflect an inclusive society, "which emphasizes social cognition, increased tolerance and acceptance of diversity, a development of personal values, friendships and social acceptance, and self concept" (Billingsley, Peterson, Bodkins, & Hendricks, 1993, p. 223). As described by Gartner and Lipsky (1987), the rationale for educating students with severe disabilities in integrated settings is to ensure their normalized community participation by providing them with systematic instruction in the skills that are essential to their success in the social and environmental contexts in which they will ultimately use these skills. According to Snell (1991), the following benefits to society should be considered in the ethical move toward instructional inclusion: "(a) the development of social skills...across all school age groups; (b) the improvements in the attitudes that nondisabled peers have for their peers with disabilities; (c) the development of positive relationships and friendships between peers as a result" (pp. 137–138).

LRE and Improved Student Performance

Many changes that have been formalized in legislation and court decisions over the years have protected the rights of exceptional learners, but laws and court decisions are subject to interpretation. Noted Kirk, Gallagher, and Anastasiow (1993): "Special educators have a unique responsibility to see that these laws and rulings are implemented as they were intended: to guarantee that all children receive an appropriate education" (p. 58). Kauffman (1995) observed that in some legal discussions, primary consideration has been given to placement, with subsequent consideration to appropriate programming. This assessment is consistent with the National Association of State Boards of Education's report (1992), which determined that most of the goals successfully attained as a result of IDEA fall into the category of increased access, not improved programming with enhanced student outcomes.

Reformers who support the move toward full inclusion argue the need for the radical restructuring of schools as well as the abolition of the law's requirement for school districts to provide a continuum of alternative instructional settings. Their blueprint for the process describes the decentralization of power and the concomitant site-based empowerment of teachers and building administrators, more cooperative teaching and learning strategies, and collaborative teaching models that reconceptualize or eliminate special education (Fuchs & Fuchs, 1994). Their opponents, who champion the preservation of the continuum, argue that even though proponents have identified factors they see as necessary for the successful process of inclusion, there is still a substantial absence of data that clearly identify factors that alter student outcomes (Hallahan & Kauffman, 1995).

Edwin Martin, the Director of the federal Bureau of Education for the Handicapped during the time that EAHCA (PL 94-142, now IDEA) was written and enacted, still finds the goals related to the provision of an individualized appropriate education for an exceptional learner in a setting with nondisabled peers to remain worthy but difficult to reach. What is needed, he maintains, is a research emphasis on the effectiveness of innovations as judged by the successful outcomes for students: "New programs designed to include all children with disabilities in regular classes should be carefully tested and replicated widely only when they are demonstrated to work" (personal communication to the *New York Times*, January 27, 1994).

Concerns about outcomes for exceptional learners were heightened by Wagner (1990), who reported in the National Longitudinal Transition Study that students with disabilities had more absenteeism, higher drop out rates, and lower grades than the general high school population. Students who spent most of their time in regular classes were 10% more likely to fail a class in the 9th grade than peers who spent only half their time there. Less individual attention from the teacher due to higher student-to-teacher ratios in regular classrooms was considered to be an obstacle.

The Ethics of Efficacy. To summarize the arguments of conservationists who claim the continuum is a useful strategy, it might be said that caution should be exercised during times of change and that innovations that hold promise should be evaluated on the merits of improving students' academic and social performance before being institutionalized as reforms. Carnine (1994b) described innovation as part of the problem-solving process, not the solution to educational dilemmas: "An innovation succeeds when a change has been made; an educational reform succeeds when learning improves" (p. 1).

In considering moves toward fuller inclusion, Cohen (1993) stated that "we face a situation where any one or all of the actors have limited knowledge and differences in opinion about what is best for the child" (p. 266). Kauffman (1992) posed the following questions regarding the ethics of moving forward armed with limited knowledge:

> Under what conditions, if any, is an approach to education (or to child discipline, medical treatment, or any other human service) "right" even if it doesn't work? Can education or treatment be morally "right" if it provides no benefit, even if it does harm? Are we to assume that what is "right" for most students is "right" for all, regardless of benefit or harm in the individual case? (Kauffman, 1992, p. xv)

Conflicting Views

"Inclusion is an issue that, in many respects, is going to be dealt with as a political issue," claimed Cohen (1993), who noted that concerned voices range from individual stakeholders to the collective interests of national organizations who take varying positions on the issue (Hallahan & Kauffman, 1995; Verstegen & Martin, 1995). In his discussion of the political arena, Cohen identifies those whom he considered to be the stakeholders within the education community: special education teachers, principals, superintendents, researchers, special programs, and students.

Special Educators. "Special education teachers are concerned about relocation, loss of work, licensing, regular education resistance to collaboration, and a fear of being used as aides in regular education" (Cohen, 1993, p. 266). Data seem to support the importance of the issues. If student placements are changed to a variety of schools within a district, the service providers would follow the action, resulting in building reassignment and the reduction in force for special educators because of reduced mandates for low student–teacher ratios. Fuchs and Fuchs (1995a) called for the maintenance of the number of special educators under these conditions so that existing ratio mandates can be met and so that special educators "can work closely with general educators in mainstream classrooms with students who are in trouble, academically or otherwise, but not disabled" (p. 373). Some studies show that special educators underestimate the willingness of general educators to collaborate for instruction (Cannon, Idol, & West, 1992), whereas others demonstrate a willingness but lack of knowledge or skills in how to individualize (Meadows, Neel, Scott, & Parker, 1994; Vaughn & Schumm, 1996). Requirements for teacher licensing and teacher preparation programs are in flux in a field unsure of whether to prepare special educators more as generalists or specialists. The possibility that special educators will serve as aides in general education is real and threatening to meaningful instructional interactions. Willis (1994) wrote that co-teaching allows special educators to have a wider impact, but he described the work of one special educator as follows: "while she used to work with only about 20 students daily, she now interacts with more than 150, giving the district more for its money" (p. 7). He said nothing of the quality of this teacher's work or how her role and responsibilities have been redefined.

Principals. "Principals have to balance concerns of parents of regular and special education kids with teacher training and promoting collaboration" (Cohen, 1993, p. 266). Literature on inclusive schools states that the principal's support is key to effective inclusionary practice (Rude & Anderson, 1992). However, administrators have little data to guide them in selecting effective practices, and thus it is difficult to present instructional approaches to parents with confidence (Fuchs & Fuchs, 1995b). Student and program evaluation designs and measures are inadequate, evaluation processes are supported by limited data, and little research is available to guide IEP development (Lipsky, 1994). In addition to these administrative issues, some studies show teacher training for inclusive schools to be inadequate (Kearney & Durand, 1992). It may be impossible to convince parents that their children's needs can be met when inadequate data are available.

Superintendents. "Superintendents and school boards are worried about money, community politics and issues, parent pressures, and liability" (Cohen, 1993, p. 266). There is a scarcity of information about the costs of providing inclusive instruction and little to support the suggestion that inclusion might save money. Studies typically fail to relate the needs of a given child to the services that he or she requires (Verstegen, 1996). Currently, superintendents have little financial data to guide their decisions. In addition, issues of violence in schools are a frequent community concern and a legal reality for the school chief. There is a real need for school systems to develop policies and procedures to ensure that all students' rights are protected (Yell, 1990, 1998).

Researchers. "University people are interested in publishing and data collection" (Cohen, 1993, p. 266). The controversy surrounding LRE has provided many theorists with the opportunity to publish widely on the topic and to attract grants to support further research. Regardless of their stance, writers in professional journals have kept the focus on needs in the nation's schools. The debate has also affected the structure of teacher education programs. Some suggest that policy statements such as that of the National Association of State Boards of Education and others calling for full inclusion feed a "zeitgeist that special education is harmful, not helpful; evil, not good" (Fuchs & Fuchs, 1995a, p. 366). Data from the Higher Education Consortium on Special Education indicate that in 1987, 39 institutions responding to a survey of 45 colleges and universities granting doctoral degrees in special education claimed special education departments. In 1992, the number of institutions with special education departments was only 25, a 31% drop in only 5 years (Fuchs & Fuchs, 1995a, p. 366). This is a disturbing trend because it comes at a time when increased research is needed to document best practices and shortages of personnel threaten effective practices already in place.

Separate Programs. "Low-incidence programs are concerned with the perception of the loss of jobs, power, and buildings, and the possible dissolution of units " (Cohen, 1993, p. 266). Students who have orthopedic or health impairments, are blind or deaf, or have multiple disabilities, autism, or traumatic brain injury are a small percentage of the special education population but often require specialized techniques and equipment and highly trained staff to meet their needs. Many programs nationwide have served their respective clientele long and well. For example, the deaf community has been outspoken against full-inclusion policies and vigorously defends the maintenance of separate schools for deaf students (Willis, 1994). According to Oscar Cohen, Executive Director of the Lexington School for the Deaf in New York, no research shows that inclusion is effective for deaf children. Although respecting that inclusion in general education might be a needed option for some, Cohen said that, "the idea of one-size-fits-all is either misguided idealism or cost cutting" (Willis, 1994, p. 7). Oscar Cohen saw a real threat to the existence of special schools in this wave of inclusion, and he understood the need to fight for their survival.

Parents. Interestingly, Matthew Cohen (1993) did not include parents in his list of stakeholders, yet protections for student and parental rights are an integral part of special education law. Initially, parents were satisfied if their children were provided with an appropriate education and not left out of the education system. Now that total exclusion from services is not the threat, some say that "in the future we can expect parents to advocate for educational placements in environments that are closer to the general educational program" (Osborne, DiMattia, & Curran, 1993, p. 98). Given the individual needs of the children, this statement is perhaps an oversimplified prediction of parental choice. Both proponents and opponents of full inclusion can produce impassioned testimony from parents who support their views. Of significance is the opportunity of a child's parent to have a say in the choice.

Researchers have studied patterns of school choice by parents of students with special needs in Minnesota, where open enrollment is an option for all students (Lange & Ysseldyke, 1994). Over 60% of the parents surveyed reported greater satisfaction with the chosen school than the previously assigned one. The most frequent reason parents expressed for wanting a change was the belief that their children would receive more personal attention. Some studies have questioned whether such school choice transfers result in better educational outcomes for children or if the families only perceive an increase in quality. Although it has not yet been documented that these children have superior educational experiences, the perception of the families is that they are in a better situation. "It may be that when parents and students are allowed to seek out the best alternative for the student, it has a positive effect on the child's education" (Lange & Ysseldyke, 1994, p. 84).

Students. "Student issues include peers, competencies, outcomes, self-esteem, fear, and responding to teacher and parent pressures" (Cohen, 1993, p. 266). These issues are relevant to students with or without special needs. Lipsky and Gartner (1997) reported that students respond overwhelmingly that they prefer being in inclusive settings, and the voices they selected as illustrative reflect this point of view. Others who have surveyed students with disabilities have reported a mixed picture, dependent on the particular context and the individual. For example, high school students with learning disabilities reported to Centra (1990) that they did not feel stigmatized by resource room support and that they had more positive feelings about their special education teachers than teachers in their general classes. Padeliadu and Zigmond (1996) interviewed a large number of elementary students, also with learning disabilities, who responded similarly, saying that they understood why they were receiving special services, liked their teachers in the resource room, enjoyed their classes there, and did not feel deprived by their absence from the regular class. Scruggs and Mastropieri (1995) suggested that, "overall, it appears that concerns for the stigmatizing effects of visiting resource rooms may have been greatly overstated, especially with reference to the very real problems in school learning evidenced by students with LD" (p. 232). Hurst (1984), using a social interactionist perspective, suggested that a deeper notion of stigma be considered in analyzing the impact of disability on students: "Policies and practices relating to the integration of physically-impaired adolescents into ordinary schools have not given adequate consideration to the full range of participants at the school and classroom level" (Hurst, 1984, p. 223). As a consequence, the impact of social norms, cultural expectations, language use, and social encounters, as well as the views of others on the development of a student's sense of self, identity, role, and status have been underplayed. Hurst reported that some teenagers with physical disabilities, who had experienced education among able-bodied peers expressed a preference for special schools.

Although educators, parents, administrators, students, and policymakers are divided on the issues of educational placement posed by the concept of LRE, there is a common ground. Improved student performance is central to most stakeholders who urge full inclusion of exceptional learners into regular classroom settings as well as to those who are moving toward inclusion but with greater caution.

DILEMMAS OF SERVICE DELIVERY

Since the passage of federal special education legislation in 1975, there have been efforts to provide appropriate classroom instruction for students with disabilities alongside their nondisabled peers. However, the absence of consistent terminology and clear communication about several critical issues has hampered effective service delivery.

Terminology

The terms *mainstreaming, integration,* and *inclusion* do not appear in federal laws or regulations pertinent to student placement (Pitasky, 1996). Each has been used in professional literature to describe the provision of services in the LRE, but none is exactly aligned with the concept. The following distinctions have been made among these three terms most commonly used to indicate the instruction of students with disabilities alongside their nondisabled peers.

Mainstreaming describes the placement of a student with a disability in a regular classroom for the purposes of social interaction or in academic or special subject instruction with nondisabled peers. Evidence from ongoing evaluations leads to the expectation that the special-needs student will achieve educational benefit in this setting with appropriate supports and coordinated programming from both general and special educators (Kaufman, Gottlieb, Agard, & Kukic, 1975).

Integration is sometimes used interchangeably with the other two terms and is characterized by three levels of involvement. *Physical integration* involves placing exceptional learners in programs designed for typical students of the same age. *Social integration* indicates placement in a setting to develop positive social interactions among students with disabilities and those without disabilities. *Academic integration* occurs when instructional goals for exceptional learners are addressed in a typical setting where instructional responsibility, resources, and planning are shared among regular and special education staff (Salisbury & Smith, 1991). Biklen (1985) refered to a fourth form—*societal integration*—more pertinent to the settings beyond school in which adults are integrated in vocational, residential, recreational, and community living environments.

Inclusion most often describes the placement of a student, regardless of the level of his or her disability, into an age-appropriate general education classroom in the local community school. According to one state's definition, all necessary supports are provided when inclusion is properly implemented, including modification of curriculum, employment of special education teachers, additional instructional and support staff, integrated related services, adaptive technology, instructional methodologies that support diversity, and team planning, which includes families, school personnel, students with and without disabilities, friends, and community members (New York State Regents Commission on Disability, 1993).

Martin (1995a) suggested that for those wishing to study it scientifically, inclusion poses a challenge, as there are many differing approaches to what bears the name. He noted that practices differ markedly from setting to setting and observed that "as a matter of public policy, a federal or state government, even a local school system, cannot responsibly adopt 'inclusion' without defining its proposed program" (p. 193). Skrtic (1991) described four models, all of which agree that a restructured and unified system of special and general education should be "'flexible, supple and responsive', a 'totally adaptive system' in which professionals personalize instruction through 'group problem solving . . . shared responsibility, and . . . negotiation', [but the models] disagree on which students should be integrated into the new system on a full-time basis" (p. 158). Some models propose the inclusion of literally all students with disabilities and define this as *full inclusion*. Others define full inclusion as regular class placement for all students with disabilities but on a part-time basis for some; still others propose the inclusion of students for whom it is "appropriate." MacMillan, Gresham, and Forness (1996) pointed out the significance of the term *full inclusion*:

> If it means that regular class placement should be available for some children with disabilities, then it has been available for years, and there is no need for a specific term "full inclusion." If it refers to the placement of *all* children with disabilities in age-appropriate regular

classes all day in their neighborhood schools, then its adoption
requires the abolition of the continuum of placements provided for in
the Individuals with Disabilities Education Act (IDEA). (p. 147,
italics in original)

Separating the Issues

Classification and Placement. Bateman (1996) made a clear distinction
among the law's components for evaluation and identification of unique
student needs, development of the individualized program to address them,
and the consequent placement of a child in an instructional setting best
equipped to support the provision of an appropriate education. By making this
explicit distinction, she demonstrated how the EAHCA/IDEA breaks with
traditional service delivery that, for years, followed the determination of
eligibility with the determination of placement and only subsequent to these
steps developed a program to address students' needs. This customary
practice resulted in categorical placements, based upon classification of
disability and often independent of individual need.

Even though federal law has prohibited this approach for more than 20
years, practices have been slow to change, and even in places where they
have, some professionals have continued to intertwine what they view as
pernicious labeling with capricious placement. The law is clear, however, and
places its emphasis on the provision of appropriate services through a
carefully and thoughtfully crafted IEP. Although there are practical problems
with evaluation and identification in determining a learner's eligibility for
special education, these are related but separate from similarly thorny
problems of placement. Confounding the issues of eligibility with the
subsequent provision of services is, to some degree, inevitable, but it can be
addressed only if the wedge between identification and placement represents
the unique educational needs of a particular child.

Diversity and Disability. With regard to learning disabilities (LD),
both Bateman (1992) and Keogh (1988) spoke to the confusion between
classification or identification of students with LD and the perplexing
learning difficulties of these students that defy even the most effective
known instructional strategies. The definition of LD is even more confusing
if it is extended to include students who are educationally needy but not
strictly defined as disabled. Many urban districts, short on resources and
long on low-achieving students, use special education as a means of dealing
with general education's nondisabled fallout. Gottlieb, Alter, Gottlieb, and
Wishner (1994) described many children in urban schools classified as LD
as "having an acquired learning deficiency in all subject areas that is

attributable to a variety of factors, but not to a learning disability the way it is conventionally defined" (p. 463).

Variance Among Students with Educational Disabilities. Disabilities vary in type and range from mild to severe. Type and severity affect how instructional interventions are approached in classrooms. In 1993, the Rehabilitation Services Administration categorized adults with LD as mildly disabled to distinguish their needs from others with severe, profound, or multiple disabilities. Mixing terms that have one meaning in habilitative services for seriously disabled adults with other terms connoting special instruction for children and youth, however, can lead to the unfortunate assumption that the educational needs of students with LD are mild and easily addressed (Mather & Roberts, 1994). Reformers laboring under this untenable assumption may conclude that all students with mild disabilities can be educated appropriately in general education.

Breaking down the term *mild disabilities* into its components better reflects the often varied outcomes of special education for students with LD, MR (mental retardation), EBD (emotional or behavioral disorders), or SL (speech–language disorders). In planning for service delivery, "disaggregating general from special education is not sufficient; students with disabilities must be disaggregated" (Kauffman, 1993, p. 11). Walker and Bullis (1991) noted that restructuring special education for inclusion "does not apply uniformly across handicapping conditions" (p. 76). This variability among groups and individuals with disabilities demands clear thinking about "how, and under what conditions, individual differences among learners can be accommodated" (Keogh, 1988, p. 20).

Differentiating Service Needs Across the Lifespan. There are marked differences in the structure and curriculum of elementary and secondary schools in mission, teacher training, professional role perception, and opportunities for flexible programming. Even more striking are the differences in time for student contact, with the typical secondary teacher spending 50 minutes per day with a given student and the typical elementary classroom teacher spending 350 minutes daily (Schumaker & Deshler, 1988). The importance of differentiating student characteristics and classroom environments developmentally is underscored in planning for service delivery. Not only do educational structures differ, but young children's inability to use social comparison and normative information in the early grades could affect their sense of competence or vulnerability in instructional settings (Butler & Marinov-Glassman, 1994).

Keogh (1994) highlighted the importance of considering the goals to achieve with students at each developmental stage, keeping in mind that various strategies addressing prevention, intervention, or both cross the lifespan. Keogh's conceptualization of services addressed four developmental periods:

infancy–preschool, middle childhood, adolescence, and adulthood. Goals appropriate to one group of students might not apply to others, whereas commonalties and linkages among goals might stress elements for smooth transitions in services from one level to another.

A PRAGMATIC CONCLUSION

Fuchs and Fuchs (1994) suggested that defining LRE as exclusive of any instructional settings except the regular classroom threatens to marginalize special education from the predominant discourse of school reform, which emphasizes, rather than downplays the importance of curriculum, academic standards, and student and teacher accountability. This specter becomes more real in the face of systematic data confirming the supposition that little substantive attention is paid to special education or to students with disabilities in reform efforts and, disturbingly, that special educators often know little about these reforms (Meyers, Truscott, Borelli, Gelzheiser, & Meyers, 1997).

Keogh (1988) called for rethinking and not just restructuring instructional settings for exceptional learners. Lloyd and Gambatese (1990) set out a thoughtful set of essential inquiries to guide this professional introspection:

- Are regular educators prepared to work with pupils who have disabilities? Do they have the expertise? Are they willing to have more students with handicaps in their classes? Do they have the requisite administrative and institutional support?

- Are many of the problems confronting atypical learners and their schools symptomatic of problems in how the larger society addresses handicaps? Does society as a whole consider people with handicaps to be less worthy, less human, less capable? Is it the responsibility of schools to blunt such an attitude? What changes are needed to make regular education more amenable to serving atypical learners?

- Do non-handicapped pupils receive a better education when they have more frequent and more direct contact with their peers who have handicaps? Does placing pupils with handicaps in regular classrooms hinder the educational progress of pupils who do not have handicaps?

- Does identifying and labeling students as handicapped cause them harm? Do labels cause stigma? Is labeling itself essentially discriminatory? Is it necessary?

- Are our systems for classifying students defensible? Are our instruments measuring what they are supposed to measure? Does anyone really know where to draw the line between normal and retarded achievement? How precise and trustworthy are test scores? Should a difference of one or two points on one test—between otherwise identical people—make the difference between labels? Do our criteria for classification take into account other factors in children's lives (abuse, poverty, hunger, sleeplessness) which may be affecting their achievement and behavior?

- Does the matter of integration depend on the type of handicap a pupil has? Should students be integrated into the mainstream regardless of the kinds of problems they may manifest? Is integration more appropriate for certain pupils during certain times of the day?

- What is the least restrictive environment? Should regular education classrooms be considered the least restrictive environment and, therefore, the recommended placement for all pupils? Under what conditions is it appropriate to use specialized settings away from regular classrooms?

- Is special education effective? Is regular education effective for learners with handicaps? On what metrics do we base our answers to these questions? How trustworthy is the evidence bearing on them?

- What is the place of evidence in making educational policy? Should policies be based solely on evidence?

- Is provision of educational services outside of the regular classroom a violation of a fundamental right? Does requiring students with handicaps to participate in regular classrooms violate a right to needed services? Is separate education on the basis of learning characteristics inherently unequal?

- Is it fair to spend more money on one child than on another? What is the source of the enormous amount of money required for special education?

- Are our special education dollars being used wisely? Would schools be more effective if they were no longer required to devote certain funds to special education and were free to allot the money to serve a wider variety of students with learning problems?[1]

---

[1] *Note:* From Reforming the relationship between regular and special education: Background and issues, by J.W. Lloyd & C. Gambatese. In J.W. Lloyd, N.N. Singh, & A.C. Repp (Eds.) *The regular education initiative: Alternative perspectives on concepts, issues, and models* (pp. 7-11), 1990, Sycamore, IL: Sycamore Press. Copyright © 1990 Sycamore Publishing Co. Used by permission of Wadsworth Publishing Company.

In examining the potential restructuring of educational services by truncating or eliminating the continuum of alternative placements essential to the notion of LRE, we employ the perspective of history and the evidence of practice in subsequent chapters. We review, but do not resolve, the multidimensional issues of instructional settings for exceptional learners presented by the LRE concept. Before considering the ramifications of law, we consider the social context that gave rise to its precepts because, as Sunstein (1996) suggested, "it is in democratic processes, not in courtrooms, that large-scale issues are usually, and best, debated and identified" (p. 195.)

3

The Viewpoint of History: Educational Environments and Social Context

I do not choose to be a common man. It is my right to be Uncommon—
if I can. I seek opportunity—not security. I do not wish to be a kept
citizen, humbled and dulled by having the state look after me. I want to
take the calculated risk to dream and to build, to fail and to succeed. I
refuse to barter incentive for a dole. I prefer the challenges of life to the
guaranteed existence, the thrill of fulfillment to the stale calm of
Utopia. I will not trade freedom for beneficence nor my dignity for a
handout. I will never cower before any master nor bend to any threat. It
is my heritage to stand erect, proud and unafraid, to think and act for
myself, enjoy the benefit of my creations and to face the world boldly
and say this I have done. For our disabled millions, for you and me, all
this is what it means to be an American. —Henry Viscardi, 1967, as
cited in Burgdorf, 1980, pp. 1-2

This chapter describes the cultural conditions that led to contemporary special
education—something that can be viewed variously as a legally prescribed vehicle
for full educational opportunity, an educational strategy for specialized instruction,
or a means by which parents of exceptional learners are brought to equal power
with professionals. We analyze through scholarly literature the history of
American social thought and schooling for students with exceptional learning
needs. We probe issues of social-political ecology, looking at beliefs and
educational placement practices for these students before and after the passage of
the Education for All Handicapped Children Act in 1975. Our emphasis is on the
development of parental advocacy, equal protection under the law, and
normalization in human services and education for individuals with disabilities.

A CALL TO SERVICE

The following are recollections of Crockett.

I was a freshman in high school when John F. Kennedy gave his inaugural
speech in January, 1961, inspiring young people to ask not what their country
could do for them, but rather what they could do for their country. I was smitten

as his words hit home. Two weeks later, along with friends who also passed themselves off as age 14, I signed up as a volunteer with the American Red Cross. While we stuffed envelopes in New York and ironed our blue striped uniforms—our teenage badges of social commitment—others older than we were similarly charged but played central roles. In New Haven, the Yale Campaign for Kennedy was run from the rooms of Thomas K. Gilhool, a graduate student and a social activist in the service of civil rights. In Washington, Donald Stedman, a prominent educator from the University of North Carolina, was assisting Rose Kennedy in planning for the future of her daughter, Rosemary.

In 1962, Samuel Kirk, a professor from the University of Illinois, along with a party that included Lloyd Dunn, was sent by the Kennedy administration to observe services for children with mental retardation in Russia. Armed with their data, President Kennedy requested federal legislation providing funds for research and training, and subsequently Congress enacted the Mental Retardation Facilities and Community Mental Health Centers Construction Act of 1963 (PL 88-164). In signing the legislation, President Kennedy announced that "we are establishing a new division in the U.S. Office of Education to administer the teaching and research programs under the act. This will be called the Division of Handicapped Children and Youth, and will be headed by Samuel A. Kirk" (Kirk, 1993, p. 28). Kirk was 59 years old when he was similarly moved to enter public service by Kennedy's inaugural challenge:

> Previous to the announcement, the commissioner of education asked that "in the public interest" I suffer the necessary cut in salary in order to start this new division. I was informed by the president's secretary that one does not refuse a request from the president and that if the country can draft men into the military service, they can request professionals to serve in Washington and help run the government. I was hesitant but the president's earlier words were ringing in my ears: "Ask not what your country can do for you; ask what you can do for your country." (Kirk, 1993, p. 28)

Kirk recalled that only three weeks after this announcement, the president was assassinated: "On my first day of the new job in Washington I attended the sorrowful funeral of President John F. Kennedy" (p. 28).

The Public Good

The American political imagination was kept alive by a movement for civil rights that was national in scope and compelling in charisma. The Students for a Democratic Society (SDS), driven by their Port Huron Statement in 1962, mobilized youth to radical social action, while Martin Luther King's biblical and historical allusions enabled individuals to see their common ground with others and recognize their kinship across color differences:

> King characterized legal disenfranchisement, poverty, and unemp- loyment as institutionalized denial of personal dignity and social participation—glaring failures of collective national responsibility. The powerful response King elicited, transcending simple utilitarian calculations, came from the reawakened recognition by many Americans that their own sense of self was rooted in companionship with others who, though not necessarily like themselves, nevertheless shared with them a common history and whose appeals to justice and solidarity made powerful claims on their loyalty. (Bellah, Madsen, Sullivan, Swidler, & Tipton, 1985, p. 254)

The moral imagination of the post-war society was receptive to issues of disability and encouraging of a public discourse that acknowledged differences and freedom. This zeitgeist, espousing a philosophy of equal opportunity, humanitarianism, a belief in education as a means of social participation, and the commitment to invest in it economically, breathed new life into the field of special education. A century earlier, Tocqueville referred to such characteristics as American habits of the heart that sustain our connection to the public good. Cruickshank (1967) described them as the philosophical foundation that undergirds American special education:

1. The democratic concept that equality of opportunity should be provided to everyone regardless of religion, race, or social standing.

2. The humanitarian ideals embodied in a heritage . . . ensuring the personal worth of the individual, irrespective of personal abilities or disabilites.

3. The belief that it is economically realistic to invest money in the education, care, and treatment of the handicapped early in life to minimize the amount of funds that would be required for their life time maintenance without such pre- adult expenditures.

4. The reflection of society's concern for the "good life," the hope that through education, every individual will participate freely in the social religious, aesthetic, and scientific aspects of his culture to the limits of his capacity. (p. 45)

As principles of leadership, they directed a course of action toward compulsory schooling and movement toward greater integration of disabled citizens into a society once concerned primarily with their survival and humanitarian care.

Social Change and Exceptionality

National revolutions and eras of great social change can be characterized by the intention and the achievement of a decisive break in both the allocation of political power and its distribution (Sarason, 1996, p. 239). Historians, said Sarason (1996), ask three questions of revolutions: "What were the precursors and why were they hardly or not at all recognized or appropriately weighted? How did these discrete precursors-barometers come together to give force to the social change? Was the . . . overthrow of the existing order inevitable or was it avoidable?" (p. 240). All too often, these shifts in power relationships are silent or unrecognizable, making it difficult to predict the future or make sense of the past. Sarason claimed, however, that there have been three revolutions in American education representing such profound political alterations and affecting every school: compulsory education, the 1954 desegregation decision of *Brown v. the Board of Education of Topeka*, and the EAHCA of 1975. In each case and in some dimension, either by state code, judicial decision, or legislation, the law made refusal to educate illegal and participation in schooling mandatory. None of these efforts achieved improved student outcomes because of the gap between policies of organizational reform and what actually occurs in the classroom.

   Education and Exceptionality. The task of providing exceptional learners with an appropriate education in the least restrictive environment has been rife with administrative arrangements that obfuscate the key ecological elements of human interactions, curricular design and instructional delivery, and classroom management. In an editorial for the *Journal of Exceptional Children* in November, 1941, Kirk directed his remarks to what was then an unresolved and troubling issue of instructional settings for exceptional learners:

> There appears to be some confusion in the minds of certain educators
> on who should care for or educate exceptional children. One group
> alleges that exceptional children should be educated in special
> classes, while the other group maintains that exceptional children
> should be educated by the regular teacher in the regular grades.
> (Kirk, 1941, p. 35)

   Fifty-three years later, Kirk's (1993) perspective continued to reflect the notion of individual differences and their consequent relevance to instruction. He reminded advocates of mainstreaming that integrating students with and without disabilities is not new. Some structured models of integration were established as early as 1913. Other programs have a long tradition of providing either itinerant services, aids and adaptive instruction, or even resource rooms long before the 1970s: He wrote, "as early as 1936, Godfrey Stevens, one of my first graduates, established such a class in South Milwaukee" (p. 31).

Kirk and Gallagher (1979) identified four historical stages that reflect changing societal attitudes towards disability: survival, humanitarian care, compulsory schooling and the relief philosophy of institutional care, and movement toward integration into society. Zigler and Hall (1986) suggested that specialized services and supports have progressed in cycles that swing from optimism to despair, dominated by trends with an average lifespan of about a decade. Progress, they advised, demands that expectations be tempered with realism and compassion.

Reynolds (1991) viewed the history of education for exceptional learners as a positive movement toward progressive inclusion:

> starting with total exclusion and neglect, then moving to segregated residential schools as the modal arrangement, progressing next to day schools, then to separate special classes in regular schools, recently to resource room and other mixed types of arrangements within integrated regular schools, and now to much more mainstreaming. The story is one of a quite steady trend, describable as progressive inclusion. (p. 13)

Richardson (1994) used a more postmodern perspective, envisaging multidimensional linkages from the beginnings of American education with what he termed the worlds of the common, the delinquent, and the special. Rather than seeing special education as a separate field, he argued for an increased isomorphism among these three elements as they have been joined by legal mandates over time:

> The reform movements to segregate and yet educate the worlds of the delinquent and special were critical antecedents to the formalization of the common school.... Universal compulsory education was possible because the caveats to this responsibility were already in place: Those conditions of unsound mind and ill-health were exempted, and those of delinquent conduct could be expelled. The prior insititutionalization of these populations purified the world of the normal and strengthened the boundaries that distinguished each from the others. Nonetheless, these caveats were ritual and procedural boundaries that, together, delineated a single, trinary system of general education. (p. 715)

With regard to instructional settings for exceptional learners, Allan (1996) asked the essential question: How did integration and not something else come to be the dominant discourse within special education?

Research on the mainstreaming of children with special educational needs has tended to concentrate on the *amount* of integration taking place, seldom moving beyond crude notions of how much time a child spends in an ordinary school or classroom, or 'inventories of human and physical resources' (Slee, 1993). Hegarty (1993) argues that integration is an unsatisfactory construct which is open to simplistic and erroneous uses and Oliver (1985) is critical of what he sees as a lack of any theoretical basis. As Fulcher (1989) points out, however, integration is a highly political process which "constructs patterns of social relations in classrooms and in the wider educational apparatus." It is important to find new ways of understanding the complex experiences of children with special educational needs in mainstream schools. (p. 219)

Allan (1996) suggested that in probing this issue, points of resistance should be sought by observing power/knowledge relations, looking for evidence of opposition or alternatives to imposed positions or identities: "groups representing individuals with, for example, hearing impairment, aphasia or specific learning difficulties, some of whom have advocated segregation, or at least separate specialist provision, need to be part of this process" (p. 225).

Because issues of student placement in the LRE have not always shown concern for the effective instruction of exceptional learners, Morse (1984) was prompted to identify the goal of such placement as finding "the most productive setting to provide the maximum assistance for the child" (p. 120). Abeson, Burdorf, Casey, Kunz, and McNeil (1975) pointed out that "translating 'least restrictive environment' into practice requires the establishment of service programs that contain a variety of alternative settings and the fewest in the most non-normal or restrictive settings" (pp. 275–276). Kauffman and Smucker (1995) posed research questions to guide the current overriding concern with student placements and to grapple with the underlying instructional issues of education and exceptionality that lie at the core:

How do we maintain sociobehavioral diversity—both within and among a diversity of social ecologies—that gives rise to and sustains desirable human behavior? What conditions and behavioral interactions are required to move the student toward desired goals as effectively and efficiently as possible? In what place are we most likely to be able to create the conditions and foster the behavioral interactions we wish to produce? (p. 34)

In reviewing the social-political context that gave rise to the notion of LRE, the nature of power/knowledge relations, along with notions of disability and serendipity, provide perspective on both how and why decisions have been made to provide an appropriate public education in the LRE for learners considered disabled in the schoolroom. Where personal interests converged with public concerns, it appears that an idea's time had come.

Personal Interests and Public Concerns

According to Cruickshank, Morse, and Grant (1990), "the growth of special education in the United States has been an arduous and slow development. Humanitarianism and education did not appear simultaneously" (p. 39). The early history of Americans with disabilities reveals society's reliance upon impulses of pity, charity, and guilt to care for, not educate, those deemed dependent in the social order.

The Colonial Era. Rothman (1971) underscored the financial bent of the colonial attitude toward disability by noting that the roster of dependents included widows, orphans, the aged and sick, and those considered to be insane or disabled. As early as 1683 in New York, the first province-wide legislation obliged local citizens to "make provision for the maintenance and support of their poor" (p. 4). To the colonists, such poverty or dependency was inevitable and was not symptomatic of a critical defect in society, nor beyond the capacity of local response. Excluded from this cadre, however, were those called rogues and vagabonds, whose behavior was seen as willful, deviant, and worthy of rebuke. To the colonists, deviancy, like poverty, did not herald a flaw in the social order but in individual behavior. Those whose actions of crime signaled human depravity often went to the gallows within earshot of a community sermon on the dangers of deviancy. Those who could or would not conform were eliminated. Those who had yet to cross over the line still had time to mend their ways (Rothman, 1971).

Colonial history also records the injuries induced by trauma of notables such as Peter Stuyvesant and Gouverneur Morris, a drafter of the U.S. Constitution. Far fewer references are made to conditions such as the cerebral palsy that caused Stephen Hopkins to remark as he signed the Declaration of Independence, "My hand trembles but my heart does not" (Shapiro, 1993, p. 33). In the wake of the Revolutionary War, the Continental Congress paid for up to 50% of the pensions for disabled veterans, representing the first time that the federal government helped the states to provide such support (Shapiro, 1993).

The 19th Century. Jacksonian America had quite another view of disability, locating the origins of insanity, crime, and delinquency within society. Fault for rampant crime was seen as stemming from inadequacies of the family to keep such vice in check in an increasingly industrial and urban era. People questioned how the social order might be stabilized and how deviancy might be kept in bounds. The root of unruliness and family dysfunction was thought to be traceable to the frightening awareness "that the old order was passing with little notion of what would replace it" (Rothman, 1971, p. 78), and such profound social change was thought to be "corrupting and provoking of madness" (p. 127). The development of asylums, penitentiaries, and institutions was the societal response to the belief that deviancy was the fault of the environment, not a permanent or inevitable phenomenon. Society could become, at once, both perpetrator and healer.

With zeal and gusto, Jacksonian America set about fixing the problem of deviance. As techniques emerged to enhance the participation of citizens with disabilities, optimism surged, and charity was replaced by energy and resources to advance their independence. Early programs led the way toward education rather than custodial care. Baltimore's school for the blind was founded in 1812, and Thomas Gallaudet's school for the deaf opened in Hartford in 1817. Samuel Gridley Howe opened the Massachusetts Asylum for the Blind, later to become the Perkins Insititute in 1832; it boasted a curriculum parallel to that of the regular schools to prepare blind youths for work and self-sufficient community living (Shapiro, 1993). Numerous states and territories established similar programs, yet despite these early efforts custodial care and limited educational opportunities were predominant. When experiments such as Howe's school for the mentally retarded, begun in 1848, failed to cure some conditions thought to be remediable, disappointment and more warehousing than schooling was the result. Cruickshank et al. (1990) observed that "although the desire to be of assistance was prevalent, the techniques to facilitate these desires were undiscovered" (p. 81). Only later in the century did advances in technology, psychology, and medicine provide effective tools. This evident lack of progress stifled society's impulse for fiscal charity, as not much more than kindness could be offered.

By mid-19th century, state sympathies were roused following the Civil War, and in 1886, 20 years after the conflict had ended, Mississippi reportedly spent 20% of its revenues on artificial limbs for disabled veterans (Shapiro, 1993). The effects of war and industrial accidents wreaked havoc, giving rise to the new field of orthopedic medicine, while European science and psychology probed the nature of exceptionality and the extent of deviancy. Breakthroughs by Louis Braille and Alexander Graham Bell brought devices helpful to blind and deaf Americans, and optimism was once again on the upswing, ushering in a progressive era for special education.

The 20th Century. Like the earlier Jacksonians, the Progressives of the late 19th and early 20th centuries saw the origin of deviancy in the social environment. However, they believed that the problem lay not with the fundamental structure of American society but with its lack of promised equity to all segments of that society. The question posed by the Progressives was how to provide "the continuity of a universal educational system: how could all be brought in and adequately educated?" (Lazerson, 1983, p. 42). Although many states had passed compulsory school attendance laws before 1900, their enforcement had been sporadic. As a result of serious enforcement, public day school enrollment increased by 55% between 1890 and 1915. Average daily attendance went up 84%, and total school expenditures climbed by 329%. Along with reorganized programs, burgeoning classrooms, and bureaucratic structures came specialized classes for students with disabilities (Lazerson 1983). In 1909, Baltimore's superintendent of schools, James Van Sickle, remarked:

> before attendance laws were effectively enforced, there were as many of these special cases in the community as there are now; few of them, however, remained long enough in school to attract serious attention or to hinder the instruction of the more tractable and capable. (Lazerson, 1983, p. 17).

Fifteen years later, in 1924, Ellwood Cubberley wrote:

> Not only have the truant and incorrigible been brought into the schools in consequence, but also many children suffering from physical defects and disorders as well as those of low mentality. As a result our schools have experienced great difficulty in handling such children, and an educational problem has been created with which we formerly did not have to deal to any such extent as at present. (Cited by Lazerson, 1983, p. 17)

Special Classes. This broadening of the scope of public education was rivaled by an even larger extension of public responsibility: "the belief that government intervention would have positive outcomes.... The state was beneficent, its agents experts. When parents were negligent, or overwhelmed by their social conditions, the state had an obligation to respond" (Lazerson, 1983, p. 20). As an overburdened bureaucratic system attempted to react, a climate of frustration was formed that embraced any solution that could effectively relieve the problems of clientele and overcrowding. When Goddard and Terman began their extensive intelligence testing in the century's second decade, a welcomed sorting system was found. Goddard, a supporter of the eugenics movement, warned the public with missionary zeal of the social depravity of the feeble minded, and Terman, placing the onus of deviancy on the individual, wrote in 1917, "only recently have we begun to recognize how serious a menace it is to the social, economic, and moral welfare of the state" (as cited in Lazerson, 1983, p. 25). It followed that children with less intelligence as measured by the Binet scale could be removed to special programs or residential institutions for the protection of the "normals." Consequently, the effective segregation of large numbers of poor and immigrant students was achieved, confirming what Lazerson (1983) described as the frequently class-based tension between humanitarianism and social control: "The latter tended to overwhelm the former, as the humanitarian concerns of special education became secondary to the desire to segregate all those the educational system found disruptive" (p. 21).

In the face of what we see today as the biased and offensive rhetoric of Goddard and Terman, it is difficult to understand that many special educators at the time genuinely hailed separate classes as a means to greater individualized instruction and prescriptive teaching (Blatt, 1987). Osgood (1997), however, noted that the Boston School Committee invested in specialized training for "some of the ablest young teachers now in the city's service" who would then be *promoted* to the special classes" (Lincoln, 1902/1903, as cited in Osgood, 1997, p. 19, italics added). He notes that in 1902 the Committee approved a year's leave of absence with pay and travel expenses for five grammar and primary school teachers to receive training at The School for Feeble-Minded Children in Elwyn, Pennsylvania. Osgood drew on documents from the Boston Public Schools, 1909–1928, to describe the requisite qualities for a special class teacher:

> Ada Fitts, a special class teacher and first Supervisor of Special Classes, elaborated on these qualifications, saying that the instructor "must be one whose sympathies are keen and whose outlook is broad, but who combines with these gifts, steadiness of purpose and the power to raise and hold her pupil to his best. A sense of humor will help out in many a situation." Professionally, special class teachers needed to be "wise and accomplished," with a sound knowledge of kindergarten teaching methods. They should know not only "how much freedom can safely be given the child," but also his or her limitations, and they should have training "along universal lines of pedagogy" as well as an awareness of "the heart of the child." Special class teachers also had to be able to act independently and use their best judgment consistently while demonstrating skill "in the recognition of remedial defect." According to a special class curriculum manual, "the supreme need of one who would teach or train a little child is the power to put oneself in his place—to go as far as the actual point of meeting with his actual need . . . [to] link her strength to her pupils' weakness, her knowledge to his ignorance, her skill to his lack of skill." (p. 18)

This perspective looks at the interactive, personal nature of specialized instruction as a palliative to the exceptional learner. The special class, to the special educator, facilitated this interaction; in this instance, the humanitarian value overshadowed the specter of social control. MacMillan and Hendrick

(1993) similarly downplayed the extent to which mental testing shaped special education, observing that the issue can be viewed from multiple perspectives:

> The concern with setting variables has preoccupied many in the field and may be linked to the assessment by scholars, journalists, jurists, and some members of the general public concerning educators' motives in establishing special classes. That is, when children are placed in a self-contained special class . . . it is possible to interpret the action as one motivated to best serve the child's interests through special instruction as well as protect the child from undue failure and ridicule. Alternatively, the action may be represented as malevolent segregation leading to negative stigma and lives of despair. (p. 34)

Special education legislation was passed in many states between 1919 and 1929, and special classes and programs grew. An interesting element of the emerging bureaucracy in special services was the rise to leadership of women to supervisory and directorial positions within major urban systems, including in Boston, Ada Fitts, Supervisor of Special Classes, and Theresa A. Dacey, Assistant in Charge of Speech Improvement Classes; and in New York City, Elizabeth Farrell, Director of Ungraded Classes (special education). Osgood's (1997) descriptions of the characteristics considered desirable in early special educators read like a catalog of traditional feminine and maternal virtues. Even from 1870 to 1930, the teaching force for the predominantly male cadre of exceptional learners was female. The placement of their special classrooms "in basements, down dark hallways, and in former closets or somewhere in the back of the main school building" (Winzer 1993) might be suggested to reflect a double indicator of low status—the disabilities of the students and the gender of their teachers.

Winzer (1993) observed that in the 1920s two major forms of Progressive education emerged: the developmental approach of Dewey and the scientific movement of Thorndike. Both espoused a focus on the individual and his or her preparation for adult life through the medium of the school curriculum. Both encouraged the practical study of science and social studies, but Dewey's developmental orientation encouraged an inductive response from the learner whereas Thorndike's progressivism emphasized a deductive reliance on the acquisition of basic skills and new tests to measure intelligence. Classroom teachers in special settings adopted the essential notions of Dewey's approach but in many cases were disappointed in its application to their students. Winzer (1993) suggested that the problem lay in the implementation of Dewey's principles, not their inapplicability to exceptional learners: "The problem was rooted in a notion that any basically good teacher could teach any group of special children" (p. 371). Writing in 1939, Grave observed that

> while we expounded progressive education theories . . . we did not practice them . . . older teachers were skeptical of the changes from formality to freedom . . . young teachers were easily convinced of the value of progressive education, but did not know enough about exceptional children to adopt their techniques wisely." (As cited by Winzer, 1993, p. 371)

Thorndike's orientation became the main influence in special education, eschewing the practical-arts curricula of the traditional special classrooms and the incidental learning of the activity-based model that had failed to hit its mark. "By the 1930s drill had become the watchword of special education" (Winzer, 1993, p. 372).

In 1920, Philadelphia featured special education as a centerpiece of its school system, yet by the mid-1930s the Philadelphia schools ceased to emphasize its importance. This became a pattern in most large cities. Special education issues that had been prominently discussed earlier retreated to marginal conversations limited to the specialized professional organizations that developed through this period and assumed the responsibility for educating exceptional learners. According to Lazerson (1983), a disassociation between general and special education began to occur: "once the current of fear had declined, replaced by other concerns, once a structure had been established to place and thus control the deviants, special education seemed to have little to offer" (p. 37). Osgood (1997) viewed this lack of affiliation somewhat differently, crediting the professionalism of special educators as a factor and carrying the disassociation into the present time:

> Teachers in the programs for students with disabilities not only met the standard qualifications but also satisfied additional ones related to their specific work. Far from being mere warehouses or dumping grounds, these instructional settings established some of the strongest professional expectations for personal character and professional skills for teachers of any subject at any level and attested to the seriousness with which the schools viewed that work.... The perception that knowledge and pedagogy related to the education of students with disabilities constitutes a substantively unique, separate body of information—a perception deeply entrenched in history and practice . . . is a fact of life in educational institutions today which interferes with efforts to move beyond the separation of special education and regular education. Overcoming this tradition of separation will be no easy task, nor should it be seen as a given, or even necessarily appropriate: professional identity of this sort has played a significant role in developing respect for the work of special educators and in strengthening knowledge, understanding, and method among teachers of children with disabilities. The extent and

> value of professional identity in special education thus must be recognized, accepted, and respected. Transcending this separation, then, requires working with rather than trying to squelch this tradition of primary professional association as an educator of children with disabilities. (p. 33)

Early attempts at educating exceptional learners have left a legacy of enduring practices that now form the heart of special education for students at all levels of schooling: individualized instruction, a carefully sequenced series of educational tasks, emphasis on stimulation of the senses, careful arrangement of the learning environment, behavior management techniques, tutoring in functional skills, and a belief that every student should be educated to the greatest extent possible (Kauffman, 1981).

Events of the first half of the 20th century significantly affected Americans with disabilities and their educational odyssey. The eugenics scare with its perils of genetic inheritance, intelligence testing, immigration, organized labor, the passage of child labor laws, technology, psychology, the First World War, and the Great Depression forced society to consider once again whether disability and difference were private troubles or public concerns. Kauffman (1981) observed that

> these factors affected how people thought about the measurement and meaning of difference, human potential, the role of children in society, the prevention and cure of diseases and defects, the causes of behavior and the social limitation imposed by physical disabilities. (p. 7)

World War II. Capable support on the homefront from women and men unfit to fight, combined with the indebtedness of society to its returning maimed and wounded veterans, once again ushered in a new commitment to address exceptionalities following World War II. Mass access to higher education was achieved through the GI Bill, and education was touted as the route to a more secure financial future. Special education similarly emphasized potential economic returns by providing vocational training and job placement as well as an increased focus on assessment, pedagogy, classroom management, and curriculum. As a consequence, special classes were promoted with new zeal.

> Although World War II provided a brief respite to the schools by lowering enrollment rates and increasing work for youth, the numbers of students soon expanded again rapidly. In 1940 a total of 400,000 children in the United States were enrolled in some type of special school or special class, although conservative estimates placed the number actually needing attention as closer to 4 million.

By 1947, 500,000 American and Canadian children in 7,000 city school systems were receiving special education from 1600 teachers and supervisors. In 1920 only three states had directors of supervisors of special education; by 1946 twenty-five states had directors of special education. In the period between 1948 and 1953 the enrollment of children in special schools and classes increased 47 percent, and the number of school districts providing special education services increased 83 percent; the number of teachers in special programs grew by 48 percent. However, still only about 18 percent of all exceptional pupils were in specially adapted school programs. (Winzer, 1993, pp. 373–374)

Twentieth century advances in medical technology were not only increasing survival rates and decreasing the potential severity of disabilities among soldiers and newborns, they were also curing crippling diseases such as polio and helping to define types of school failure such as specific learning disabilities. At this point, disability became more of a White, middle-class issue than it had ever been, and as a result, the political clout and aspirations of disabled citizens assumed a different character. The post-war population boom affected special education rosters significantly. From 1948 to 1968, the number of children with disabilities in public schools went from 357,000 to 2,252,000, or from 1.2% to 4.5% of the K–12 population (Lazerson, 1983). By 1976, this number had become 3,837,000, and as middle-class parents called for better access and quality in special programs, their voices were joined by those reflecting the interests of African Americans and other minorities who suspected that their children were being separated from the mainstream based more on bias than on educational necessity. The civil rights to choice and opportunity were their common ground, and their efforts resulted in the passage of major disability rights legislation in the span of the last quarter of the 20th century.

This cursory glance backward includes a variety of images of how Americans have responded to disability over time and from multiple perspectives. Points of action and change often reflect the convergence of societal impulses—pity, guilt, responsibility, optimism—with the particular interests of the disability community. Rarely have these points been the result of linear or enlightened progression. Rather, they often have reflected discontinuity or gaps and disjunctures in the historical discourse. Foucault suggested that historical events are not really intentional but rather are unmotivated and unintentional, not internally rational or irrational (as cited in Allan, 1996). Extending this thought, social change and public policy seem typically to emerge from a convergence of personal interest and public concern.

SOCIAL THOUGHT AND POLITICAL ACTION

Significant parables in the recent history of special education are best told by those whose wits and political savvy helped to combine traditional scholarship about exceptionality and difference with contemporary political realities. James Gallagher, Edwin Martin, and Frederich Weintraub, who were called to public service in the 1960s along with Thomas Gilhool, Donald Stedman, and Samuel Kirk, must be brought on the scene to best explain the development of federal special education policy during the last decades of the 20th century. Examining their parables requires us to resume the narrative and return to a still impassioned Washington following the death of John Kennedy.

Political Parables

Within a brief six months after President Kennedy's assassination and Kirk's first day on the job, the new Division of Handicapped Children and Youth distributed 14 million dollars in personnel training grants to universities and state education departments. In June, 1964, Congressman John Fogarty of Rhode Island reported to the legislature that requests for aid submitted in response to the Act amounted to three times the appropriation, and Congress doubled the appropriation for the following year. Ironically, 18 months after its creation, this division was abolished when the White House authorized the reorganization of the Office of Education into four bureaus. Kirk (1993) remembered national concern about this absorption of the special division into the Bureau for Elementary and Secondary Education because it threatened cuts in resources similar to those begun in 1959 when categorical funding for research in the field of mental retardation was removed.

In response to this dissolution, Representative Hugh Carey of New York spearheaded a Congressional subcommittee in 1966 to investigate issues related to the provision of educational services across the United States for children then described as having handicapping conditions. Carey charged his assistant, Edwin Martin—a young speech clinician with a doctorate from the University of Pittsburgh, then teaching at the University of Alabama and the Alabama Medical College—to assemble a professional advisory panel to assist the Congress. The group comprised notables in the field of disability, including Dr. Frances Connor, Chair of the Department of Special Education of Teachers College, Columbia University. The work of this panel portrayed the fractured status of schooling for children with special needs and the incredible financial costs assumed by their parents. It made recommendations for an amplified voice to remind the general education community and the larger society of the needs of exceptional learners. In its suggested model for a state plan to provide services, the panel called for civil rights protections to be guaranteed to persons with disabilities and for educational services to be provided to "handicapped children" in settings that emphasized affiliation with neighborhood children. When this was not possible, efforts should be made for connections between separate and regular environments:

> There must be free and easy movement to and from each and every one of these facilities, depending on the particular needs of a particular individual at a particular time. What every one of these facilities needs above all are bridges that join rather than walls that divide. (Education and Training, 1966, p. 1063)

To convince Congress that a categorical bureau to address the education of exceptional learners was needed, Kirk presented charts of the financial data showing the reductions in support when categorical funding was removed.

> In analyzing the grants made for the mentally retarded, I found that when the categorical appropriation of funds was removed, the Federal grants to researchers decreased from year to year. In 1957, 61% of one million dollars appropriated went to research on the mentally retarded. In 1959, when categorical funding was revoked, the grants were 36%. Funds deceased gradually until in 1963 only 5% of the appropriations was allotted to research in mental retardation and that 5% was for the continuation of previously granted research. Actually, no new grants for research were made in 1963. (Kirk, 1993, p. 26)

In his testimony at the hearings, Kirk called for two actions: "(1) the creation of a Bureau of Education for the Handicapped (BEH), and (2) the creation of an advisory committee of citizens to advise the bureau and to protect it against itself and against onslaughts by others" (Kirk, 1993, p. 29). In 1967, Congress created the Bureau. James J. Gallagher of the University of Illinois was appointed as director and Edwin W. Martin, Congressman Carey's aide, as assistant director. J.J. Gallagher (personal communication, November 22, 1996) recalled the controversy surrounding his appointment as a bureau chief, underscoring the need in politics to have a platform from which to speak:

> Let me give you a good example of how someone who knows the system can make it work for you. I found this out after the fact. I went to Washington to head up a bureau in the Office of Education (now it is the Department of Education.) It was a bureau because the Congress said it would be a bureau. The administration did not want a *bureau* of the handicapped. They fought against it. John Gardner went up and fought desperately to do this. The administration said, what is the legislative branch doing organizing the executive branch?

From an organizational standpoint they were right. What business does Congress have coming in and telling them how to organize themselves?

But, essentially . . . they knew very well what would happen if it became a bureau. If it became a *bureau*, then I, as the bureau chief, would testify before Congress. If it were a *division,* I would not. If I were the head of a division, then all of the testimony and all of the discussion about the needs of handicapped children would come through the Bureau of Elementary and Secondary Education. Well, that Bureau has so many fish to fry that this issue [handicapped children] becomes a very minor thing from their standpoint. Now as chief of a Bureau of the Education for the Handicapped, I am able to go up and testify before Congress. See, the only way they have of controlling us is really to keep us quiet, not to have any platform to speak from. I don't know whether that's true now. But at that time, if I said let me tell you about these handicapped kids, and let me tell you about these families, and here is what we are doing, and here are their needs, then I was able to go into the appropriations committee and to say this is the money we want, and this is why we want it, and these are the serious needs that we are trying to take care of. When you do that, it's awfully hard for them to say, "No," to handicapped children. But they can arrange it so they do not have to say "No." They can just not say anything because the subject won't come up. That is what is happening at the local levels. You ask who is on this commission that knows anything about disabilities? The answer is nobody. Who is on this local committee, who is on the school board that knows anything about this?

Gallagher spoke to the need for a special education presence even in an era whose zeitgeist was fueled by high achievement and social action on behalf of the public good.

By the mid-1960s, Lyndon Johnson's Great Society was drawing talent to service across the United States and attracting educators to Washington in the years of the first major federally sponsored educational programs. Fred Weintraub, a doctoral student at Teachers College, Columbia University, came to Washington on the advice of his doctoral advisor, Frances Connor, and stayed in the nation's capital to play a central role for the next 30 years for the Council for Exceptional Children. Although society was receptive to issues of equity for minority groups in the mid-1960s, funding appropriations were never guaranteed. F.J. Weintraub's description (personal communication, January 7, 1997) of his inauspicious entrance into governmental affairs is characteristic of the political realities facing the established field of special education newly merging its services and scholarship with public advocacy:

I started work in June, and I guess now it was December, 1967. We had the first amendments to the Elementary and Secondary Education Act and people were putting through a little amendment to Title III of the ESEA which provided money to school districts for model programs. What we were doing was earmarking 15% of Title III for special education. It was one of the first of the earmarks. And I didn't have anything to do with this. I didn't know anything about this. I was busy out there with state laws, but I was in town, and it was days before Christmas. I was the only senior-type person in the office, everybody else was out for Christmas break. We got a call at CEC that there was a move to try to get this amendment dropped from the bill and that somebody has to go up and save this. So I called Bill Geer, the Executive Director, and I gave him the message. He said go take care of it. The last time I had been to the capitol was on my high school class trip and I wouldn't know a congressman if I fell over one. Here I am, it's late at night, a couple days before Christmas, it was snowing, and the Senate is going to vote on this bill, and I'm up there wandering the halls of the Congress, having no idea what to do. I don't even know how to find the senator to talk to. I was standing in the hall—as long as I live, I'll remember this—I was standing in the hall, and I'm crying because we're going to lose this thing, everybody's going to blame me, nobody's telling me what to do (and I'm also only 25 years old). I'm just beside myself, and this guy comes down the hall, he's eating an apple, and he puts his arm around me and says, "What's the matter?" I tell him [in tears] and he says, "Don't worry, kid, I'll take care of it," and he hands me his apple and he goes off. It was Senator Everett Dirksen who was the minority leader of the Senate. We won the set-aside amendment!

The players assembled, and "the stars came together in many ways at that time," recalled D. Stedman (personal communication, November 22, 1996). What followed was a confluence of timing and talents that culminated in the enactment eight years later of PL 94-142, known as the Education of All Handicapped Children Act of 1975 (EAHCA).

The Social Origins of the EAHCA

According to Turnbull (1990), the EAHCA originated with the articulation in American society following World War II of political, legal, and human-service values and principles embued with the notions of "equal protection, due process, egalitarianism, normalization, and integration" (p. 290). Kirp (1995), considering a raft of changing conceptions of educational equity, noted that equity became an advocate's weapon, "a good thing being contrasted with something less good. It's instructive that no one favors inequality of opportunity, at least not out loud.

Equity has this much in common with excellence—it has to be appreciated as a protean and politicized concept" (p. 99).

In the 1960s, American education moved into the compensatory period best captured by Coleman (1968), who encouraged disadvantaged students with the words, "We'll give you crutches, we'll give you remedial reading, we'll help you run the race" (p. 17). This notion of equity championed equal access to differing resources in order to achieve equal objectives. It seemed the natural segue from *Brown v. the Board of Education of Topeka,* the decision that claimed for all children the emancipatory right to a racially integrated public education. Ten years later, the Civil Rights Act of 1964 was passed, establishing a statutory basis for the civil rights of students in public schools. Title VI of this Act prohibited discrimination of students on the basis of race, color, and national origin in schools receiving federal funds. Congress sought to speed up the slow process of integration moving through the courts by providing a financial disincentive for segregation: Schools found in violation of Title VI would lose their financial support. According to Gerry and Benton (1986), "In the first six years of the statute, HEW's Office of Civil Rights focused virtually all of its resources on a massive effort to desegregate almost 4,000 southern school systems once enmeshed in *de jure* segregation" (p. 44). The Elementary and Secondary Education Act of 1965 targeted schools in general and provided funds calculated to benefit collectively children at risk of failure. E.W. Martin (personal communication, November 12, 1996) recalled the genesis of this federal support:

> It is interesting to note that in 1965 the most massive amounts of education legislation had passed the Congress in the history of the country. There was the Elementary and Secondary Education Act which focused on not only improving education for low income and minority children in Title I but providing services to both public and private schools through Title II library funds. There was a third title for innovation and exemplary programming in education which gave grants to schools with interesting ideas across the country, and all sorts of regional laboratories.... There was a title on research and innovation, and there was a title that strengthened state departments of education. So that bill which started with the billion dollars for Title I for compensatory education to assist low income and minority children was an incredible break-through and it broke down long-time barriers that had prevented federal aid to education. Major barriers at that point had been the refusal of the chairman of the committee in the House, Adam Clayton Powell, to give federal funds to segregated schools, and the refusal of primarily Southern legislators to vote for education legislation unless it did, and debates between the National Education Association (NEA) and representatives of the Catholic Church concerning aid to parochial

school children (Title II resolved this issue along with language in other titles to "benefit" children in parochial schools).

An interesting coda to these federal incentives are two provisions of Title VI of the Civil Rights Act of 1964. One offered an unsuccessful attempt at parental participation, and the other considered the effects of the education provided in the integrated setting. In an effort toward voluntary integration, those who espoused parental freedom of school choice held optimistic views, imagining that "if parents of all children were simply given the right to choose a school for the child to attend (among formerly Black and White schools), equal educational opportunity could be achieved" (Gerry & Benton, 1986, p. 44). The reality of the power relations, however, confronted many minority parents with a nonchoice: "Many felt that the hostility, or at least the cultural exclusiveness, of the formerly White schools would create a socially and educationally disadvantaged school environment for their children" (p. 44). In the absence of true choice, many children continued to attend the traditionally Black schools attended by their parents.

The second prescient aspect of Title VI lay in what is described as a little-noticed provision that provided "basic reinforcement for the radical proposition which would follow both in the Section 504 regulations and in PL 94-142—that the effect of educational practices on the learning of children is itself a major civil rights issue" (Gerry & Benton, 1986, p. 45). Long before the term was applied, issues of educating students in the LRE were permeating discussions of student placement as schools struggled with justifying the separation of minority students on instructional grounds (Gerry & Benton, 1986). Absent from the discourse at this point were exceptional learners and a nuanced notion of equity to emerge in the 1970s. According to E.W. Martin (personal communication, November 12, 1996):

> What was missing, in 1965, was any focus on children with disabilities. They were not seen as one of these at-risk groups like poor children and minority group children, and they did not participate. There was one small exception to that: Pat Forsythe, a very effective mother and lobbyist, who influenced Congressman John Fogarty of Rhode Island, who, himself, had enormous influence at that time. Pat had a deaf child and was familiar with the kinds of [state] schools [serving children with disabilities]. She saw that children, even poor children, in those schools, could not participate in Title I because these schools were run by state education agencies rather than local education agencies. All of Title I funneled money to local education agencies, so later in the 89th Congress, a small amendment was passed which allowed the states to count children in state-operated or state-supported schools for Title I grants

[PL 89-313]. But there was a fight over that—whether the children were really going to be eligible just because they were disabled, or whether they had to be poor, first, and disabled. The passage of the Elementary and Secondary Education Act was so tenuous that the Senate . . . decided to pass the House version and just go along rather than run the risk of making changes that would defeat the very narrow majority in the House. The Carey hearings in 1966, for which I was staff director, organized the sub-committee hearings and helped coach the [congressional] members on what the issues were. Those hearings collected 1,000 pages of testimony and demonstrated that only about 1 in 5 children with disabilities were enrolled in special education. Nobody really knew, by the way, because states were not counting the numbers of children and they certainly did not count the ones that they were not serving. The federal government had no grant-in-aid programs so it did not count handicapped children either. So the best we could do was get estimates and we did that from various small studies of incidence and we patched them together. Then we talked to the experts and we finally came to the conclusion that about 10% of the school-age population had a disability. Then as we went on and began talking with people about learning disabilities, we added another 1 to 3% percent for children with learning disabilities although they were not covered. The resistance, primarily from Pat Forsythe, was that she felt the LD would dilute the funds available to deaf and others. There was some feeling that maybe LD kids were just another version of poor kids who could not read and they should really be served under Title I. Interestingly enough, it was not until 1975 that children with learning disabilities were really fully incorporated into disability law. Now, about half the children in special education are identified as LD, so that tells you what a difference that made. The 10-12 % figure has still pretty much held up, and was written into 94-142 with states being unable to be compensated for children counted above that number.

In 1966, Congress created the Education of the Handicapped Act (PL 89-790), which served as the foundation for the federal role in special education (Weintraub & Ballard, 1986). Seven years later, disability issues were codified in Section 504 of the Rehabilitation Act of 1973, aimed at securing the rights of all citizens by preventing discrimination against individuals considered to be disabled. Section 504 covered all individuals with disabilities who were served by agencies receiving federal funds. Following the reasoning that "rights run with revenues" (Turnbull, 1990, p. 290), two years later the EAHCA of 1975 (PL 94-142) provided states with federal funds to cover the excess local costs of educating exceptional learners. The regulations for both of these Acts were written simultaneously and jointly to ensure coherence between the civil rights protections of Section 504 and the distributions of funds through the EAHCA supporting these students with a free appropriate education in the LRE. Both pieces of legislation required a focus on the individual learner and advanced a new meaning of equal educational opportunity: "equal access to differing resources for differing objectives" (Weintraub & Abeson, 1972, p. 1056).

A Model Statute. The groundwork for PL 94-142 was laid in activity a decade before enactment of the law. F.J. Weintraub (personal communication, January 7, 1997) described his 1967 assignment, as an intern at CEC, to a federal project in which he traveled across the country reviewing state special education laws and their relation to practices in schools. He regarded this experience as a realistic primer in special education law at a time when few others were concerned or knowledgeable about the topic:

> The notion was to try to find out what worked, what didn't work, what made some things work.... I mean, it was down to things like how do you come up with state transportation policies that will work in urban centers and work in rural areas and suburban areas. We would study the laws of the state, spend some time in the state capital. Then we would go out on the road and we would visit, let's say, six school districts and we would interview everyone from kids, to administrators and teachers, to parents, to school board members. We would do research in that district and then we would get in our car and drive on to the next district.... That year I traveled 70,000 miles. You're looking at somebody who had never been west of Pittsburgh and in that first year I was on Indian reservations in Arizona, I was in Florida, I was in Hawaii, I was in Illinois, I was all over the country, driving from one town to another.

These efforts led to a model statute developed by CEC in the late 1960s and promulgated nationwide in 1971 (Weintraub, Abeson, & Braddock, 1971). The model statute was designed as a supplement to regular state education codes, and the text begins with a brief acknowledgment of compulsory attendance laws. "This is included because one of the most serious problems in attempting to secure education for the handicapped is the tendency to excuse children with special problems from the requirements of regular school attendance" (Weintraub, 1976, p. 195). Weintraub (personal communication, January 7, 1997) pointed out the early blend of legal and educational prescription: "Section 102 of the model statute sets out a preference for regular programs based upon the notion that there was a continuum of services. That came from the professional literature of Maynard Reynolds and Evelyn Deno."

The model statute was adopted by the Council of State Governments and in-service training for state legislators was funded by the United States Office of Education through the Education Commission of the States. Weintraub (personal communication, January 7, 1997) noted, in another political parable, that in the early 1970s states were changing their laws based upon this model statute, ultimately facilitating the passage of PL 94-142:

> What happened was that while we were passing PL 94-142, when the Senate sent letters out to all the governors asking for their opinions, the governors all wrote back and said we support this legislation because it's just like, it's modeled after, our state law! (Well, because it was all modeled after the model statute.) It's part of the notion that federal law never leads, it brings things together.

The Right to Education.   In 1970, despite compulsory education laws in 49 states, U.S. Census Bureau data analyzed by the Children's Defense Fund revealed that nearly two million children aged 7 to 17 years were not enrolled in public schools. This was considered to be only the surface of the problem, and one compounded by the frequent exclusion from the schoolhouse of children with disabilities. It was not unusual for school districts to exclude or excuse children who were blind, deaf, "feebleminded," or seriously emotionally disturbed on the grounds that there were no educational programs to meet their needs or because the provision of homebound or hospital-based services were not specifically mentioned in state codes. Education was provided to some exceptional learners who met strict definitions. For example, children considered to be educable would be served, but not those classified as trainable. Often, behavioral or physical requirements had to be met, as in the 1971 North Carolina regulation stipulating that for admission to public schools students needed to be "trained in toilet habits" (Zettel & Ballard, 1986, p. 12).

In the same year, Nancy Beth Bowen, along with the Pennsylvania Association for Retarded Children (PARC), sued the state of Pennsylvania. How, they asked, given Pennsylvania's constitutional guarantee of an education to all of its citizens, can we be denied free public schooling? On November 12, 1971, a three-judge panel presided over a consent decree between the parties that established not only the right to an education for citizens of Pennsylvania who were mentally retarded but schooling that was "appropriate to their learning capacities" (*PARC v. The Commonwealth of Pennsylvania*, 1971). In its decree, the court set out a continuum of alternative placements in which such learning could occur, blending once again law and education.

The push behind these right-to-education cases, epitomized by *PARC v. The Commonwealth of Pennsylvania* (1971), is often credited to parental advocacy, spearheaded by such pioneers as Elizabeth Boggs, and professional advocates, including Gunnar Dybwad. Although this advocacy was contributing to progress in Pennsylvania, a more complex process was also at work, allowing for a powerful convergence of parental and institutional interests, one that linked many of the players introduced earlier in this chapter. Public instructional options, especially for children with mental retardation, were restricted. Many private schools for these exceptional learners, paid for by parents, were provided by groups such as the National Association for Retarded Children (NARC), now called simply the ARC. F.J. Weintraub (personal communication, January 7, 1997) commented:

> One of the things most people do not know is that the Pennsylvania Association for Retarded Children had to be pressured into supporting the PARC case. They did not want to be associated with it; they did not want the case. They did not want the right to education [because they] . . . ran all of these little schools. Basically, they knew this would put them out of business, and so they did not want to support it. They were also afraid if they participated in suing the state, then the state might cut off support to these schools. What happened was that there was an institution called Pennhurst, and what happened was that several young people had died at Pennhurst—one, if I remember correctly, had fallen into the sewage system and one died from being scalded in the showers. Dennis Haggerty, a Philadelphia lawyer, had a child with mental retardation and was on the Board of the PARC. He and I were doing some work together, and he found this young Tom Gilhool, a civil rights lawyer who was looking for something to do. So we decided the issue was how do you deal with Pennhurst. Well, why were people in Pennhurst? They were in Pennhurst because, if you were mentally retarded, you couldn't go to school. We also knew that if you were going to try to fight these issues that there was probably an equal protection argument for the right to go to school, and at that period of time we could not come up with a concept that there was a right to treatment. That was a harder fight, so the issue was let's take on the schools. Dennis took the autopsy slides from the kids killed at Pennhurst, and made the Board of the PARC sit and watch them. They ended up lending their name to the suit.

Burgdorf (1980) credited Gilhool with legal insights in this case that "are difficult to overestimate" (p. 90). Gilhool (1976) wrote of the consent agreement forged with the Commonwealth of Pennsylvania and the contributions made by eminent educators who gave testimony on behalf of the educational benefits to children with mental retardation. Those testifying included James Gallagher, then at the University of North Carolina; Ignacy Goldberg, from Columbia Teachers College; Burton Blatt of Syracuse University; and Donald Stedman, the first Associate Director of the John F. Kennedy Center for Research on Education and Human Development, Chairman of the Division of Human Development in the School of Education at the University of North Carolina,

Associate Editor of the *American Journal of Mental Deficiency* (now the *American Journal of Mental Retardation*), author or co-author of some 30 publications on the mental retardation, and a permanent consultant to the President's Committee on Mental Retardation (*PARC v. The Commonwealth of Pennsylvania*, 1971). Gilhool (1976) noted:

> On August 10, some 10 days before the trial, we served on the Attorney General, as is the custom in Federal litigation, the list of witnesses we intended to call. The Attorney General called together Mr. Ohrtman, Director of the Bureau of Special Education, and his deputy at that time, Mr. Lantzer, and their counterparts in the Department of Public Welfare and said to them, "Who are these people?' The answer was that they were the very best in the profession. The Attorney General asked, 'What are they going to say?' Mr. Ohrtman and Mr. Lantzer and the others replied, 'They are going to say that all children are capable of benefiting from an education.' The Attorney General said, 'What do we say?' Our friends said, 'We say they are right." (p.18)

In recalling his participation in the PARC case, J.J. Gallagher (personal communication, November 22, 1996) remembered the judge asking him a question during his testimony:

> The judge got tired of it [the lawyer's line of inquiry] and leaned over and said, "Dr. Gallagher, can these children learn something useful in the schools?" I said, "Yes, sir." Okay—and essentially that was it, because "all" really meant "all" . . . and if you have people [expert witnesses] saying, "Yes, they can learn," then that's it. It was a simple decision, I remember . . . from the legal standpoint, but it really tore up the pea patch.

In addition to operationalizing the continuum of alternative placements, D. Stedman (personal communication, November 22, 1996) also attributed the PARC case with establishing the concept of "at risk," "pushing schools to acknowledge a higher incidence for all kinds of problems in poor and lower income groups" (p. 5), as well as acknowledging the importance of early intervention as a key educational strategy.

Origins of the Term LRE

D. Stedman (personal communication, November 22, 1996) remembered the concept of least restrictive alternative (LRA) emerging from the PARC case. LRA was a term with which most lawyers were familiar, but one foreign to educators: "I'd never heard it, but it seemed like an apt way to frame the issue." Stedman pointed out that initially parents wanted some relief and advocated for better institutions. Many went along with professionals who thought that deinstitutionalization was the right thing to do: "Some parents were almost embarrassed, maybe they were not doing the right thing for their child if they did not go along with this change." Essentially, parents wanted relief for themselves and a better education for their children. J.J. Gallagher (personal communication, November 22, 1996) added that the poor quality of institutions probably pushed greater integration, especially for children who were mentally retarded. Gallagher observed that the issue of deinstitutionalization became the issue of mainstreaming. He recalled the application in the 1970s of the term LRE as both an educational strategy and a legal principle:

> Mainstreaming was widely accepted as a concept and method of putting students in the regular program. The least restrictive environment was an attempt to use a term that said that it was what we hope will happen, but we know it doesn't happen with all kids. And we have to have a term that would fit this diversity of kids, some of whom may need specialized help beyond the regular classroom. So it means we're aiming for mainstreaming but we know we can't make it with all kids, and so we have to have a term that leans in that direction but which recognizes the reality of the situation. Then it got included as one of the six key points in PL 94-142. I remember the first time I saw that bill. It was Senate Bill 6, and I said there's no way on God's earth they're going to pass that law. It's such a radical bill. It still is a radical bill! But what I underestimated was the pressure put on the states which were under attack by the courts at the time.... The Pennsylvania case was dramatic enough because they chased down 11,000 kids that were out of school, but the one in Alabama [*Wyatt v. Stickney*] is the one that really got the attention of the states. In that case, the parents were told by state officials that they had asked for more money and the legislature had turned them down.... The judge said, you have state property, sell it. You have timberland, sell it, if you need the money. This money has to be provided for these kids and if the state legislature is not willing to do that, then you take other assets of the state and get rid of them. Well, that really got the attention of a lot of states and they said—this could happen to us.... Essentially, the governors and the state legislatures came down on senators and congressmen from their states and said, "Hey, you have to help us here!"

"Well, that's part of it," said Stedman (personal communication, November 22, 1996), who added that parental advocates went through different stages and in their newfound proximity to power brought about many of these right-to-education class action suits across the country:

> Parents had their associations and their friends. I mean they ran around with people like Pearl Buck and Hubert Humphrey, and people in high places who had children and grandchildren with disabilities. They found advocates in Congress like John Fogarty and they pulled strings in the federal and state legislatures to get things done.... They initiated the concept of these class-action "friendly lawsuits"—suing administrators and governors who had been helpful. There are no friendly lawsuits, and some of these got dirty.

Said Gallagher (personal communication, November 22, 1996): "We always put a premium on parents becoming active, writing letters, and going to see their congressman—that sort of thing. But there is absolutely no substitute for having one or two influential people in the right place at the right time."

Civil Rights. Gallagher noted, "Civil rights—you never get a change like this out of any one thing. It has to be a combination of forces to make it the right time." Gallagher's words echo Turnbull's (1990) observation that the civil rights movement was remarkable for the interaction of the social belief in egalitarianism, constitutional doctrines supporting equal educational opportunity, and the developing special education and human-service concepts of normalization and integration in the LRE. The societal embrace of egalitarianism, or the belief that all citizens are inherently equal and entitled to equal treatment, is the corollary to the constitutional principles of equal protection and due process. "Equal protection and due process hold, respectively, that governments may not treat essentially similar people differently or arbitrarily (i.e., without sufficient reason to make the distinctions)" (Turnbull, 1990, p. 278). In education, these social and legal doctrines came to mean that children with disabilities may not be excluded from schooling. Additionally, it is considered arbitrary to deny exceptional learners educational opportunities considered less than comparable to those provided to others.

Normalization. The principle of normalization, imported from Scandinavia and articulated in the United States by Wolfensberger (1983), sought to provide services that were as normal as practicable for the clients served in human-services systems. The notion of social role valorization grew from its second formulation, seeking to create and support valued social roles for people at risk of being devalued (Wolfensberger, 1983). According to Turnbull (1990), both principles attempt to "reduce or prevent the overt signs and differentness that may de-value a person in the eyes of others and to change societal perceptions and values in regard to such a person so that his or her disability is no longer devalued" (p. 279). Lisa Walker (1987), legislative aide to Senator Williams, who introduced the EAHCA legislation, recalled that, "Congress was interested in the normalization of services for disabled children in the belief that the presence of a disability did not necessarily require separation and removal from the regular classrooms, or the neighborhood school environment, or from regular academic classes" (p. 99). Zigler and Hall (1986) raised concern that "underlying the very idea of nomalization is a push toward homogeneity, which is unfair to those children whose special needs may come to be viewed as unacceptable. We must face the fact that normalization can entail nonacceptance of an individual's differences" (p. 2).

Reflections on the Roots of LRE

Both normalization and civil rights have been, at times, misapplied to instructional settings for exceptional learners. Kauffman and Hallahan (1993) noted that, "both ideologies have been of considerable value to special education, but both have been invoked inappropriately in attempts to justify proposals that undermine its conceptual foundations" (p. 79). They observed that some educational reformers distort the concept of educational equity for exceptional learners:

> Some calls for radically restructured special and general education assume an isomorphism of ethnicity and disability, which yields the conclusion that separating exceptional children for instruction is unfairly discriminatory as maintaining schools segregated by ethnicity. Some have used the argument that separate education is inherently and unfairly unequal when children are segregated by skin color or ancestry to justify the conclusion that grouping children for instruction based on their performance is inherently and unfairly unequal, particularly when children differing in performance are instructed in different classrooms. This line of reasoning ignores the fact that racial segregation was the total separation of children for instruction according to the dichotomous and, presumably, instructionally irrelevant variable of skin color, whereas schools separate children into groups for special education for varying amounts of time (relatively small amount of the school day for most) based on assessment of their academic performance and instructional needs. (p. 80).

Kauffman and Hallahan (1993) argued that the notions of normalization have been misconstrued by radical reformers to imply that instruction for all students must be provided in general education settings only (see also Kauffman & Lloyd, 1995). They noted that Wolfensberger's formulations address the issues of societal integration and, in doing so for clients requiring psychiatric services, make use of 15 different small residential living arrangements varying in separateness according to the characteristics of those to be served. For Wolfensberger (1972), this principle had realistic boundaries: "Normalization does not mean that only normative human management tools and methods are used—merely that these be as normal as feasible" (p. 238).

EDUCATIONAL EQUITY AND PRODUCTIVE LEARNING

To Reynolds (1991), the history of special education is progressive, or gradual, and it is inclusive, or integrated: "That history is also describable in terms of a gradual shift, within a cascade model, from distal to proximal administrative arrangements and from segregated to integrated arrangements" (p. 14). Reynolds (1989) thought the time had come to conceive of the continuum of alternative placements as existing within a school building:

> It is well demonstrated that we can deliver special education and related services within general school buildings and at a continuum level no higher than the special class. Thus, we can foresee the undoing or demise of special schools (day and residential) as delivery mechanisms for special education—at least in the United States. (p. 8)

Kirk, in a letter to Reynolds, reflected a less sanguine perspective and an admitted regret that issues of student placement had not developed past the status quo in the 44 years between this letter and his 1941 editorial:

> I think what we have missed in our arguments for mainstreaming is the fact that special education has developed a large number of innovative approaches that gradually seep into regular education. Behavior modification was used primarily by special education but now it has moved into many of the classrooms. Mental testing was started by Binet on the mentally retarded and has led to the use of tests for all children. My point here is that when we can transfer the special methods that have been developed for handicapped children to the repertoire of skills of regular teachers we can then request them to do more work for handicapped children in the regular grades. I do not think that we have reached that point yet. (Kirk, personal communication, May 1, 1985)

Dorn, Fuchs, and Fuchs (1996) avoided the assumption that an essential quality adheres to any one instructional setting and suggested that those who emphasize its primacy in special education are focusing attention on the wrong issue:

> In some schools, for example, resource teachers with wonderful skills and a quiet environment may provide the best learning opportunities for many children. In other schools, however, a hard-working regular classroom teacher may provide the best instruction for a child whose skills are close to those of the other students. We are reluctant to make generalizations about place. (p. 17)

These authors warned that society's contemporary retreat from principles of broad public concern threatens a backlash to the rights gained for exceptional learners through PL 94-142. If integration continues to dominate the special education discourse, these authors predict the risk is real that social goals of equal opportunity will distract us from the appropriate educational means to achieve productive learning.

Since the passage of PL 94-142, special education has increasingly become a tool for implementing governmental policy in the pursuit of social equality (Kauffman, 1981). Kauffman (1981) described the field of special education as influenced by two strands in America's social history: the civil rights movement and the culture's discomfort with differences in educational performance. He predicted that special education services would continue to be considered an equalizing agent only if the purpose of education remained centered on student performance:

> As long as performance deficits are seen as differences in need of reduction or elimination, there will be need for massive efforts to normalize the handicapped. But if educational opportunity loses its identification with performance and is redefined in terms of the amount of educational resources allocated to children, the case for special education as we know it today may be lost.... It may someday be considered unfair to average children to give very many extra resources to the handicapped.... One could argue that equal opportunity means equal allocation of resources, even if outcomes are different.... And to the extent that special education cannot meet the goal of equality of performance, public policy is likely to shift to one of guaranteeing the handicapped little or nothing more than access to equal educational resources. (p. 15).

PL 94-142 has its roots in the 1964 Civil Rights Act, which prohibits discrimination in federally funded programs. Halpern (1995) noted the intent of social movements throughout the 20th century to improve education for children of racial minorities but suggested that the court in *Brown v. Board of*

Education of Topeka in 1954 and the Congress in Title VI of the Civil Rights Act a decade later shifted the emphasis from crafting an education with meaningful substance to assuring the means of equal access to the school house. Halpern (1995) examined how an emphasis on compliance with resulting legal procedures in order to retain federal funds affected the subsequent educational opportunities of African American youngsters for whom both laws were initially intended:

> The history of the constitutional litigation seeking to enforce Brown v. Board and the history of the litigation seeking to enforce Title VI are strikingly comparable. In each case, the litigation became misdirected, losing sight of the educational objectives that were its original goal.... Litigation focused on ensuring that a routinized set of procedures existed for investigating complaints of racial discrimination...[and] counting the distribution of children by race throughout a school system, rather than by evaluating the skills, services, and training that schools provided to black children." [2]

Eventually, the constitutional protections of *Brown* and the civil rights provisions of Title VI were applied to children with disabilities, for whom Halpern's analysis of educational access mistaken for educational substance reads like a cautionary tale. Implicit in the analogy is the need not only for integration but for the recognition and acknowledgment of relevant differences and the mobilization of energies to address them. Halpern's observation that meaningful and equal educational opportunity remained elusive for African American students in the wake of *Brown* and implementation of Title VI of the Civil Rights Act of 1964 suggests that physical integration as the central discourse in educational equity falls short of the mark.

FOCUS ON THE PURPOSE OF LEARNING

At the heart of the issue of providing exceptional learners with an appropriate education in the LRE is the inescapable element of difference and how that difference dynamically interacts with instructional factors. Concerned that some members of the professional community have limited the possibilities for productive learning by redefining disabilities as merely social constructions, Jacobson, Mulick, and Schwartz (1995) suggested that this unflattering

---

[2] *Note.* From *On the limits of the law: The ironic legacy of Title VI of the 1964 Civil Rights Act* (p. 316), by S.C. Halpern, 1995, Baltimore: Johns Hopkins University Press. Copyright 1995 by Johns Hopkins University Press. Reprinted with permission.

sociological description "says more about the limitations of Western society than the limitations of people" (p. 761). They responded to this approach by asking a central question:

> Are all organic and functional deficits to be redefined as cultural sequelae, incapacities with meaning only as they relate to the fit with societal demands?... Or, is there an objective foundation to disability that can be defined, quantified, and measured, a foundation that has something to do with unusual characteristics and features of the actual development and performance of an individual? (pp. 761–762)

Barth (1993) reflected on diversity within the educational discourse, remarking that:

> I would prefer my children to be in a school in which differences are looked for, attended to, and celebrated as good news, as opportunities for learning.... The question I would like to see asked more often is, "How can we make conscious, deliberative use of differences in social class, gender, age, ability, race and interest as resources for learning?" (pp. 220–221)

Although Barth's vision is laudatory, it should not be taken to suggest that all differences are equal. Hungerford (1950) probed with greater depth the differences posed by exceptionality: "Only the brave dare look upon difference without flinching" (p. 417). In reality, both teachers and exceptional learners struggle daily with the hard reality of differences that are directly relevant to instruction. Both must cope with "the tendency to avoid confronting the reality of difference and venerate the appearance of sameness" (Kauffman, 1997a, p. 131). Low (1996) observed that, for students with disabilities, the negotiation of environments, disabled identities, and nondisabled identities are interconnected and frequently contradictory:

> In order to be seen as "normal", students with visible disabilities strive for independence and make efforts to reduce stigma by concealing their disabilities. Yet, in order to have access to the course materials and other rights of a "normal" student they must ask for concessions, thereby disclosing their disabled identities to their professors and/or classmates. (p. 246)

It is no easy task to address these differences boldly with an informed understanding of methods to ameliorate their negative effects, but it is essential to providing and securing support that neither minimizes nor oversimplifies the impact of educational exceptionalities. Teacher and pupil are each required to make an important instructional discrimination: When is a difference to be celebrated as a manifestation of human diversity, and when is the courage called for "to confront exceptionality for what it is—difference that demands an extraordinary response" (Kauffman, 1997a, p. 130)?

Dynamic Reciprocity

Several authors have advanced Bronfenbrenner's (1979) ecological model of human development as a practical means to conceptualize the interconnected subsystems at work in negotiating identities of sameness and difference (Guralnick, 1982; Odom et al., 1996; Zigler & Hall, 1986). Odom et al. (1996) depicted this approach in a useful model, adapted by them to the issue of instructional settings for exceptional learners.

The first level depicts the *microsystem* and contains factors within a student's immediate environment that directly affect him or her or are, in turn, affected reciprocally. These factors include classroom practices such as curriculum, instruction, and social interactions. *Mesosystems* encompass interactions among two or more settings, such as the relations between a student's home, school, or neighborhood peers. Relationships between collaborative professionals also fall into the mesosystemic level. Bronfenbrenner (1979) described the *exosystem* as moving to settings that "do not involve the developing person as an active participant, but in which events occur that affect, or are affected by, what is happening in the setting containing the developing person" (p. 25). These factors include the organizational structure and policies of agencies responsible for instructional service delivery. Finally, the macrosystem envelops the micro, meso, and exosystems, with social and cultural values consistent with each sublevel (Odom et al., 1996).

Imagined in this way, instructional settings for exceptional learners can be analyzed with the complexity they deserve. Implicit in the notion of LRE is a dynamic reciprocity that exists not within any one setting but between and among a student, classroom practices, professional and parental collaboration, organizational structures, and social values. The notion of progressive inclusion advanced by Reynolds (1991), although perhaps positive and visionary, suggests a march toward an instructional utopia—the neighborhood school. The concept of LRE envisions somewhat more the complexities that surround the realistic provision of appropriate services in the company of nondisabled peers. Bronfenbrenner's (1979) model captures this complexity nicely, and Odom et al.'s (1996) application of it helps to articulate what must be heeded and addressed in providing meaningful inclusive settings.

Productive Learning

Speaking from years of practice at the interface of politics and pedagogy, Gallagher (1984) credited Kirk with having taught him an important lesson about social policy, "that it is necessary to have a clear sense of your goals and a determined persistence in pursuing them if you want a change to succeed" (p. 214). Like compulsory schooling and racial integration, the social virtues of physical integration for exceptional learners have been articulated but not clearly aligned with the goal of enhanced student outcomes. Sarason (1996) pursued this notion of clarity and purpose with the conviction that "if changes are not in the service of a clear and concrete conception of productive learning, we end up confirming that the more things change, the more they remain the same" (p. 257). He sagely observed that "people are not in the habit of scaling the purposes of schooling" (p. 259). Unlike the university ethos of teaching, research, and service, Sarason maintained that the public school does not have a central purpose to protect but, in fact, protects the status quo: "It has learned nothing from its past and it has no conceptual basis for an alternative future" (p. 260).

Although his verdict is harsh, Sarason (1996) proffered a remedy: "a riveting on productive learning, on the social contexts that are necessary to arouse and sustain a combination of intellectual curiosity and striving, a sense of personal worth and growth, and a commitment to the educational enterprise" (p. 261). Productive learning, so defined, subsumes the concept of progressive inclusion, provides a powerful sense of instructional purpose, and contributes toward a nuanced notion of equal educational opportunity. Refocusing the discourse of special education on productive learning as described in these words allows for the dynamic reciprocity inherent in the provision of an appropriate education in a variety of instructional settings, any one of which, for any particular student, might be determined to be the least restrictive environment.

4

The Viewpoint of the Law:
Environment and Liberty

This is the essential nature of equity; it is a rectification of law in so
far as law is defective on account of its generality.... An irregular
object has a rule of irregular shape, like the leaden rule of Lesbian
architecture: just as this rule is not rigid but is adapted to the shape of
the stone, so the ordinance is framed to fit the circumstances. —
Aristotle, trans. 1976, p. 200

In this chapter we explain and interpret the concept of the least restrictive
environment (LRE) from the perspective of law, with its long-celebrated
language and tradition of settling the score of human accounts. We attempt to
determine whether the underlying assumptions about LRE in relation to free
appropriate public education (FAPE) have changed, thereby placing more
emphasis on instructional integration for exceptional learners. If such changes
have occurred, has the cause been shifting legal interpretations of LRE, new
understandings of the underlying principles of LRE, or imprecise
implementation of legislation? We have drawn the thoughts of lawyers, legal
scholars, and developers of legislation from the texts of judicial decisions,
federal directives, legal analyses, and personal conversations. The result is an
examination of the meaning of *restrictiveness of an environment* for exceptional
learners within the purview of legal reasoning and interpretations of case law.

LEGAL REASONING AND SOCIAL CONFLICT

"The IDEA is a fascinating law and a difficult federal mandate that touches on a
contemporary American problem—the successful integration of historically
excluded and disparate groups" (Siegel, 1994, p. 134). Halpern (1995)
suggested that submitting such a problem to legal analysis and resolving it
through the lens of legal rights limits the questions we ask and the solutions we
consider: "Framing a social problem as a legal issue produces a transformation
of the issue itself—a reconceptualization of the problem, yielding unique
questions and concerns that first become the focus of the legal debate and
subsequently tend to dominate public discussion" (Halpern, 1995, p. ix, see

footnote 2). Perhaps this is so because judges employ a particular form of reasoning that emerges from their role in settling social conflict involving particular people and particular circumstances. Sunstein (1996) observed that courts consist of highly diverse people with limited fact-finding capacity "who must render many decisions, live together, avoid error to the extent possible, and show respect to each other, to the people who come before them, and to those affected by their decisions" (p. 6). Their best approach, he contended, is one that produces agreements on particular outcomes, leaving fundamental decisions for the political rather than the judicial arena.

In these kinds of settlements, which Sunstein (1996) termed *incompletely theorized agreements*, "what accounts for the opinion, in terms of a full-scale theory of the right or the good, is left unexplained" (p. 5). Participants may be clear on the result without concurring on the general theory that accounts for it. For example, lawyers, in thinking about equal protection, do not in every case theorize about the meaning of equality in a democracy. Instead, "they ask what particular sorts of practices seem clearly to violate the Fourteenth Amendment or the principle of equality, and then whether a measure discriminating against . . . the handicapped is relevantly similar or relevantly different" (Sunstein, 1996, p. 49). In this analysis, lawyers and judges try not to engage in abstract political theorizing in every case or judicial decision because it is time consuming and often unnecessary. According to Justice Holmes, "general principles do not decide concrete cases" (*Lochner v. New York*, 1908).

Judges attempt to blend statute and judicial precedent into a coherent framework that allows decisions on the details to be considered with more or less regard to both fit and justification. A more rule-bound conceptualization of law, associated with Supreme Court Justices Hugo Black and Antonin Scalia, places a premium on "the creation and the application of general rules avoiding open-ended standards or close attention to individual circumstances" (Sunstein, 1996, p. 10). Such formalism can be characterized as impersonal in its principles and its policies (Tate, 1997). In contrast, Justices Holmes, Frankfurter, and Harlan valued "law-making at the point of application" (Sunstein, 1996, p. 11), eschewing a broader reach and paying keen attention to the details before them. Although a case-by-case approach is far from a foundation for law, any judgment rests upon the use of principles or reasons broader than the particular circumstances for its decision.

"The content of law should turn a good deal on the consequences of law. Sometimes reasoning in law, or elsewhere, is simply a way of discovering the actual effects of legal rules and of figuring out the best means of achieving given ends" (Sunstein, 1996, p. 19). This statement is as true in special education law as elsewhere, and those rules and ends will be experienced by different actors in the legal arena those persons or institutions that issue the provision, those subject to it, and those charged with its interpretation. At the heart of the legal discourse is the relative threat to justice of too many or too few rules.

The Language of Legal Reasoning

Educators as well as justices demonstrate a proclivity for clarity or ambiguity of rules, and the application of their preference greatly affects their opinion of the relation between FAPE and LRE. Some school reformers are troubled by the relativity of the LRE concept and seek a more explicit, less ambiguous legal directive to ensure that exceptional learners are placed only in regular classes. However, the practice of legal reasoning in areas of social conflict suggests that two questions be asked before legislation is written or judicial decisions are interpreted (Kauffman, 1991): Should laws or rules be written so that there is only one interpretation, or should they allow for some ambiguity? Should laws or rules be interpreted as strictly or as literally as possible, or should courts consider the purposes or intent of laws and interpret them in the light of particular circumstances?

For many of us less familiar with the strategies of lawmaking, there is an assumed polarity between indiscretion and rules. Within the legal tool kit, however, a continuum of discretion exists between the two and includes presumptions, factors, standards, principles, and guidelines (Sunstein, 1996). Interestingly, all these terms have been used to define LRE. The professional literature reflects usage of the terms LRE *principles*, LRE *guidelines*, LRE *standards*, LRE *mandate*—even the LRE *doctrine*, a term struck from the first draft of the federal regulations (Bureau of Education for the Handicapped, 1976). The varied usage of the term LRE warrants a closer look in light of Halpern's (1995) observation that in translating a social issue into legal language, "lawyers must frame their analysis in terms of contrived concepts, issues, questions, and remedies that the legal system recognizes and deems legitimate. In that translation, as in any translation, there are constrictions and distortions" (p. ix, see footnote 2). It is useful to examine briefly these semantic distinctions because shadings in the degree of discretion these terms allow within the legal discourse could be significant, suggesting that a specific legal intent might be distorted by a layman's linguistic imprecision.

Rules are usually understood as having mandatory authority. "A key function of law is to assign entitlements—to say who owns what, to establish who may do what to whom. If this is so, a rule can thus be defined as the full or nearly full before-the-fact specification of legal outcomes" (Sunstein, 1996, p. 22). In the strictest form of rule-bound judgment, only the facts need to be found: People under sixteen may not drive. The law need not be interpreted. What of rules of thumb as opposed to mandatory rules, and even rules with exceptions? Much depends on the specificity of the exception. "People under sixteen may not drive, unless their last name begins with *s'*—this is a rule. 'People under sixteen may not drive, unless they can show that they are competent to do so'—this is not a rule at all" (Sunstein, 1996, p. 26). We can readily replace these examples with statements about instructional settings for exceptional learners. For example, "All children will be educated in regular settings, unless their last name begins with *s*" is a rule. "All children will be educated in regular settings unless there is a good reason not to do so" is not a rule at all.

Exceptions to rules are sometimes thought permissible only in the face of something understood as extraordinary. The law may presume one thing, but upon rebuttal of specific nature or sufficient strength, that presumption can be overridden. For example, soldiers can be conscripted in time of war because constitutions allow abridgments of individual liberties in cases of emergency. The thin line between a rule with exceptions and a presumption depends upon what counts as the rebuttal and whether its nature is specific or vague, or its scope broad or narrow.

In attempting to set the degree of proof upon which a rebuttal hinges, the legal system employs a hierarchy of standards instead of establishing a flat numerical percentage. Standards are frequently identifiable by the usage of such words as *excessive, reasonable, competent, appropriate*, or *satisfactorily* and are used when a formulaic response is senseless. The essential point is that a standard, once defined, allows for adaptation to individual contexts and circumstances. Once we define the term, "we may well end up with a rule . . . or we may instead end up with a set of factors, or a presumption" (Sunstein, 1996, p. 27). For example, it might be presumed that travel over 60 miles an hour is excessively fast, unless special circumstances show otherwise.

"If a statute says that whether speed is excessive will be determined through an examination of weather conditions, time of day, and popularity of the relevant route, we have a system of factors" (Sunstein, 1996, p. 29). Factors differ from rules more in degree than kind. Like standards, they do not determine outcomes in advance, but unlike standards, they enumerate the types of considerations that might be applied to particular instances. They do not offer less discretion than standards, and often decisions based on factors result from the interpretation of standards. Frequently, courts rely on a test of "the totality of the circumstances" in which three or more relevant factors are considered. Such tests leave room for discretion, as no list of factors can be exhaustive and additional ones can be proffered that have the sound of relevance yet the result of justifying a judge's preferred outcome. Resulting decisions are vulnerable to the vagaries of personnel and circumstances; the decisions may shift without the ballast of principles for support.

Principles involve the justifications behind the rules—the reasons for the rules. "They bear on moral issues, but by themselves they do not resolve particular cases" (Sunstein, 1996, p. 30). For example, the speeding driver violates the principle of public safety; the breaker of contracts violates the principle of trust. This notion positions principles as background ideas more flexible than rules because they bear on cases without disposing of them. Another view situates principles as relevant factors in the resolution of disputes. In this case, a particular decision is said to turn on a principle. When this approach is applied, a standard and a principle become indistinguishable.

In the United States, principles of liberty can only be abridged for good cause in particular cases. At times, the law will employ guidelines, either mandatory or suggestive, to assist the decision maker in determining the limits of discretion. Guidelines provide a stricter discipline than standards and closely resemble presumptive rules. Their purpose is to set boundaries and to require explanation if limits are to be exceeded in particular cases. There is often pressure to convert guidelines into rules, ignoring the fact that some guidelines are rigid and others more responsive to the particular context (Sunstein, 1996).

Interpreting statutes requires the ability to use analogies, to measure the relevance of prior cases and to base new judgments on legal reasoning employed by others in similar situations. In examining previous opinions, or precedents, often a standard emerges elucidating the case at hand. Decision by precedent is at the heart of legal casuistry, or law at the point of application, because no rule is specified in advance of the analogical process (Sunstein, 1996). The incompletely theorized decisions that result from reliance on precedent, as is true of decisions that rely on the other discretionary tools, provide for agreement on particular practices if not abstract principles.

These various tools of jurisprudence can be employed to help avoid a constant struggle over basic ideals in the face of pluralism. Silence with regard to abstract theories can enable decisions that provide for some predictability, fairness, efficiency, and constraint on discretion. "If judges disavow large-scale theories, then losers in particular cases lose much less. They lose a decision, but not the world.... Their own theory has not been rejected or ruled inadmissible" (Sunstein, 1996, p. 41). In fact, these deeply held convictions may be essential elsewhere in law. This logic, which embues the application of law with the power of the particular, reduces political costs while supporting social stability and respect.

The Power of the Particular

There is a seduction in believing that rule-bound justice will reliably settle all conflict in advance. There is also another attraction. Some rules can be described as having an expressive function, giving voice to a desirable posture and governing responsible social action. "Many people argue for rules because they think that the statement in those rules will make good 'statements' or have good social consequences, by pressing social attitudes and norms in the right direction" (Sunstein, 1996, p. 109). The catch is that, by their very generality, such rules can abridge equality. By ignoring particular circumstances, relevant differences can easily be disregarded. For example, "a familiar understanding of equality requires the similarly situated to be treated the same; a less familiar but also important understanding requires the differently situated to be treated differently, also in the interest of equality" (Sunstein, 1996, p. 132). This is a feature of the civil rights movement for Americans with disabilities. Federal disability legislation that guides our collective behavior—including the Individuals with Disabilities Education Act (1997), Section 504 of the Rehabilitation Act of 1973, and the Americans with Disabilities Act (1990)—reflects the principles of this democratic social movement.

Federal special education legislation, in particular, is replete with standards and factors, suggesting less than a social consensus within the law-making body and a consequent need in the law for "purposeful ambiguity" (cf. Kauffman, 1991). Applying rules to issues of equity in disability cases might be less acceptable because of both rapid social change regarding people with disabilities and the fact that each case most often stands on its own (Sunstein, 1996). It follows that decisions acknowledging relevant differences require nuanced rather than rule-bound responses. To employ legal reasoning in the settlement of social conflict—in this instance, to choose wisely from its elaborate system of analogy and discretionary tools in successfully integrating exceptional learners into instructional settings—requires a tolerance for ambiguity and a keen attention to detail:

> we need to know a great deal about the context, and in particular about the likelihood of bias, the location and nature of social disagreement, the stakes, the risk of overinclusiveness, the quality of those who apply the law, the alignment or nonalignment of views between lawmakers and others, and the sheer number of cases. (Sunstein, 1996, p. 163)

LEGAL REASONING AND LRE FOR EXCEPTIONAL LEARNERS

The basis for legal reasoning about LRE for students who receive special education rests with the federal legislation and regulations of the Education for All Handicapped Children Act of 1975 (EAHCA), renamed the Individuals with Disabilities Education Act (IDEA) in 1990 and amended in 1997, and Section 504 of the Rehabilitation Act of 1973. In addition, state codes and regulations related to the EAHCA/IDEA often provide significant prescriptions for services and funding that in many cases exceed the federal mandates and direct the law's implementation in one state differently from that in another (Katsiyannis,

Conderman, & Franks, 1995; E.W. Martin, personal communication, November 12, 1996; Weintraub, personal communication, January 7, 1997). In this section, we examine the statutory and regulatory elements of LRE and the roots of the concept of LRE in the U.S. Constitution. We review litigation securing the right to an education for all children based on Constitutional claims with a focus on the development in law of both access and appropriateness of this new educational opportunity for students with disabilities.

Federal Legislation: EAHCA/IDEA

"Like most laws, the IDEA's LRE provision is deliberately brief and vague, and left wide open to interpretation (Pitasky, 1996, p. 1). Bateman and Chard (1995) describe LRE as "a complex concept that includes both absolute mandates and qualified requirements" (p. 294) "Far from being a place or a placement, the LRE is the decision that results from following a set of procedural requirements in the IDEA" (p. 291). According to Fred Weintraub, who directed governmental policy for the Council for Exceptional Children (CEC) at the time of the development of the EAHCA/IDEA, this statute was "largely CEC's ball game" (p. 15) and that of Ed Martin and the Bureau of Education for the Handicapped. This legislation was developed not by lawyers but by representatives of an unholy alliance of educational organizations (F.J. Weintraub, personal communication, January 7, 1997). Evident from the social history presented in chapter 3, PL 94-142 had its roots in earlier legislation enacted over the previous 10 years. In May, 1974, 8 months after the passage of the Rehabilitation Act of 1973, Representative John Brademas (D-Indiana) introduced H.R.7217, the House bill designed to support states in providing an appropriate education for their children with disabilities. Senator Jennings Randolph (D-West Virginia) entered the Senate's bill, S-6, in January, 1975. Later that summer, both were blended and renamed, following significant tussles with funding formulae. The reconstituted S-6 was passed in Congress, through the aegis of Senator Harrison Williams (D-New Jersey) and his assistant, Lisa Walker, and signed into law as PL 94-142 by President Gerald Ford on November 29, 1975 (Weiner, 1985).

Federal Statutory Language. Edwin W. Martin knows his way around the original EAHCA/IDEA legislation. As Chief of the federal Bureau of Education for the Handicapped and then Deputy Commissioner of Education from 1969 to 1980, he was deeply involved in developing the legislation, writing the law, and creating the regulations that would govern its implementation. In our 1996 conversation, Dr. Martin did not refer to the federal regulations at all. Rather, he very deliberately walked through text of the statute that had remained unchanged since 1975. (Amendments to the EAHCA in 1990 retitled the Act as the IDEA but did not substantially alter the sections addressing student placement. The IDEA was amended and reorganized in 1997. Significant provisions were added to the law, and the original nine subchapters were consolidated into four parts to facilitate understanding [Yell, 1998]. We have chosen to set forth the original sections noted by Martin [personal communication, November 12, 1996] in order to illustrate the historical evolution of the legislation. For clarity, we have referenced these sections as coming from the EAHCA, 1975/IDEA, 1990.)

Martin pointed out references to varied settings in the text and indicated that "LRE was an important element of the law, but it was down the list of elements. The most important element was 'free appropriate public education.'" He noted that the phrase *least restrictive environment* is not in the original text of the law but that the reference to a continuum of placements was built into the law from the start:

> The assumption was not that all children would be educated in the regular classroom with non-handicapped children, although a statement including the word "appropriate" does appear. There is an underlying philosophy that supports that inclusion, or mainstreaming, but the intent was not "all"—just where "appropriate." Appropriate placement is based not on the philosophy of the school but on the individual IEP under the law.

Prior to the 1997 amendments to the IDEA, the first reference to the notion of a continuum of placements appeared in the initial section of the statute entitled Definitions: "'special education' means specially designed instruction, at no cost to parents or guardians, to meet the unique needs of a child with a disability, including—instruction conducted in the classroom, in the home, in hospitals and institutions, and in other settings" (EAHCA, 1975/IDEA, 1990, Section 1401(16)(A)). Related Services were defined next as enablers of special educational services, followed by the definition of FAPE:

> The term "free appropriate public education" means special education and related services that: (A) have been provided at public expense, under public supervision and direction, and without charge; (B) meet the standards of the State educational agency; (C) include an appropriate preschool, elementary, or secondary school education in the State involved; (D) are provided in conformity with the individualized education program required under Section 1414(a)(5) of this title." (EAHCA, 1975/IDEA, 1990, Section 1401(18))

This section provides a clear priority for some standard of quality in educational programming, and Martin referred to the importance of explicitly defining these services as both being free and meeting the standards of the state education agency (SEA): "A lot of programs were run by private groups other than the SEAs, and they didn't have standards."

Martin indicated that where items appeared in the original statute signified their importance, and closely following the definitions of special education, related services, and the provision of FAPE came the means to document that a student was, indeed, receiving them. An *individualized education program* (IEP) was defined as a written statement developed by a representative of the local school district or an intermediate educational unit who "shall be qualified to provide or supervise the provision of specially designed instruction to meet the unique needs of children with disabilities, the teacher, the parents or guardian of such child, and, whenever appropriate, such child" (EAHCA, 1975/IDEA, 1990, Sec. 1401(20)). He noted:

> We defined that rather carefully—what it should mean; how it would be not too precise; it would not be a federal control of education, yet at the same time, it would guarantee the simple statements. It has been made much more of by state regulations, making it cumbersome. Basically, it was a statement of present levels, a statement of annual goals, a statement of specific educational services to be provided to such a child, and the extent to which each child would be able to participate in regular education programs. (There is the first, I would say, philosophical underpinning of LRE.) The effective date of initiation and the appropriate objective criteria and evaluation procedures. That's it.

Placed at the front of the statute, this Definitions section recognized that special education and related services might be received in a variety of settings but required that the educational program for the exceptional child be free and appropriate as considered by both the objective standards of the SEA and the subjective criteria stipulated in the child's IEP. "Our concern about having something on LRE [in the original statute] was not to eliminate any part of the continuum but to assure that there would be a continuum. That's why, in the definition of special education, the continuum was there" (F.J. Weintraub, personal communication, January 7, 1997). In 1975, the EAHCA made a shift away from the substantive policy approach used in the states, which was based on the notion that placement was dependent on category of disability: children with mental retardation went to the school for those who were so classified; children with physical disabilities went somewhere else. Most legislative developers shared a belief that the general category of the learner's disability did not define the delivery of service, and the decision was made to adopt an individualized approach in the EAHCA dependent upon a set of procedures rather than a specific outcome:

> In other words, by taking an individualized approach, then you had to presume that each student was an individual, and required a unique set of decisions based on their unique needs. We focused on a *process* of determining what was appropriate for the student. What we didn't want was something that simply said that there is only one choice. We wanted to break that tradition. If one were to say what is the revolutionary part of PL 94-142 (EAHCA), it was the shift from substantive to procedural policy, so that supposedly we were making the decision individually, not by classes or groups of individuals. The IEP is the vehicle for holding procedural law together... We could not have had this law without an IEP because you cannot have compliance unless you have a document.

In this fashion, the EAHCA went beyond a simple, equal access civil rights statute and directly addressed the issue of a meaningful educational opportunity for each child with a disability.

Essentially, the EAHCA/IDEA is a funding statute that stipulates how disbursements are made and who is eligible to receive them. Martin (personal communication, November 12, 1996) called attention to what he termed the priorities of PL 94-142 in Section 1412: eligibility requirements. To be eligible to receive funds, a state had to have in effect a policy assuring all handicapped children the right to FAPE. In addition, the state had to develop a plan that showed in detail the policies and procedures that the state intended or already provided to assure that

> there is established (i) a goal of providing full educational opportunity to all handicapped children, (ii) a detailed timetable for accomplishing such a goal, and (iii) a description of the kind and number of facilities, personnel, and services necessary throughout the State to meet such a goal. (EAHCA, 1975/IDEA, 1990, Sec. 1412 (1)(2)(A))

"Hear that?" asked Martin, "'The kind and number of facilities, personnel, and services necessary throughout the State to meet such a goal.'"

Originally, Section 1412 (5)(B)(C) referred to placement and to assessment, two issues that affect individual civil rights of students with disabilities. Item 5(B) of Section 1412 is the statement upon which most placement decisions have hinged. It is here in the original statute "that you do find essentially the philosophical underpinnings to LRE" (E.W. Martin, personal communication, November 12, 1996). Section 1412 requires each state to establish procedures to assure that

> to the maximum extent appropriate, children with disabilities, including children in public or private institutions or other care

> facilities, are .educated with children who are not disabled, and that special classes, separate schooling, or other removal of children with disabilities from the regular educational environment occurs only when the nature or severity of the disability is such that education in regular classes with the use of supplementary aids and services cannot be achieved satisfactorily. (EAHCA, 1975/IDEA, 1990, Sec. 1412(5)(B))

Martin noted that "this phrase was added later at the insistence of some of the people who worked on the [right-to-education] court cases that were happening at the same time this bill was being studied, from late 1971, and passed in 1975."

In analyzing the original text of the statute, Martin referred to Section 1414 and its prescriptions for application of the law at the local level as another example of reference to educational setting. This section indicated that states may provide educational services in separate intermediate educational units in certain circumstances (1414(d)) but should be establishing a goal of providing special services that allow exceptional learners to participate in regular education "to the maximum extent practicable and consistent with the provisions of Section 1412(5)(B) of this title" (Section 1414 (a)(C)(iv)). This item referred directly to regular education, but it did so with a caveat and another cross-reference that seemed to speak to two levels of decision making: a practical one on behalf of the district—"to the maximum extent practicable"—and an appropriate one on behalf of the child—"consistent with the provisions of Section 1412(5)(B) of this title," referring back to the key statement in the law requiring states to establish procedures to assure the appropriate educational placement of each student with a disability. When this cross-reference appears, it is within the greater context of establishing a goal of full educational opportunity for all children with disabilities. In more straightforward language, the IDEA of 1997 affirms the responsibility of the states to provide exceptional learners with FAPE and permits states to provide, under certain circumstances, services in alternative locations, including regional or state centers (IDEA 1997, Sec. 1413(h)).

The IDEA Amendments of 1997 retain the wording in the definitions of special education and free appropriate education, but the items were renumbered within Section 1401. Mobility training and Braille use have been added to the list of related services available to assist a child to benefit from special education. The IDEA of 1997 defines the IEP as "a written statement for each child with a disability that is developed, reviewed, and revised in accordance with Sec. 1414 (d)" (IDEA, 1997, Sec. 1401 (11)). This restructured section of the statute explicitly requires changes in the IEP that address student progress. According to Yell (1998), "Congress believed that the IDEA had been extremely successful in improving students' access to public schools, and the critical issue in 1997 was to improve the performance and educational achievement of students with disabilities in both the special education and general education curricula" (p. 87).

The amended text also expands the definitions in Sec. 1401 and reorders the topics alphabetically rather than in a conceptual sequence. Supplementary aids and services are defined for the first time in the statute; specific reference is made to their use in enabling children with disabilities to be educated in "regular education classes or other education-related settings" with their nondisabled peers (IDEA, 1997, Section 1401 (29)). No definition is given in this section for the term *least restrictive environment*, but a cross-reference is made to Sec. 1412 (a)(5) where the term now appears, for the first time, within the text of the law.

With the 1997 amendments to the Act, the term LRE has officially been transferred from the federal regulations into the statute. The IDEA of 1997 retains the original language of Sec. 1412 (5)(B) but specifically calls this provision "Least Restrictive Environment" in the text at Sec. 1412 (a)(5)(A). According to the Office of Special Education and Rehabilitative Services (U.S. Department of Education, 1997a), "the emphasis on LRE has not diminished under the IDEA 97" (p. 8-3). The newly authorized law additionally requires that states employ a placement-neutral funding formula that does not violate the LRE requirements.

In Sec. 1412, the IDEA of 1997 continues to ask states for evidence of policies and procedures ensuring FAPE, a full educational opportunity, and IEP provision. Child-find efforts must be continued and extended to students currently in private schools and in need of special education and related services. The 1997 amendments to Sec. 1412 do not require children be classified by disability, as long as they meet the federal definition for eligibility. This section of the amended law also addresses the issue of cessation of services and clarifies that most students will have a continued right to FAPE during disciplinary periods. The element of the original legislation extending the benefits of special education and related services to children in private schools and facilities has been retained in the IDEA of 1997 and moved to Sec. 1412, clarifying the rights of private school students and limiting the exposure of public agencies to pay for their private placements.

Efforts to determine performance goals and indicators for students with disabilities are now tied to general school reform initiatives under Sec. 1412. Waivers may be sought to comingle or supplant funds to accommodate state or local school-improvement efforts, but states may not reduce fiscal efforts in other disability programs related to the IDEA (Turnbull, Rainbolt, & Buchele-Ash, 1997). To facilitate coordination with instruction in regular settings, a provision allowing general education students to benefit incidentally from special education services has been added at Sec. 1413 (a)(4).

The Comprehensive System of Professional Development (CSPD) provision, embodying personnel standards, has been moved from Sec. 1413 in the EAHCA, 1975/IDEA, 1990, to Sec. 1412 of the IDEA, 1997. This places the CSPD within the section of the law that addresses the establishment of state goals for the performance of children with disabilities and their participation in state-wide assessments. In the original statute, Sec. 1413 was significant because it set a priority for the preparation of personnel to educate students with disabilities in order to satisfy the terms of the law. According to Attorney T.K. Gilhool (personal communication, December 12, 1996), the CSPD is "the state of the art imperative" and a provision that has for too long been ignored by the states. Gilhool remarked that "Justice Rehnquist in the *Rowley* decision calls this section of the statute a clear statutory directive and places it at the heart of the Act." Said Gilhool, "It's time for us to turn toward directly enforcing this 'state of the art' imperative of the Act."

The 1997 Amendments to the IDEA retitle Sec. 1414 as *Evaluations, Eligibility Determinations, Individualized Education Programs, and Educational Placements*. Changes to the text assume that exceptional learners have gained educational access; consequently, the amendments target a relation with the regular education environment and curriculum. In addition to defining supplementary aids and services to support exceptional learners in settings with nondisabled students, the IDEA of 1997 amends the contents of the IEP to "weave in an emphasis upon student involvement in the general curriculum" (U.S. Department of Education, 1997a, pp. 8–7). Some IEP components have been rephrased to underscore the presumptive nature of regular programming for students receiving special education. For example, IEP content has changed from explaining how much the child will participate in regular education to a provision that reads "an explanation of the extent, if any, to which the child will not participate with non-disabled children in the regular class and in the activities described in clause (iii)" (extracurricular and nonacademic activities); Sec. 1414(d)(1)(A)(iv)). Sec. 1414 of the IDEA of 1997 explicitly requires involving parents on any team that makes decisions about the educational placement of their child.

Section 1418 in the original text, *Evaluation and Program Information*, addressed funding for students in different settings and annual progress reports, with cross-reference to procedures for determining appropriate placement at Sec. 1412(5)(B) and providing full educational opportunity in Sec. 1414. The 1997 amendments to the IDEA reordered this section, placing emphasis on collecting and examining data to determine if significant disproportionality based on race occurs in the identification or educational placement of students within the states.

Comments from the Committee on Education and Labor in the 94th Congress as it developed the EAHCA illustrate the statute's original intent to provide special education and related services in a variety of instructional settings yet simultaneously emphasize the regular education classroom:

> The Committee understands the importance of providing educational services to each handicapped child according to his or her individual needs. The needs may entail instruction to be given in varying environments, i.e., hospital, home, school, or institution. The Committee urges that where possible and where most beneficial to the child, special educational services be provided in a classroom situation. An optimal situation, of course, would be one in which the child is placed in a regular classroom. The Committee recognizes that this is not always the most beneficial place of instruction. No child should be denied an educational opportunity; therefore, H.R. 7217 expands special education services to be provided in hospitals, in the home, and in institutions. (U.S. Congress, House, June 26, 1975)

Comments from the U.S. Senate Committee on Labor and Human Resources (1997) in reauthorizing the IDEA illustrate the intent of the amendments to emphasize the regular classroom yet simultaneously acknowledge that the needs of an individual child might call for another setting:

> Prior to the enactment of PL 94-142 in 1975, the opportunity and inclination to educate children with disabilities was often in separate programs and schools away from children without disabilities. The law and this bill [S. 717] contain a presumption that children with disabilities are to be educated in regular classes.... This committee recognizes that every decision made for a child with a disability must be made on the basis of what that individual child needs.... Nonetheless, when the decision is made to educate the child separately, an explanation of that decision will need, at a minimum, to be stated as part of the child's IEP. (pp. 20–21)

Martin, in reflecting on the amendments addressing LRE, suggested that although some analysts might see new requirements such as placement-neutral funding as strengthening ties to general education, others might suggest that this provision simply allows for fairer funding based on child need rather than administrative convenience. "Congress did not remove LRE," he remarked. "Progress that could be made for child-benefit would be very welcome, but caution is required. There are not the necessary and sufficient conditions for educational change" (E. W. Martin, personal communication to J. B. Crockett, May, 24, 1998).

The Wording of Federal Regulations. Contentious debates concerning instructional settings for exceptional learners are most often argued with reference to the guidelines that fall under the chapter heading of *Least Restrictive Environment* in the federal regulations to the EAHCA/IDEA statute (34 C.F.R. Sec. 300.550-552). Bateman and Chard (1995) referred to six regulatory provisions that guide placement decisions. They considered three of the LRE guidelines as "mandatory, absolute, binding, and without an 'escape clause'" (p. 291): (1) A continuum of alternative placements must be made available by a school district; (2) consideration must be given to any potential harmful effect on the child or his or her quality of service by a district making placement decisions; and (3) placement must be based on the IEP and determined at least annually. Three more LRE requirements are considered "qualified"; that is, "they are preferences to be implemented to an extent indicated" (p. 291): Students with disabilities must be educated with their nondisabled peers to the maximum extent appropriate; students' removal from the regular education environment can only occur when the nature or severity of the disability is such that education in regular classes with the use of supplementary aids and services cannot be achieved satisfactorily; and unless the IEP requires otherwise, the student should attend a neighborhood school. If a non-neighborhood placement is indicated, it should be as close to home as possible.

Bateman and Chard (1995) argued that, ironically, these qualified provisions are the focus of much philosophical and ideological debate surrounding LRE: "The central issue in the controversy has to do with when, if ever, education cannot be 'achieved satisfactorily' in the regular classroom. When it cannot, removal from that classroom is legally appropriate" (p. 292). In their analysis, LRE is not a location but a procedural process in which a greater weight is given to the standard of FAPE than to the requirements of the LRE guidelines. "LRE is also a policy preference of the law that must take a secondary role to the primary purpose of the law, that is, to provide a free appropriate public education to every child who has a disability" (p. 294). At the time of this writing, regulations to guide the implementation of the 1997 amendments to the IDEA have not been finalized.

Constitutional Basis of the Least Restrictive Alternative (LRA)

Turnbull (1990) suggested that legislation and litigation play different roles in addressing social problems, including conflicts over student placement. The legislature enacts laws and appropriates funds to implement them; the courts interpret and apply the law. Early legal literature, as well as the first draft of the federal regulations, referred to the least restrictive alternative (LRA)—a less situational term than LRE and one that in this analysis is used interchangeably with LRE. Application of this concept to the education of children has followed an interesting route through both legislation and litigation.

The concept of LRA has been applied to a variety of government regulations, including interstate commerce (*Toomer v. Witsell*, 1948). For example, South Carolina, in order to conserve its shoreline resources in 1948, imposed a shellfishing fee of $25 on residents but a licensing fee of $2,500 on nonresidents. The Supreme Court decided that the state could meet its legitimate conservation goals by using a less oppressive strategy, or a less restrictive alternative, than a prohibitive fee. This decision allowed for less of an impact on the private right of nonresidents to earn a living. A classic metaphor vividly illustrates the concept of LRA: Use a fly-swatter instead of a bazooka to kill a fly (Burgdorf, 1980; Turnbull, 1990).

The concept of LRA has its legal basis in the U.S. Constitution and serves to accommodate individual and state interests to one another.

> As long ago as 1819, Chief Justice Marshall of the United States Supreme Court, in the early landmark case of *McCullock v. Maryland*, indicated that regulation affecting citizens of a state should be both 'appropriate' and 'plainly adapted' to the end sought to be achieved. (Burgdorf, 1980, p. 278)

This principle has been phrased in various judicial forms, including "less drastic means for achieving the same basic purpose" (*Shelton v. Tucker,* 1960), "least restrictive means" *(Smith v. Sampson,* 1972), and "the least burdensome method" *(Ramirez v. Brown,* 1973). Burgdorf (1980) summarized the issue:

> These majestic-sounding phrases have a fairly straightforward meaning. In very simple terms, the principle of least restrictive alternative means that state laws and state officials (and here would be included public education officials and public school teachers) should be no nastier than they absolutely have to be. (p. 279)

Essentially, even if the purpose of a governmental action is legitimate, such as regulating commerce or providing education, the purpose may not be pursued by means that curtail personal liberties if it can be achieved less oppressively or restrictively. The constitutional principle of procedural and substantive due process, embodied in the 5th and 14th Amendments, undergirds the concept of the LRA. The right of equal protection is similarly guaranteed, as no state may deny to anyone within its jurisdiction equal protection of the laws. The right to due process protects citizens from unfairly incurring the loss of a benefit provided by the state. Procedural due process requires two things: that the state prove its action is necessary and that the affected individual be given the opportunity to show the government a less restrictive (or less drastic) means of achieving its goal. Substantive due process prohibits the state from using more restrictive means than are necessary to accomplish its purpose (Turnbull, 1990).

Right-to-Treatment and LRA. T.K. Gilhool (personal communication, December 12, 1996) referred to the concept of LRA as a frequent ingredient in First Amendment cases, and he added that LRA has been put to use most notably with regard to inmates in public institutions. In a long line of cases addressing personal liberties and procedural rights, the courts provide clear directives: "Deprivation of liberty solely because of dangers to the ill persons themselves should not go beyond what is necessary for their protection" (*Lake v. Cameron,* 1966); "Absent treatment, the hospital is transformed into a penitentiary" (*Wyatt v. Stickney,* 1972).

Because of its relevant precedence in determining that residents of institutions have the right to the least restrictive conditions under which they can be habilitated, Bancroft (1976) saw the case of *Wyatt v. Stickney* (1972) as "an absolute blockbuster of a judicial decision within the field of special education" (p. 15). This class action suit represented the interests of adults, some of whom were mentally retarded and others who were geriatric patients at Alabama hospitals. The plaintiffs charged that the hospitals provided treatment that was both substandard and inhumane. In deciding for the plaintiffs, the court established three principles of treatment that subsequently reemerged in the EAHCA/IDEA legislation: an environment that is both psychologically and physically humane, a qualified staff in sufficient number to provide adequate treatment, and individualized treatment plans (Bancroft, 1976).

Bancroft, an attorney, summarized the outcomes of this case, paying attention to the court's limited knowledge, its necessary reliance on the sound judgment of professionals, yet its breadth of power to monitor the state system:

> A little judge in Alabama named Johnson, was able to express all of his feelings about the needs in these hospitals for exceptional persons, in language which is trenchant, sharp, and revealing, and which is based primarily on the expert testimony of special educators, physicians and mental-health professionals who know how these institutions should operate and how the individuals within them should be dealt with. (p. 15)

In order to ensure funds for proper treatment, Judge Johnson went so far as to threaten to sell the property on which the hospitals stood. James Gallagher, the first director of the federal Bureau of Education for the Handicapped, punctuated the end of the story well in his resonant voice as he recalled the pressure Johnson applied, informing the state of Alabama that lack of money was no excuse for failure to maintain adequate conditions: "You have state property, sell it. You have timberland, sell it" (J.J. Gallagher, personal communication, November 22, 1996).

The phraseology in *Wyatt v. Stickney* (1972) is significant because it clearly makes the point that the deprivation of liberty is secondary to the primary purpose of securing individually effective treatment. It follows that LRA, in legal terminology, is not a rule but is considered to be a rebuttable presumption: "when it is not possible to grant total liberty and at the same time provide effective treatment, the doctrine allows the state to deprive the citizen of his or her liberty but only to the extent necessary to provide the treatment" (Turnbull, 1990, p. 146).

Right-to-Education and LRE. F.J. Weintraub (personal communication, January 7, 1997) remembered making the analogy of the LRA concept to special education after reading an account of a harmless 60-year-old woman picked up one night by police and brought to St. Elizabeth's psychiatric hospital in Washington, DC. In this case, *Lake v. Cameron* (1966), the court decided the nocturnal wanderer's need for safety and habilitative support could be met less restrictively in a supervised community residence that would care for her at night. The continuum of choices for her ranged from outpatient care to foster care, "thereafter half-way houses, then day hospitals, then nursing homes, all the way to full-time hospitals" (Bancroft, 1976, p. 16). Legally, the degree of restriction for her depended on the severity of the problem and the skillful use of professional techniques available for her supervision. To Weintraub, the parallels with educational practices for exceptional learners were clear. Some students might require a separate instructional placement from the regular classroom; others might not. A mechanism was needed to ensure the protection of a student's liberty while assuring an education that provided him or her with a meaningful educational opportunity.

T.K. Gilhool (personal communication, December 12, 1996), who called LRE a "nefarious concept," attempted to set the record straight about the application of the LRA/LRE concept to education. Gilhool noted that the phrase did not arise from the right-to-education cases, which were based on the constitutional principle of equal protection, but rather from the very different cases that emphasized the right-to-treatment within mental health institutionalization. Because "schools are not a closed institution like the institutions to which people are involuntarily committed" he views LRA/LRE as misapplied. Said Gilhool: "Equality and integration are the imperatives of the Act."

The Role of Litigation. According to Gilhool (1976a), disability litigation provides four functions, including securing a substantive right, ensuring that right through due process, advancing relevant issues in the public eye, and allowing petition for redress. As lead council for the prosecution in *Pennsylvania Association for Retarded Children (PARC) v. The Commonwealth of Pennsylvania* (1971), described in chap. 3, Gilhool successfully challenged the total and functional exclusion of students who were mentally retarded from school by using an equal protection argument as well as by advancing a due process claim based upon the stigma or "badge of disgrace" theory. To provide a remedy and to ensure the right to a meaningful education, the parties to the consent decree agreed to the provision of a continuum that allowed the Commonwealth of Pennsylvania

> to place each mentally retarded child in a free, public program of education and training appropriate to the child's capacity, within the context of the general educational policy that, among the alternative programs of education and training required by statute to be available, placement in a regular public school class is preferable to placement in a special public school class and placement in a special public school class is preferable to placement in any other type of program of education and training. (*Pennsylvania Association for Retarded Children (PARC) v. The Commonwealth of Pennsylvania*, 1971)

The *PARC* case placed a clear value on regular class placement for students who were mentally retarded, but in transferring children from private to public programs when applying the remedy, the decree also called for emphasis on the appropriateness of these programs for particular children. In this sense, the court demonstrated a judicial preference in its remedy (Burgdorf, 1980).

The case of *Mills v. Board of Education* (1972) secured education in the public schools of Washington, DC, for all exceptional students, not just those who were mentally retarded, regardless of the nature or severity of their disability. *Mills* expanded upon the *PARC* case but similarly required alternative educational placements designed to meet individual needs. Burgdorf (1980) observed that, even though the Mills case followed *PARC*, "the D.C. court was the first to apply to handicapped individuals the phraseology of 'equal educational opportunity'—the equal protection clause in its application to public school education'" (p.109). Nationwide, similar cases clamored the state courts for redress of the exclusion of handicapped children. Between 1972 and 1974, 46 similar cases were heard in 28 different states (Zettel & Ballard, 1986).

LRE and Values: Personal Liberty and Individual Needs

In trying to reconcile the relation between LRE and FAPE, a fundamental question is generated: "Does appropriateness drive placement, or is placement the starting point for any consideration of an appropriate education?" (Siegel, 1994, p. 134). Turnbull (1990) described the LRA concept as a means by which to balance the values surrounding the provision of an "appropriate education (the student's right to and need for an appropriate education) with the values of individual rights of association. It is supported by, and implemented through, the constitutional principles of procedural due process, substantive due process, and equal protection" (p. 148). As applied to education, LRA seems at first blush to have its roots in *Brown v. the Board of Education* (1954) in which the Supreme Court found no reason for the racial segregation of students in American schools. The repudiation of educational segregation by race became fused in the 1960s with sociological theory and the views of some special educators claiming that educational separation could reinforce stigma. This perspective holds that by separating children "into isolated groups and labeling them 'mentally retarded,' 'mentally deficient,' 'untrainable,' or even some of the more avant-garde terms such as 'exceptional' or 'special,' has a stigmatizing effect upon those children" (Burgdorf, 1980, p. 91).

These views coalesced in a 1969 right-to-education case in Utah involving two students, 18-year-old Richard Paulsen and 12-year-old Joan Wolf, who are described in *Wolf v. Legislature of the State of Utah* (1969) as "mentally retarded, having IQs in a range defining them as trainable, and [who] have been denied admission to the regularly constituted common school system of the State of Utah." Both students were enrolled in private daycare centers at parental expense. The decision in this case, relying heavily on *Brown*, speaks directly to society at large but addresses less precisely the quality or character of education that students with learning differences receive in the classroom:

> Today it is doubtful that any child may reasonably be expected to succeed in life if he is denied the right and opportunity of an education. In the instant case, the segregation of the plaintiff children from the public school system has detrimental effects upon the children as well as their parents. The impact is greater when it has the apparent sanction of the law for the policy of placing these children under the Department of Welfare and segregating them from the educational system, can be and probably is usually interpreted as denoting their inferiority, unusualness, uselessness and incompetency. A sense of inferiority and not belonging affects the motivation of a child to learn. Segregation, even though perhaps well intentioned, under the apparent sanction of law and state authority has a tendency to retard the educational, emotional and mental development of the children.

A tendency to retard a child's development was not a *fête accompli*, however. Legal reasoning has long made room for ambiguity. "While segregation or separation is generally harmful, it may sometimes be appropriate. The law has never stated that equal treatment means identical treatment for different types of persons" (Burgdorf, 1980, p. 280; see also Semmel, Gerber, & MacMillan, 1994).

As interpreted in the later right-to-education cases for children with disabilities, the equal protection principle evolved beyond what had emerged as "the equal access doctrine" in *Brown*—"that when a school system provides facilities to white children, exactly the same facilities (not an equivalent separate set of facilities) must be made available on the same terms to black children" (Turnbull, 1990, p. 33). A more fully developed theory of equal access views the variable of disability, unlike race, as educationally relevant and establishes claims for exceptional learners "to *differing* resources for *differing* purposes" (p. 71). Equal educational opportunity for any particular child at any particular time might consist of any of the following:

> being treated *exactly equally . . . equal treatment plus accommodations . . . different (but favorable) treatment.* There is an important reason that equality means something different for handicapped children than it does for nonhandicapped children, thus, one major reason that the new equal access doctrine was worthy of being recognized and legitimized by the courts. The major reason is *the child's disability is a distinction that justifies a different approach.* (Turnbull, 1990, p. 71, italics in original)

To allow for access to appropriate services, courts deciding the class-action right-to-education cases in the early 1970s borrowed the notions of using an individually focused treatment perspective in applying remedies and employing the device of a continuum of placements from the right-to-treatment cases such as *Wyatt v. Stickney* (1972), and *Lake v. Cameron* (1966). LRA, in the right-to-education cases, was similarly considered to be a presumption of how things would take place, not a hard and fast rule.

LRA as a Presumption.   Turnbull (1990) pointed out that, in these cases, LRA was "no more than a *preference* in favor of regular educational placement; it was not an inflexible rule. It was a guide for conduct, not a rule of conduct. As a guide, it did not prohibit alternatives to regular class and regular school placement" (p. 149, italics in original). Yet it simultaneously encouraged placement in regular settings as a means to counter contemporary stereotypes that children with disabilities were not only different but deficient and should not be schooled alongside nondisabled youngsters. The flexibility of the LRA concept allowed for the redress of total exclusion by requiring access to a public education as well as of functional exclusion by providing a meaningful education in an appropriate program. In short, it addressed both types of exclusion for exceptional learners, "with an emphasis on the latter" (p. 149).

In Turnbull's (1990) legal analysis, LRA is a rebuttable presumption or "a rule of conduct that must be followed in every case unless; in a particular case, it can be demonstrated that the general rule will have unacceptable consequences for the affected individual" (p. 163). LRA, then, is not an immutable rule but a rebuttable presumption favoring integration but allowing separation: "Presumptively...segregating placement is more harmful than regular school placement. Only when it is shown that such a placement is necessary for appropriate education purposes in order to satisfy the individual's interests or valid state purposes is the presumption overcome" (p. 163). Turnbull viewed rebuttable presumptions as positive policy tools that offer affected parties greater "*freedom of choice*" (p. 163, italics in original) and protection from having no alternative to something perceived as harmful. Ambiguity, however, is embedded in the complexity of determining what constitutes a suitable rebuttal. In this instance, "LRA is inextricably tied to the notion of appropriateness, which makes it all the more complex because appropriate education itself is difficult to define" (p. 161). This analysis distinguishes sociological considerations from educational concerns by establishing LRA as both a legal principle and an educational strategy. Although the constitutional basis of LRA requires the government, when it has a legitimate interest, to take actions that least drastically restrict a citizens' liberty, "it is another thing altogether to answer the question: What is an unwarranted or unnecessary restriction of a handicapped child when the state is required to educate him or her appropriately?" (p. 162).

Integration as a Rule.   The individualized focus of the EAHCA/IDEA legislation inhibits class action suits like those of the early 1970s, which forged the right to an education on constitutional grounds to a group of children—those with disabilities—who had been totally excluded from public education (Osborne, 1992b). LRE suits brought under the statute and regulations of the EAHCA/IDEA can be forwarded only on behalf of an individual child. "One of the things that drives advocacy groups nuts about 94-142 is that generally there is no class advocacy," said Weintraub (personal communication, January 7, 1997):

> The alternative was to say that what we will do is follow the model
> of traditional '60s advocacy, that we will put the power in the hands
> of the few, so that they can do what they believe is right for the
> many. And that we were not about to do. That's why this law is like
> no other. That is where this law was revolutionary because it
> dramatically changed how the game was played.

In contrast, civil rights advocate T.K. Gilhool (personal communication, August 11, 1998) took the position that "an exclusive focus on individuals allows schools to avoid recognizing and implementing strong systems of teaching which work for very many children." Gilhool suggested that the opposite of individual due process is not "groups" but substance. He also contended that an appropriate education, integration, and best teaching practices represented equal and substantive statutory imperatives:

> The appropriate education imperative (FAPE is an education program reasonably calculated to yield real educational benefits, usually grade to grade progress); the integration imperative (children who are handicapped will be educated with children who are not); and the state-of-the-art imperative (i.e. every state and district must acquire knowledge of, disseminate, and adopt promising education practices which have a track record of success).
>
> Individualization, whether IEPs, due process, evaluations, or whatever, is a means of getting there in service to the substantive objectives. Too many districts have avoided substance altogether—put another way, they have avoided knowledge, and in particular, pedagogical knowledge—in favor of processing families and children to death.

His current thinking seems to be consistent with his earlier position expressed in a letter to Edwin Martin, then Director of the Bureau of Education for the Handicapped in the U.S. Office of Education. Gilhool (T.K. Gilhool, personal communication, September 27, 1976) referred to children who are severely and profoundly retarded, suggesting that separate settings for them perpetuate vested interests and equating integration with an appropriate education:

> At root is the understanding . . . that severely and profoundly retarded children, let alone others, do not *require* segregation, and indeed are harmed, as are the rest of us, by segregation... Little is achieved if the segregation of the institution is traded for the segregation of the "special center" . . . Equally, while everyone would concede some children who for some time require homebound or other isolated instruction (as Congress recognized in speaking of grades of isolation, "special classes, separate schooling, or other removal of handicapped children from the regular educational environment"), educators of the severe and profound . . . who are free of administrative or other interests in the maintenance of "special centers," say clearly that most severely and profoundly retarded children will profit in their education from being with children who are not handicapped and indeed that *appropriate* education requires integration. (emphasis in original)

Attorney Mark Weber (1992) took a position similar to Gilhool's. Weber, an attorney, viewed LRE as an equal partner of FAPE because, in his opinion, failure to do so would eliminate pressure on school districts to increase the provision of services in the general education setting for exceptional learners. He equated this push as equivalent to the one that spurred racial integration of schools in words that bring to mind those offered by the court in *Wolf v. Legislature of the State of Utah* (1969):

> Forced separation of children with disabilities, like forced separation of minority children, fosters inequality. In fact, the history of legal exclusion of children with disabilities from school places them in an inferior position quite similar to that of black children who were legally barred from schools attended by whites. Courts have ordered school authorities who excluded children on the basis of race to provide special, enhanced services to permit the previously excluded children to take full advantage of newly integrated public school programs, as a means of eliminating the inferiority previously imposed by separate schooling. The comparison to children with disabilities would suggest that the schools should affirmatively provide the services to enable children with disabilities to prosper in mainstreamed settings from which they previously would have been barred. (Weber, 1992, p. 9:5)

In this analysis, Weber considered children with disabilities as a class or a group that, by virtue of their commonality as exceptional learners, is similarly situated with regard to the general education environment. In this approach, there is no sense of dynamic relativity or tension in the relation of FAPE and LRE; they are separate from one another and of equal weight. The LRE is defined as an integrated setting in which the best instructional practices are employed to address the individual educational needs of a child. It follows from this conceptualization that FAPE, as defined by the goals of the IEP, could only be provided in the setting for children without disabilities. To do otherwise would be considered discriminatory, not appropriate. This approach also uses the standard of FAPE but seems to rely on a different background principle in defining educational benefit. Normalization is the principle that gives greater weight to collective placement of exceptional learners with nondisabled peers than to the restrictive or enhancing instructional properties the regular class setting might provide to an individual learner. In this analysis, LRE is not a subset of FAPE. It is an independent variable, based on the principle of societal normalization and freedom of association. Integration becomes the rule of placement. LRE is consequently seen as an educational product rather than an administrative strategy (Turnbull, 1990).

Weber's (1992) view, written 23 years after the Utah decision, raises anew questions of equal educational opportunity. The concept of LRE has be controversial since the writing of the federal regulations in 1976, with some people, like Gilhool, objecting to its deemphasis on integration. It is interesting to note that a section from the first consolidated draft of the proposed federal regulations (Bureau of Education for the Handicapped,

1976) requiring states to submit deinstitutionalization plans was deleted, as were federal requirements for criteria and procedures in the construction of new, local educational facilities. In recalling the development of the statute itself, E.W. Martin (personal communication, November 12, 1996) referred to the controversy surrounding the insertion of what would become the pivotal Sec. 1412(5)(B). He pointed out that the qualifier referring to the removal of children with disabilities from regular classrooms, only when their progress "cannot be achieved satisfactorily," was added later at the insistence of advocates who had worked on the contemporary right-to-education cases. At the time of the EAHCA's development from 1971 to 1975, the issue of institutions was a key variable in civil rights litigation, stemming from cases like *PARC* that were brought on behalf of retarded citizens and children who were excluded from public schools. This emphasis was precisely why the drafters of the law inserted the caveat, "to the maximum extent appropriate" into the beginning of Section 1412(5)(B):

> LRE really grew out of the interests in institutionalization and de-institutionalization. Civil rights attorneys, particularly Tom Gilhool, I would think, were very committed to that principle and extended it and wanted to extend it to the everyday life of the school. At the same time, parents, and teachers who were working in the special education system, never really conceived that there would only be a mainstreamed environment for children with disabilities. That is why, right through the law, there are so many references to other settings. So these two clash a bit in their philosophy and have—although even this phrase says, (and this was important, and I can remember the discussion that put this phrase in) "to the maximum extent appropriate." I was arguing, based on my work with deaf children and emotionally disturbed children, that it would not be appropriate for every child to be in the regular class, and it had to be clear that these options existed for children for whom it would not be appropriate. At the same time, we also knew that many children were unnecessarily segregated and, therefore, we wanted to put as much emphasis as possible on having children go into the programs that were maximally appropriate for them. In many cases, for mildly handicapped children, there was no reason they could not be in regular classes full-time or part-time. So, I would say, the larger context of this law was, in its early development and even in its current state, a law that emphasized service to children, free appropriate public education, finding the children, educating them in the environments that were appropriate to them, and, within that context, encouraging their participation in regular education. Some of the court rulings . . . seem to have gone beyond that, taking this

phrase that I just read you very literally and, if you take it too literally, it would mean that children would have to fail in an educational environment in order to be able to demonstrate "that the education in regular classrooms with the use of supplementary aids could not be achieved satisfactorily." If you do not demand an actual trial and failure, then you are back to using the best judgment of the professional education staff during the IEP process (which is happening), or (what is happening in state or local law or policy) essentially insisting on including students—which is, in a sense, overriding the question of "to the maximum extent appropriate. (Martin, 1996).

Dimensions of the LRA Policy

Turnbull (1990) attempts to synthesize competing conceptualizations of LRA through examination of value assumptions that are both based on legal principles in the U.S. Constitution, and on educational strategies that produce social effects. His analysis is depicted in a matrix of educational and sociological values that interact with underlying value assumptions about the right to an appropriate education and the right of association.

TABLE
Dimensions of the LRA Policy

	Value Assumptions	
Value Assumptions	A. That individuals and societies benefit when all are educated to our fullest potential.	B. That individuals and society benefit when all its members are free to associate with each other.
Produce: Legal Principles & Educational Strategies	1. Right to Education 2. Appropriate Education	4. Right to Association 5. Integration
Resulting in: Social Effects	3. Enhanced Individual Potential	6. Decreased Stigma

Source: From *Free Appropriate Public Education: The Law and Children with Disabilities.* H. R. Turnbull (1990), p. 165. Reproduced by permission of Love Publishing Company.

According to this analysis, one conceptualization of LRA arises from values that emphasize the right of association, whereas another is grounded in values that assume the right to full educational opportunity. Turnbull (1990) saw the EAHCA/IDEA as embodying all six elements. Although this schematic analysis provides a helpful distinction between theories originating from educational or sociological goals, for practical application Turnbull relied on the LRA as a rebuttable presumption in order to determine "how these goals are to be implemented and how the value conflicts embedded in the goals can be resolved in practice" (p. 166).

Also an attorney, Siegel regards the IDEA as "inherently a law of placement" (Siegel, 1994, p. 36). He took issue with Gilhool's emphasis on generic integration in the law and Weber's equalizing conceptualization of FAPE and LRE, arguing that changes in the language throughout the legislation suggest that greater relativity and practicality are implicit in LRE. "IDEA uses the phrase 'the extent' to which a child '*will participate*,' then shifts to the 'maximum extent *appropriate*,' and finally, in Section 1414, turns 'to the maximum extent *practicable*'" (p. 36, italics in original). Siegel (1994) made a practical suggestion that the language of both the original statute and its regulations establishes a distinction between levels of decision making with regard to the provision of FAPE and LRE—one at the district level and another at the level of the learner. He suggested that *practicable* speaks to the needs of the provider (the school district), whereas *appropriate* speaks to the needs of the student. "What is practicable may very well be less than appropriate for the child, and what is appropriate may very well be impracticable for the district. Practicable gives the administrator leeway, appropriate nudges the balance toward the child, and 'possible' narrows the school's flexibility" (p. 37).

To emphasize the inherent relativity and practicality of the concept, Weintraub (personal communication, January 7, 1997) leaned across his desk during our interview and said with conviction:

> LRE exists only in a context of individual decision-making...
> I believe in inclusion. I also believe in special schools.... But as soon
> as government steps in and says there will not be these choices, then
> the whole principle is gone. So if I argue for a special school, I am
> not arguing because I believe in special schools. I do not believe in
> them any more or less than I believe in integration. I am just not an
> ideologue on these issues. I am only an ideologue about the power of
> people who know a child, who are concerned about a child, to make
> choices about the child without some other advocacy group, be they
> private or governmental, who do not know the child, coming in and
> telling them—telling them what is right. This is not an issue you are
> going to win by engaging in the great philosophical debate about
> integration. This is not about integration. This is about an

opportunity to learn.... My point is that it is all within the context of
where you are, and where you live, and this child, and this family.

Rebutting the Presumption

Bateman and Chard (1995) noted that the federal regulations to the original
EAHCA/IDEA statute place the focus clearly on a child's need for an
appropriate education and the school district's or local educational agency's
(LEA) responsibility to provide special education and related services along a
continuum of service alternatives including: "instruction in regular classes,
special classes, special schools, home instruction, and instruction in hospitals
and institutions; and [that] make provision for supplementary services (such
as resource room or itinerant instruction) to be provided in conjunction with
regular class placement" (34 C.F.R. 300.551(b)(1)(2)). A note to the regulations clearly establishes an overriding rule that placement decisions must be
made on an individual basis with the availability of various alternative
placements in order to ensure that each school-age or preschool child with a
disability receives an education that is appropriate to his or her individual
needs (Note to 34 C.F.R. 300.552).

The Standard of FAPE. "The lack of a fixed standard of 'appropriate'
education has certainly allowed educators to make decisions that have led to
appeals, litigation, and an overabundance of legislation concerning special
education" (Sage & Burello, 1994, p. 105). In the early 1980s, courts
determined that appropriate meant tailored for a child's individual needs, not the
needs of the school district (Osborne, 1992b): "During the first few years the
IDEA was in force...a majority of courts reasoned that appropriate meant more
than simple access to educational programs but fell somewhere short of the best
that could possibly be provided" (p. 489). Following the Supreme Court case of
Hendrick Hudson District Board of Education v. Rowley (1982), cases
addressing FAPE in the LRE have hinged on the provision of an individually
appropriate education defined as instruction reasonably calculated to provide
educational benefit, developed in a manner procedurally consistent with the law,
and designed for the unique educational needs of the child. To the
disappointment of many, including several justices in their dissenting opinions,
educational benefit was not substantively defined by the Supreme Court as an
opportunity equal to that of nondisabled children. Siegel (1994) observed that
Chief Justice Rehnquist, in writing for the Court, emphasized that "Congress
had not intended a 'precise guarantee' or a 'basic floor of opportunity' for
disabled children. Congress intended equal protection of disabled children, but
nothing more than 'equal access' and certainly nothing that would 'maximize'
their potential" (p. 121).

Most states define an appropriate education according to the federal standard set by the Supreme Court; however, some have set higher standards. Osborne (1992b) observed that, although some courts have interpreted Rowley's "some educational benefit" standard to mean more than trivial progress, the degree of benefit varies according to state regulations and circuit jurisdictions. In these cases, "courts have held that these higher state standards are controlling within their own jurisdictions" (p. 491). Consequently, North Carolina, in 1982, held that FAPE for a student with disabilities was an equal educational opportunity to achieve personal potential commensurate with that provided to other students (Osborne, 1992b). *Hall v. Vance County Board of Education* (1985) allowed courts to make decisions regarding the substantive standard of an appropriate IEP on a case-by-case basis throughout the 4th Circuit. In 1985, the 1st Circuit upheld a Massachusetts state standard requiring an IEP to be designed to maximize the child's potential. The 3rd Circuit, in a 1986 New Jersey case, held courts to a standard of appropriate that required "educational services according to how the student can best achieve success in learning" (Osborne, 1992b, p. 491). In 1988, a federal district court upheld the Michigan standard requiring IEPs to be designed to develop a child's maximum potential but determined that "maximum potential did not mean utopian or the best education possible.... Noting that the proposed IEP provided for education in the least restrictive environment, the court placed the burden of proof on the plaintiff" to show that the proposed IEP was inadequate in meeting the higher Michigan standard (Osborne, 1992b, p. 491).

The tenets of the *Hendrick Hudson District Board of Education v. Rowley* case procedurally address the law's requirement for the provision of a free appropriate public education program; the issue of placement in the LRE is considered a component of an IEP reasonably calculated to provide educational benefit (Osborne, 1992b). Martin (1991) described the questions set forth by the Supreme Court in the *Rowley* case, which formed the criteria for determining a free appropriate education:

> What are reasonable expectations for the child's performance this year, based on individual learning capacity? And what program (specially designed instruction tailored to the unique needs of the student, plus related services without which the child could not benefit from the specially designed instruction) is needed to enable the child to reach that reasonable goal? (p. 31)

Acknowledging that the Supreme Court clarified some ambiguity, Osborne (1992a) noted that courts, in the absence of a formulaic directive, have proceeded to determine Rowley's educational benefit standard on the individual merits of each child's case, with close attention paid to the written IEP.

FAPE in the LRE. Underwood and Mead (1995) suggested that "it might be best to say that a child has the right to the least restrictive appropriate placement" (p. 98). Placement decisions are to be child centered, not system centered. Underwood and Mead made an interesting distinction: "The IEP team cannot select an option that is inappropriate just because it occurs in the presence of nondisabled peers. Equally true, they cannot select an option that is more segregated because it offers a more than appropriate education." (pp. 101–102). In addition, considerations of FAPE in the LRE are to extend to participation in nonacademic and extracurricular services and activities. "Students with disabilities are to have access to meals, recess periods, counseling services, athletics, transportation, health services, recreational activities, special interest groups, and clubs" (Turnbull, 1990, p. 153). The extent to which each child participates in academic or nonacademic activities is to be specifically prescribed for the child in his or her written IEP so that he or she can benefit from instruction in the least restrictive appropriate placement. Underwood and Mead (1995) presented a three-step decision-making sequence for determining the LRE: develop an appropriate program as outlined by the child's IEP, determine in which settings that program can be implemented, and choose the option that maximizes interaction with nondisabled peers.

LRE and the IEP. The Supreme Court, in *Rowley,* referred to the IEP as a "written record of reasonable expectations." Bateman (1996) described the IEP process as the heart and soul of the IDEA, essential to the formulation of appropriate programming and the determination of the LRE for the child. Consequently, meaningful IEPs, with truly individualized goals and objectives, which are used to guide instructional decisions, are integral to service delivery. As the law suggests, only when such a program is designed, with collaborative input, can appropriate instruction follow. No doubt this law is what prompted Champagne (1992) to remark, "you can fight over placement all you want, but if you want to win, you need to control the content of the IEP" (p. 14).

Bateman (1996) provided a thorough guide to the creation of better IEPs that are both legally correct and educationally useful. (Although new requirements for IEP development were added in the 1997 IDEA amendments, they in no way invalidate Bateman's earlier analysis.) In her analysis, she presented a model for decision making that clearly separates and sequences three phases of deliberation within the IDEA: eligibility and identification, development of special education and related services to be included in the IEP, and placement. Bateman saw these three processes as conceptually separate. Issues of eligibility and identification for services, as well as those of placement, are surrounded by due process protections so that professionals do not tread on parental or student rights.

Bateman's (1996) model is a triangle that, properly used, gives clear indication of the correct sequence for making decisions related to the provision of special education and related services that ensure FAPE in the LRE. Too often, Bateman observed, this sequence is confounded, confusing issues of eligibility with placement, both subordinating and diminishing the appropriateness of a child's education in the process. Separating decisions of eligibility, development of the IEP, and placement is a safeguard against procedural negligence that can frequently undermine substantive issues of appropriate placement for exceptional learners: "Many of the serious disputes that arise under IDEA are about placement. This has been true and is becoming ever more so. Often the sequence of procedural 'technicalities' is vital in the resolution of these disputes" (Bateman, 1996, p. 22).

The content of IEPs also needs to be put to good use in judicial decisions of LRE. According to Osborne (1990), "courts must assure that mainstreaming decisions are made within the framework of the EAHCA and that handicapped students are not being segregated simply because they are handicapped.... Thus the mainstreaming question must be viewed in terms of its relationship to the entire IEP" (p. 454). Huefner (1994) pointed out that many courts have not given close consideration to students' educational needs, goals, and objectives when deciding placement cases. Instead, they have restricted their judicial analysis to the administrative section of the IEP dealing with the amount and frequency of recommended services. This situation needs to change, as most placement disputes are attempting to balance FAPE and the mainstreaming preference of the law. To Huefner (1994), "the concept of LRE, as opposed to pure mainstreaming, represents the balance" (p. 43).

Champagne (1992) generally rejected a balancing approach in favor of one that sequences the decision-making process. He developed a flow chart that "preserves the core notion that placements are based on the educational need of the individual, rather than on presumptions-based categories of disabilities, traditions of resource allocation, or administrative convenience" (p. 3). This sequence model depends on detailed, informative, and well-chosen educational goals and objectives in order to ensure appropriate placement. In short, it relies on a meaningful IEP. This model is recommended for use at the district level so that LRE decisions can be based not on ideology but on conscious and explainable rationales.

LRE COURT DECISIONS AND FEDERAL DIRECTIVES

Courts traditionally hesitate to meddle in educational decisions about appropriate placements and programs for specific students, bearing out the legal tradition of judicial deference to professional expertise (Burgdorf, 1980; Sunstein, 1996). However, constitutional provisions and statutory limitations have resulted in a steady increase of cases dealing with issues related to the provision of an appropriate education in the LRE. Osborne (1990) observed that "although the U.S. Supreme Court has tried to narrow the definition of an appropriate education the term is still difficult to interpret. An appropriate education for most handicapped students has many components. The least restrictive environment provision is only one of those components" (p. 454).

Maloney and Shenker (1995) reported a tremendous increase in special education litigation in the 1990s. In analyzing the frequency of special education issues under litigation between 1978 and 1994, these legal analysts drew information from all federal and state decisions interpreting the EAHCA/IDEA, Section 504 of the Rehabilitation Act, and other federal laws affecting special education, such as interpretive directives published by the federal Department of Education's Office of Special Education and Rehabilitative Services (OSERS) and its Office of Special Education Programs (OSEP). According to their data, "more than 60 percent of the more than 1,200 decisions since 1978 have been reported in the past six years" (Maloney & Shenker, 1995, p. 1). The tally has slipped since the early 1990s, when a record number of 166 decisions was reported for 1992 alone, but the trend shows no indication of falling to the lower levels reported for the 1980s. "'Due process has gotten much more adversarial over the years, and that's reflected in the number of lawsuits. It's gone from an informal procedure to a judicial one. The only thing we're missing is a robe for the hearing officer'" (Maloney & Shenker, 1995, p. 1).

Decisions on LRE cases account for 9.4% of the total judicial activity related to special education, with LRE ranking fifth out of 28 categories— behind general litigation issues, including procedural issues and burden of proof (14%), attorneys' fees, allowable since 1986 (11.1%), damages (9.8%); and responsibility for provision or funding of services (9.6%) and ahead of issues of FAPE (8%). These six categories account for almost 62% of the judicial concerns over these 16 years.

Frequency rates are high for categories that have an indirect impact on issues of student placement, such as those addressing the responsibility for providing or funding special education and related services (at 9.6% of the total) and liability and negligence actions (at 9.8% of the total). Suits in this latter category "run the gamut from personal liability for refusing to implement an IEP to whether or not schools have a constitutional duty to protect students from harm inflicted by other students" (Maloney & Shenker, 1995, p. 1). Current litigation related to eligibility, or who can be served in special education, runs at a lower rate (6% of the total). This percentage could escalate if federal and state regulations eliminate the 13 disability categories in favor of a single functional definition of disability.

The Evolution of Special Education Law

The evolution of special education law reveals new areas of litigation as well as perennials considered so important that parents and school districts, over time and in multiple localities, have sought their judicial solution. Gorn (1996) observed that "the evolving nature of educational philosophy and the constant need for individual consideration of each student means there will always be new permutations to consider . . . [but] the same types of issues assuredly will continue to be litigated in the future" (p. ix).

LRE and Separate Placements. Not all cases of LRE involve consideration of a mainstreamed or inclusive placement. Some involve various transitions on the continuum, including movement from a day school to a residential center or from hospital to homebound instruction. Huefner (1994) differentiated between LRE cases related to regular class placement and those disputes involving the issue of "which of two nonmainstream special education placements is the LRE in which FAPE can be provided" (p. 52). Furthermore, cases involving placement in a separate day class or center or a residential facility are frequently not LRE disputes but rather are conflicts over the ability of an instructional setting to provide the student an appropriate education. "If only one setting can offer FAPE, *a fortiori* it is the LRE. In such cases, neither of the parties is asserting a need for interaction with nondisabled students" (Huefner, 1994, p. 52). Bateman and Chard (1995) concurred with Huefner (1994) that many cases involving separate day and residential schools address only these and not LRE issues. These cases of appropriateness, or FAPE, are analyzed under a framework quite different from those used to determine LRE. They are derived from the Supreme Court's decision in *Rowley* (1982), and they are dependent on the IEP: Was the individualized program developed in a procedurally correct manner, and is it reasonably calculated to allow the student to receive educational benefit (Bateman & Chard, 1995)?

> Nowhere is the 'continuum' concept more important than in educational placements of students labeled SED ["seriously emotionally disturbed" in federal parlance; since the 1997 amendments of IDEA, more simply "emotionally disturbed"]. Interestingly, far less is heard about full inclusion in regular classes of students who have emotional and behavioral disorders than about any other category of disability. (Bateman & Chard, 1995, p. 302)

Many of the placement cases for these students involve instruction in separate day or residential settings.

> Perhaps educators, parents, and other advocates intuitively recognize
> that some of these children would be impossibly disruptive absent
> extraordinary behavioral management skills and/or that they need
> intensive treatment, structure, or continuity that is beyond the
> capacity of the more ordinary educational settings to deliver.
> (Bateman & Chard, 1995, p. 302)

Ironically, although there is often pressure to exclude students with SED
("emotional or behavioral disorders" is now preferred by most professionals in
the field; see Kauffman, 1997b) from regular instructional settings, many
parents complain that states do not provide enough separate or special facilities
(Bateman & Chard, 1995). In 1986, the federal Office of Special Education
Programs (OSEP) clarified the justification for separate placements, stating that
the creation of a separate school for students with emotional and behavioral
problems would not violate the law so long as placement of an individual
student in the separate facility is based on the student's individual educational
needs, not administrative convenience, and meets the LRE requirements of the
EAHCA/IDEA (*Sachais*, 1986).

LRE and Regular Class Placements.   The extent to which Congress
intended to emphasize the integration of students with and without disabilities
has long been confounding courts, as revealed in this footnote from a 1984
judicial decision:

> The Education Act shows that Congress preferred regular classroom
> placement. It is not as apparent that once beyond a regular classroom,
> that Congress had a preference. Both *PARC* and *Mills* set up a
> hierarchy: regular classroom, special classroom, separate school. It is
> not clear from the Act that Congress also adopted this hierarchy.
> Section 1412 merely lumps special classes, separate schooling, and
> other settings together. *(St. Louis Developmental Disability Treat-
> ment Center Parents Association v. Mallory*, 1984*)*

Although there is evidence for the acceptability of a variety of alternative
instructional settings to meet the educational needs of individual students, there
is no explicit indication in the law that any one setting enjoys an objective,
preferential point along a continuum based on its proximity to the regular
classroom. Such preference can only be made subjectively, with reference to a
particular child and his or her individualized educational program (IEP).

In directives from both OSERS and OSEP, this point has been consistently expressed over the years, dispelling any notion that placement decisions
could be based on "category of disability, configuration of the service delivery
system, availability of educational or related services, availability of space, or

administrative convenience" (Bateman, personal notes, April, 1996). As early as 1979, an OSEP directive clarified the intent of the LRE requirement: "that handicapped children will benefit from education in regular classes if it is in the best interest of the child and that child is able to participate" (*Mordick*, 1979). Twenty-six years later, in 1995, a letter from the same agency reiterated the same point, that "there is no requirement that every student with a disability be placed in the regular classroom regardless of individual abilities and need" (*Letter to Anonymous*, 1995). This more recent notice, however, expanded on the directive and shifted the focus to educational practices, suggesting that instructional approaches might ameliorate the need for altered placement: "Problems associated with placement of some students with disabilities in regular classes can be improved if teachers are appropriately trained, and consideration is given to the full range of supplementary aids and services to facilitate regular class placement" (*Letter to Anonymous*, 1995).

LRE CASE LAW RELATED TO INCLUSIVE PLACEMENTS

Comprehensive canvassing of LRE judicial decisions by legal scholars reveals an equivocating answer to the question of whether placing a child with a disability in a regular classroom is, indeed, placement in the LRE (Zirkel, 1996). The ambiguous answer, in each case, is that: it depends. "Courts have not used a per se, or automatic, 'yes' answer any more than they have used a per se 'no' answer" (Zirkel, 1996, p. 5). Decisions and dicta reflect a common core of criteria including comparison of educational benefits with an overall preference for placement in the regular classroom. "The judicial outcomes appear to vary according to the individual circumstances of the child in relation to common criteria and the effectiveness of each side's advocacy, i.e., evidence and arguments" (p. 5).

Judicial outcomes also vary across the 13 federal judicial circuits—11 circuits covering the states, one circuit for Washington DC, and one to handle specialized matters such as patents. The United States has three levels of judicial review. The first level is the U.S. District Court, the second is the U.S. Court of Appeals, and the third is the U.S. Supreme Court. In brief, circuit courts have controlling authority over the lower courts within their jurisdiction. "The lower court cannot question the validity of that precedent" (Yell, 1995a, p. 181). This controlling authority of the circuit courts, however, does not cut across jurisdictions and applies only to courts in the several states that comprise its range. For example, a Fourth Circuit court ruling that applies in Virginia is not compelling in California, which falls within the jurisdiction of the Ninth Circuit. A circuit court ruling may carry great influence and its reasoning may be adopted in different parts of the country, not because its authority is controlling but because it is persuasive. Decisions of the U.S. Supreme Court, however, are controlling throughout the country. To date, the high court has yet to consider a case that specifically addresses the issues presented by LRE.

The following historical analysis is intended to be illustrative, not definitive, of court opinion regarding placement of students in the LRE from the early 1980s through 1996. With these decisions and directives, consideration is given to the nature and severity of a student's disability and, when indicated, to his or her age and level of schooling. These brief synopses represent a trove of human dramas played out in courtrooms across the United States. Some of the judicial decisions upon which these synopses are based contain elegant and instructive prose about the development of special education jurisprudence, and others are distinctive for their painstaking descriptions of children protected by the law. Where feasible, we have included some of these excerpts (also see the appendix for summaries of notable cases).

The 1980s

Early judicial decisions placed great emphasis on the unique educational needs of a student and frequently concluded that these could not be met in the regular education environment (Pitasky, 1996).

Mental Retardation. In *Roncker v. Walter* (1983), citing lack of significant progress during the previous 18 months, a school district proposed to move 9-year-old Neill, who was labeled "trainably" mentally retarded, from a separate class in a public school to a county program where he would have no interaction with nondisabled children. The federal court refused to intervene and instead, developed a feasibility test for the district to use in determining whether the proposed placement violated the LRE requirements. This case is considered the first significant placement case, and its analytic framework established that a decision concerning LRE "depends on the feasibility of providing, in a nonsegregated setting, those services that make a segregated facility 'superior'. If it is feasible to duplicate those services, then placement in the segregated setting is inappropriate" (Turnbull, 1990, p. 174). In developing this standard, the court acknowledged that a learner's need for an appropriate education might conflict with preferences for integration and that certain factors could be considered in determining whether education in the regular class could be provided satisfactorily.

In *Daniel R.R. v. State Board of Education* (1989), the Court of Appeals for the Fifth Circuit upheld a Texas district's proposal to remove Daniel, a 6-year-old boy with Down syndrome, from a regular prekindergarten class and place him in a special education class. During the 3-month trial period, teachers had to spend an inordinate amount of time attending to Daniel's needs at the expense of other children in the class, and his curriculum had to be totally modified.

Because the school district could show meaningful affirmative attempts to make integration succeed, the court found that the district's action of removing Daniel from regular education for a substantial portion of the day was legitimate (Champagne, 1992).

The attorney for Daniel's family, Reed Martin—a veteran of such conflicts, developed the two-pronged test used by the court to reach its decision. The first consideration asks whether education in the regular classroom, with the use of supplementary aids and services, can be achieved satisfactorily for a given child and, if not, whether the school has mainstreamed the child to the maximum extent appropriate. Although the decision went against Martin's client in this particular case, the analytic framework has had tremendous impact on deliberating placements in the LRE. Pitasky (1996) said that "Daniel R.R. instructed that academic achievement was not the sole consideration of mainstreaming and access to regular education could not be denied just because the progress of the student with a disability will not equal that of the regular education student" (p 4). In summing up the court's opinion, Yell (1995b) wrote that the court acknowledged that the imprecise nature of IDEA's mandates was deliberate, that Congress had chosen to leave educational policy and methods in the hands of local school officials, realizing that the tension between the preference for mainstreaming and the provision of an appropriate education made alternatives to the regular class necessary at times. "Essentially, the Daniel court said that when the provisions of FAPE and mainstreaming are in conflict, the mainstreaming mandate becomes secondary to the appropriate education mandate" (Yell, 1995b, p. 393).

Multiple Disabilities. In *Mark A. ex rel. Alleah A. v. Grantwood Area Educational Agency* (1986), the court held that the LRE for a preschooler with multiple disabilities, including crossed eyes, oscillation of the eye, abnormally small head size, and cerebral palsy was a public school self-contained program. The court found that it was not necessary for the district to provide a private, integrated preschool, as the mainstreaming provision could be satisfied in ways other than by providing instruction in the presence of nondisabled students. There would be students without disabilities in the public school, if not in the immediate class.

Autism. In *DeVries v. Fairfax County School Board* (1989) the LRE for Michael, a 17-year-old with autism, was a vocational center 13 miles from his home that was able to provide him with necessary structure and one-to-one instruction. Based upon his functional performance, which is richly described in this case, the court found that if Michael were to attend his home school of 2,300 mostly nondisabled students, he would in effect be monitoring classes rather than participating in a program geared to his future. The court concluded that mainstreaming was not appropriate for Michael, nor for every child, and must be contingent upon individual appropriateness.

Physical Disabilities. In *Wilson v. Marana Unified School District No. 6* (1984) the LRE for Jessica, a second grader with cerebral palsy, was a school in a neighboring district with a teacher trained in educating students with physical disabilities. The court in its opinion sympathized with the Wilsons' position favoring the continuation of her program at the local school with a teacher certified in learning disabilities but also understood the district's desire to address Jessica's lack of progress as effectively as possible. The court expressed judicial restraint in refraining to substitute its own notions of educational policy for those of the school district. The court held that, although the mainstreaming requirement is important, "it must be balanced with the primary objective of providing an appropriate education, and accordingly, removal of a child from the regular education environment may be necessitated by the nature or severity of the disability" (Pitasky, 1996, p. 5).

Emotional and Behavioral Disorders. In *Vander Malle v. Ambach* (1987), residential placement was the LRE for a high-school student with serious emotional disturbance. The court considered psychiatric evaluations recommending a highly structured residential setting to meet and support his needs and determined that his outbursts and antisocial behavior precluded him from attending regular public or private day schools.

Hearing Impairment. In *Lachman v. Illinois State Board of Education* (1988) the LRE for 7-year-old Benjamin, who was profoundly deaf, was placement in a self-contained classroom in a regional program where he would be instructed along with other hearing-impaired children using a total communication approach. Although the boy's parents sought full-time cued speech instruction in a regular neighborhood classroom, the district was not required to establish such customized instruction. To the court, the issue of LRE was embedded in the context of what was deemed appropriate methodology— cued speech—by Benjamin's parents. Consequently, the Lachmans had the burden of challenging the district's recommendation for instruction in total communication, which was provided at the regional center. The court held that

> we must establish the nature of the mainstreaming obligation created by
> section 1412(5)(B) and clarify the relationship of that statutory
> language to the general section 1412(1) requirement that handicapped
> children be provided with a free appropriate public education. The
> degree to which a challenged IEP satisfies the mainstreaming goal of
> EAHCA simply cannot be evaluated in the abstract. Rather, that

laudable policy objective must be weighed in tandem with the Act's principal goal of ensuring that the public schools provide handicapped children with a free appropriate education.

According to Pitasky (1996), the court concluded that "the mainstreaming preference of the IDEA is not unqualified and that the educational program for a particular child must be one that can be effectively implemented in a regular classroom before the Act's preference for a regular education can be accomplished" (p. 5).

In *Visco v. School District of Pittsburgh* (1988), a verdict that similarly balanced FAPE with LRE was reached regarding two high school sisters who were deaf. The court, in holding that the LRE for Jennifer and Rene was a private placement rather than a local hearing-impaired program, eloquently stated its decision: "Mainstreaming that interferes with the acquisition of fundamental language skills is foolishness mistaken for wisdom.... Nescient [ignorant] educational mainstreaming defeats the very purpose for which mainstreaming was conceived. The ultimate goal is to adequately prepare individuals for the mainstream of life."

The Early 1990s

The Americans with Disabilities Act was enacted into law in October, 1990, and represented society's political acknowledgment of civil rights for people often handicapped by architectural and attitudinal barriers. Several court decisions regarding student placement in this era gave hope to some advocates that a greater premium was being placed on the integration of students with disabilities into regular classrooms than had been in previous years. The following cases, heard from 1991 to 1994, serve as examples. Some analysts suggest that "the courts looked back at earlier inclusion cases and used the foundation they established to arrive at the opposite conclusion—that regular education placements were necessary to comply with the IDEA's LRE requirement" (Pitasky, 1996). Others maintain there was no pendulum swing, just continued application of individualized criteria in the making of placement decisions (Zirkel, 1996).

Mental Retardation. In *Greer v. Rome City School District* (1991), the parents of Christy Greer, an elementary student with Down syndrome, favored her placement in a regular class in the neighborhood school. The district proposed placement at another school in a self-contained class with mainstreaming in nonacademic areas. The court did not determine what constituted the LRE for Christy because it was unable to do so, based upon the insufficient information provided by the district on Christy's IEP. Relying on the test established in the case of *Daniel R.R.* (1989), the court found that the district failed to consider the critical inquiry demanded of the test's first prong; it had failed to consider whether Christy could progress in the regular classroom if provided with the appropriate aids and services. The minutes of IEP meetings indicated that minimum consideration had been given to other options for her and revealed damning evidence that Christy's IEP had been written without parental input and placement decided before due consideration of her needs. The district was ordered to reconsider its recommendation (Yell, 1995b).

In *Oberti v. Board of Education of the Borough of Clementon School District* (1993), the LRE for Rafael, an 8-year-old boy with Down syndrome, was the regular classroom, following the school district's failure to provide him with appropriate aids and services in a part-time regular kindergarten. Once again, the *Daniel R.R.* (1989) test was used. The court determined that despite Rafael's serious and aggressive behavior problems directed toward his teachers and peers, no plan to manage his behavior was incorporated into his IEP, and no consultation was provided to his regular educator. In contrast, his afternoons in a special class were free from such behavioral outbursts. Based on the district's failure to support his integrated education, the court determined that it had not been established that Rafael could not succeed in a regular class. Significantly, the court held that more than academic progress must be used to justify a special placement, stating that parallel, not identical, instruction might be required for him. The court placed the burden of proof on the school district for the following year and stressed, in doing so, that it was not embracing the full-inclusion concept. The court held that Rafael's IEP could be implemented within the regular class but that the district had not made an adequate attempt to support him there (Yell, 1995b).

In *Sacramento City Unified School District v. Rachel H.* (1994), the LRE for 11-year-old Rachel Holland, a student with moderate mental retardation, was the regular classroom for the full day with appropriate aids and services, rather than the district's proposed placement in special classes for academic subjects with mainstreaming for art, music, lunch, and recess. This arrangement was determined through a four-pronged test established by the court in this case. Differing from the other frameworks used in *Roncker* (1983) or *Daniel R.R.* (1989), this test did not require balancing the benefits of special or regular class instruction but considered only the benefit of regular education for Rachel with appropriate support, the nonacademic benefits of the regular class, her effect on other students within that class, and the financial costs of her inclusion. The court held that "mainstreaming is the starting point . . . placement in other than a regular class is a fall-back choice made only after it is determined that placement in regular classes will be unsuccessful." In holding for the Hollands in this instance, the court "by emphasizing a test for (as opposed to an absolute right to) inclusion . . . implicitly sanctioned inclusion and removal" (Siegel, 1994, p. 48). The court instructed that all future appropriate placements for Rachel should be similarly determined by this four-pronged framework.

Multiple Disability. In *Teague Independent School District v. Todd L.* (1993), a public school placement rather than a residential psychiatric institution was considered the LRE for a 17-year-old student whose condition was characterized by a variety of behavioral, learning, and speech disorders. Despite his low frustration tolerance and outbursts in reaction to stress, the court held that the public high school placement allowed him the chance to interact with nondisabled peers and to participate more fully in his community.

Learning Disability. *Amann v. Stow School System* (1992) determined that both FAPE and LRE could be provided in a public setting that afforded interaction with nondisabled peers to a 14-year-old student with learning disabilities. This placement obviated the need for the state to provide a private program maximizing his academic benefit. The court held that federal law does not require a maximizing view of the IDEA but rather requires one that provides the lower standard of a minimum floor of opportunity (Pitasky, 1996).

The Mid-1990s

Court decisions on LRE from 1994 to 1996 give evidence of a continued emphasis on the unique needs of individual learners and the dominance of an appropriate education when FAPE and LRE cannot be achieved in the same setting. Recent trends indicate that when the two conflict, LRE must be sacrificed, eliminating the possibility that LRE means regular class placement in every instance (Pitasky, 1996). In some cases, the student profiles reflect a noticeable increase in the degree of disability. Several decisions involved programming for students with severe and profound disabilities, unlike cases earlier in the 1990s that concerned the needs of students who were less severely disabled. Other cases reflect the increasing prevalence of students with attention deficit hyperactivity disorder (ADHD) and the challenging behaviors of students with Tourette Syndrome.

Mental Retardation. In *Kari H. v. Franklin Special School District* (1995/1997), the LRE was a special class with mainstreaming for nonacademic subjects for a 16-year-old girl with Cri du Chat syndrome, a severe form of mental retardation characterized by persistent cat-like mewing. The circuit court, considering her low functional performance in a previous inclusive setting as well as her measured IQ of 21, upheld the district court's decision that benefits in regular classes were marginal for her compared to her chances to learn and comprehend in a setting where the teacher and students could communicate with her at a language level more conducive to her development. In addition, the court found that her disruptive behaviors—including hand clapping, making noise, and walking around the classroom—were disruptive to the regular classroom environment (Pitasky, 1996). Judge Wiseman wrote in the concluding statements to the district court decision:

> Congress has expressed a preference for providing that individualized education in the regular classroom. But the preference is not outcome-determinative. The question remains: What will be the least restrictive environment for Kari to realize her goals and potential. Framed this way, "least restrictive environment" is not the same as "inclusive."

In *Hudson v. Bloomfield Hills Public Schools* (1995/1997), the LRE for a 14-year-old student who was "trainably" mentally impaired with an IQ of 42 was a special education class with part-time mainstreaming instead of a program of parallel instruction in a regular class at her local middle school. The district court's reasoning was based on evidence that although she was placed in a regular class she worked alone and was reliant on a personal aide who provided her with the first- or second-grade level instruction she required. The court found that past inclusionary placements demonstrated that no amount of aids or services could provide her with appropriate support in a regular setting, nor could she achieve her IEP goals for independent living and social skills there (Pitasky, 1996). The Sixth Circuit Court upheld the lower court's opinion that neither the IDEA nor its regulations require a neighborhood placement. The decision rested on evidence that the student was unable to derive academic benefit from the regular setting because the subject matter exceeded her ability level.

In the previous two cases, the academic demands of a secondary class placement in regular education outweighed the social interests of students in the mainstream.

Autism. Two recent cases resulted in very different outcomes for students with autism, one of whom has mental retardation as well as autism.

In *Student v. Somerset County Board of Education* (1996), a self-contained, special education classroom with opportunities for mainstreaming in nonacademic areas was the LRE for a 10-year-old boy with autism. His intelligence was determined to be in the profoundly mentally retarded range.

In *Hartmann by Hartmann v. Loudoun County Board of Education* (1996/1997), the Fourth Circuit Court determined that partial mainstreaming met the LRE requirement for Mark, a middle-school student with autism, reversing a district court's determination that the LRE for him was the regular classroom. In the initial proceedings, both a hearing officer and a state review officer upheld the school district's proposed IEP which called for partial mainstreaming. Upon appeal from Mark's parents who desired a fully inclusive program, the district court determined that the Loudoun County school district's attempts to include him were inadequate, citing insufficient staff training, lack of staff experienced with autism, failure to follow advice from properly trained consultants, and inconsistent staffing and consultative services. The lower court noted the child's intelligence and that his primary difficulty was in the area of communication. To arrive at the decision, the lower court relied on testimony from Mark's private tutor and videotaped evidence of Mark's performance in a regular classroom in another school district.

In its reversal, the circuit court found that the district court did not give "due weight" to the previous administrative hearings, failing to consider the district's discretion when determining appropriate programming for one of its students. The circuit court held that (a) mainstreaming is a preference not a mandate; (b) overwhelming evidence was ignored that Mark made minimal if any progress in his inclusive placement; (c) the inclusive accommodations of the second district need not be replicated because they approached a "potential maximizing standard" exceeding the *Rowley* (1982) educational benefit standard; (d) the district court failed to consider the disruptive effects of Mark's behavior in the regular classroom; (e) Loudoun's IEP was appropriate because it provided Mark with both educational benefit and opportunities for mainstreaming. Yell (1998) described the three-part test used by the Fourth Circuit Court in reaching its decision. This test determines that mainstreaming is not required when

> (1) a student with a disability would not receive educational benefit from mainstreaming in a general education class; (2) any marginal benefit from mainstreaming would be significantly outweighed by benefits that could feasibly be obtained only in a separate instructional setting; or (3) the student is a disruptive force in the general education classroom. Finally, the circuit court stated that the LRE provision of the IDEA only created a presumption, and the presumption reflected congressional judgment that receipt of social benefits is a subordinate goal to receiving educational benefit.

Dupre (1998) notes that

> The court of appeals sharp;y criticized the district court for substituting its notions of educational policy for those of school authorities and, in essence, instructed lower federal courts to defer to the professional judgment of educators making decisions regarding inclusion when those educators have made a "reasonable pedagogical choice." The

court stated categorically that "IDEA does not deprive these educators of the right to apply their professional judgment." Moreover, "local educators deserve latitude in determining the individualized education program most appropriate for a disabled child," and their professional judgment is "deserving of respect." (p. 442)

Multiple Disability. In *McWhirt by McWhirt v. Williamson County Schools* (1994), the LRE was a separate class with mainstreaming opportunities for a severely disabled fourth-grade student with multiple disabilities that negatively affected her health and social and emotional development and limited her verbal skills and ambulation. After all the school personnel testified that resource room support had not met either her physical or her educational needs, the court held that the regular classroom was incapable of meeting her needs.

Courts in two additional cases involving students with multiple disabilities, in Indiana and in Maryland, did not require that a student fail in a regular class setting before removal. In both instances, it was permissible to give serious consideration to the potentially negative consequences of such a setting before placement. Both districts were able to justify their decisions based upon the students' previous performance in limited mainstream settings *(D.F. v. Western School Corporation* (1996); *Student v. Somerset County Board of Education (1996)).*

Hearing Impaired. In *Poolaw V. Bishop* (1995), the LRE for Lionel, a 13-year-old student who was profoundly deaf and whose communication skills were described as primitive, was a state residential school for the deaf. Lionel, whose parents moved residences frequently, had been previously mainstreamed with appropriate aids and services in several states, yet he could neither read nor write. Based upon his records from multiple schools, the court held that to receive an academic benefit, he required intensive instruction in American Sign Language, which was provided in Arizona only at the state school. The court held that Lionel's currently profound academic needs outweighed the social benefits of a regular setting, including peer interaction and the influence of his Native American culture.

Visually Impaired. In *Carlisle Area School District v. Scott P.* (1995), placement in a physical support class at a public high school was the LRE for a 20-year-old student who had sustained injuries in an accident that left him with brain injuries and blindness. Although his parents sought a residential setting for him, the court held that the district's placement, with academic, social, and vocational instruction with other students who were blind, would provide him with educational benefit in a less restrictive setting.

Learning Disability. In *Ft. Zumwalt School District v. Clynes* (1997), the Eighth Circuit Court determined that a district elementary school offered FAPE in the LRE to an elementary student with learning disabilities, invalidating an earlier district court's decision (*Ft. Zumwalt School District v. Missouri State Board of Education*, 1996). Although this case might be considered one primarily regarding parental reimbursement, it is remarkable for the district court's controversial interpretation of LRE.

In 1996, a separate school placement was determined the LRE for Nicholas, a fourth grader who could not write a complete sentence and whose grades were declining. The district court, seeking to keep him from harm, held that the student's "self-esteem and behavior were aggravated by his associations with students from whom he felt 'different' and that, consequently, his academic progress was hindered." The court considered Nicholas' consistently poor performance in regular classes, finding the district's strategy of increasing resource support time without changing teaching methods to be inadequate in meeting his needs. Nicholas' parents were entitled to financial reimbursement for private school tuition based upon the greater probability of the school's ability to provide him with FAPE and also because the court found that the school district violated its own provision of FAPE by not preparing an IEP for him until one month after the school year had begun. The court's view in this particular case departed from the prevailing view—that regular class instruction breaks down the stereotypes that make students with disabilities feel different from their nondisabled peers. "To date, the basic premise underlying mainstreaming has been that self-esteem and morale have the greatest chance to flourish when students with disabilities are given optimal opportunities for interaction with their nondisabled peers" (Pitasky, 1996).

In its 1997 reversal, the Circuit Court determined that the lower court erred in providing reimbursement for the private school on the basis that FAPE in the LRE had been denied. Citing Nicholas' progress and passing grades as well as his opportunities to interact with nondisabled peers, the court supported the school district's IEP for placement in a regular class with part-time special education instruction for reading and math. "The statutory goal is to make sure that every affected student receive a publicly funded education that benefits the student," wrote the court. Although the district court held that only a segregated setting would assist Nicholas to accept his disability, the circuit court recalled that earlier decisions by a state level review officer attributed his poor behavior to difficulty in academic classes, not to his interactions with nondisabled students. In its decision, the Circuit Court found that "the hearing panel indicated that Nicholas should not be segregated from non-disabled students."

Emotional and Behavioral Disorders. In *MR v. Lincolnwood Board of Education* (1994), a therapeutic day school was the LRE for a 13-year-old student described in the decision as one who disrupted the mainstreamed setting by barking, making noise, biting his thumbs, pulling his hair, hitting adults, throwing temper tantrums, and telling his teacher he was going to kill her. The court, after viewing videotaped evidence of classroom performance, held that despite attempted instruction in a separate class for students with behavioral problems and mainstreaming to the maximum extent possible for him, the student still engaged in inappropriate behaviors presenting a risk of danger to others in the regular setting.

In *Clyde K. ex re. Ryan D. v. Puyallup School District* (1994), placement in an off-campus self-contained program was the LRE for Ryan, a 15-year-old with Tourette Syndrome and ADHD who was failing in his mainstreamed setting and disrupting the environment with taunts and profanity directed at students and teachers. The court, employing the *Holland (1994)* test, determined that Ryan derived no academic benefit from his regular class placement and was, in fact, regressing. In addition, his nonacademic benefits were minimal. The cost of a personal aide was irrelevant in determining whether Ryan would be included in a regular class because the court determined that this service would not be of benefit to him. Most important to the court was the overwhelmingly negative effect of what it termed Ryan's "dangerously aggressive" behavior and the reality that his explicit taunts could initiate a Title IX sexual harassment charge:

> These are not incidents school officials can dismiss lightly; they have a special obligation to ensure that students entrusted to their care are kept out of harm's way.... While school officials have a statutory duty to ensure that disabled students receive an appropriate education, they are not required to sit on their hands when a disabled student's behavioral problems prevent both him and those around him from learning.

In an interesting coda to this decision, Judge Kozinski remarked on the length of time Ryan spent in what should have been a temporary, part-time placement. He wrote passionately in his notes about the negatively preemptive advocacy supposedly taken on behalf of Ryan and his parents by their attorney:

> Hardball tactics are seldom productive even in ordinary civil litigation, and are particularly ill-advised in this context. Working out an acceptable educational program must, in the end, be a cooperative effort between parents and school officials; the litigation process is simply too slow and too costly to deal adequately with the rapidly changing needs of children. In addition, litigation tends to poison relationships, destroying channels for constructive dialogue that may have existed before the

litigation began. This is particularly harmful here, since parents
and school officials must—despite any bad feelings that develop
between them—continue to work closely with one another. As this
case demonstrates, when combat lines are firmly drawn, the child's
interests often are damaged in the ensuing struggle.... This is
surely a case where the lawyers would have better served their
clients—and the interests of the society—had they concentrated
their efforts on being healers and mediators rather than warriors.

Osborne (1992a) summed up the state of judicial decisions related to
inclusive placements, which have held into the mid-1990s: "The weight of the
case law indicates that the least restrictive environment mandate is secondary
to the provision of appropriate services and may not be used to deny a student
access to needed services" (p. 370). Twelve years earlier, Burgdorf (1980)
had remarked that "ideally, the law ought to set up a framework and some
broad guidelines, within which public educators can exercise their
professional discretion in selecting an educational program and placement
designed to meet the needs of each individual handicapped student" (p.273).
Since that time, several significant cases have surfaced that have devised tests
or analytic frameworks by which to evaluate whether a student is achieving
satisfactorily in the regular classroom. The major frameworks include the
Roncker (1983) standard, the two-pronged test from *Daniel R.R.* (1989), and
the four-pronged *Holland* (1994) test. Currently, no national framework is
employed in such decisions. The Supreme Court has denied hearing any LRE
cases to date, and, consequently, each circuit has its own preferred test or
framework to decide cases related to LRE. Activity has varied among the
circuits, with the Second Circuit seeing the most activity (Maloney &
Schenker, 1995).

Analytic Frameworks

Roncker Standard (Roncker v. Walter, 1983). The Sixth and Eighth Circuits
apply a similar standard. The Fourth Circuit is moving away from this analysis
(see *Hartmann by Hartmann,* 1996/1997). This framework uses a feasibility or a
"portability" test to determine whether services that make a separate placement
superior could be feasibly provided in a regular class setting. This is called the
"portability standard" (Huefner, 1994). Feasibility is defined by three exceptions:
whether any marginal benefits of mainstreaming are outweighed by the benefits of
the separate setting; whether the child with a disability is disruptive in the regular
class; and whether the cost of mainstreaming one child would deprive others with
disabilities. Cost is only a consideration if the district has available a full
continuum of alternative placements. This framework developed a new standard to

determine when mainstreaming was occurring "to the maximum extent appropriate" as required by the EAHCA and, with its portability standard, seemingly allowed courts considerable discretion in determining the LRE for a given student (Huefner, 1994).

Daniel R. R. 2-Prong Test (Daniel R.R. v. State Board of Education, 1989). The Third, Fifth, and Eleventh Circuits use this standard. Recently, the Fourth Circuit has applied this standard. This framework is widely used and requires less judicial intrusion. It "explicitly rejects the portability standard stating that it does not give enough deference to the 'educational policy choices' of state and local education agencies'"(Huefner, 1994, p. 31). According to *Daniel R.R.* (1989), the feasibility of transporting services to a more integrated setting is an administrative decision, dependent on the contextual circumstances at the state and local levels. This statutory framework requires an "individualized, fact-specific inquiry" (Bateman & Chard, 1995, p. 293) that asks two key questions. First, can education be achieved in the regular classroom satisfactorily? Four additional questions qualify this broad issue. 1) Has the school taken steps to accommodate the child in the regular class with appropriate aids and services? Not every conceivable aid or service needs to be provided, and undue teacher time and undue curricular modification are not required. In making this determination, the school must consider more than token attempts at modifying instruction but need not offer every conceivable service nor completely alter the program. 2) Can the child benefit from regular education? According to the court, "this inquiry necessarily focuses on the student's ability to grasp the essential elements of the regular curriculum." 3) On balance, will this child benefit more from regular or special education? And 4) What effect will this child have on other children and the quality of their education? The second key question is whether, if this child's education cannot be achieved satisfactorily in regular education, he or she is being offered mainstreaming to the maximum extent appropriate. (Bateman & Chard, 1995; Huefner, 1994; Yell, 1995b).

The Holland 4-Prong Test (Sacramento City Unified School District v. Rachel H, 1994). The Ninth Circuit applies this standard. This framework is notable for the absence of the consideration of balancing special and regular education benefits in determining if a child can receive education in the regular classroom satisfactorily. This analysis addresses the educational benefits of placing the child in a full-time regular education program, the nonacademic benefits of such a placement, the effect the child would have on the teacher and other students in the regular classroom, and the costs associated with this placement.

Comparison of the Frameworks

The cases upon which these analytic frameworks are based vary in their particular circumstances, but the factors considered in each provide clarification of the LRE guidelines. Advocates favoring a more active judicial response tend toward the *Roncker* standard's portability criterion (e.g., T.K. Gilhool, personal communication, 1996; Weber, 1992). Yell (1995b) regarded the *Daniel R.R.* test as the preferred statutory standard, as did Bateman and Chard (1995). In an effort to synthesize the various frameworks as an aid to placement decision makers, the following guiding elements emerge (Yell, 1995b).

1. *Determination of the LRE is based on the individual needs of the student.* In making this individualized determination, each test requires that both the academic and the nonacademic aspects of regular class placement be considered. "It is inappropriate for an IEP team to make a placement based on a priori district policy. To determine that all students must be educated in integrated settings is as discriminatory as educating all students with disabilities in segregated settings" (Yell, 1995b, p. 400).

2. *Good-faith efforts are required to maintain students in integrated settings.* Schools must consider reasonable efforts to maintain students in regular classrooms and may consider more restrictive placements "only when it is determined that efforts to include the student in the mainstream will not result in his or her receiving an appropriate education" (Yell, 1995b, p. 400). There is controversy in the literature about a district's need to place a student in a regular classroom or set him or her up for failure there before recommending a separated placement. Directives from both OSEP and OSERS refute this approach, advising that although there is no fail-through requirement, districts should be ready to justify that they arrived at their decisions through careful consideration of the needs of individual students (*Richards*, 1987; Will, 1986a). Huefner (1994) addressed this controversy by recalling the procedural nature of the IDEA:

    > Some may wonder if Daniel R.R. infers that a school must try supported mainstreaming for all students with disabilities or else be violating the act. If so, it would represent a broader reading of the mainstreaming preference than that of Roncker. The answer is no. A careful reading of Daniel R.R. suggests that the court meant to create an obligation to use supplementary aids and services only when education officials had placed students in mainstream classrooms. The opinion states that placement of a child in other than a regular classroom does not raise a procedural issue whereby

the school district can be held in noncompliance for not placing all children in the mainstream initially; instead it raises only a substantive issue as to whether a given child was placed in the LRE (Daniel R.R., 1989, p. 1043). (p. 33)

Yell (1995b) noted that, traditionally, courts have restricted their purview to these procedural concerns, leaving educational issues to the schools. However, in some cases, courts faced with imprecise data have required proof to rebut the presumption that an exceptional learner should be educated in a regular instructional setting. Consequently, schools are advised to keep impeccable records concerning their educational decision-making process as well as data-based decision models to monitor results for students (Yell, 1995b).

3. *Each school district must make available a complete continuum of alternative placements to meet the needs of each of its special education students.* Placement outcomes for students have varied with each standard, indicating at times regular and at other times separate placement. Case law as well as a recent federal directive continue to emphasize alternatives to the regular instructional setting to ensure that students derive educational benefit (*Letter to Anonymous*, 1996).

4. *When students are placed in separate programs, they are to be integrated in regular settings to the maximum extent appropriate to their needs.* This process demands careful professional judgment and decisions that comport with the student's IEP goals.

5. *The needs of nondisabled peers may be considered in determining placement in the LRE.* All the tests consider the potential disruptive effect of the student with disabilities upon the instructional environment. Courts also consider whether accommodations to ameliorate disruption, such as behavior management plans, have been considered (Yell, 1995b).

There is less consensus with regard to cost, although both the *Roncker* and *Holland* frameworks allow it as a factor in considering the child's impact on the provision of educational benefits to other students with disabilities or his or her effects on nondisabled students. Although cost is not a factor in the provision of FAPE, it is permissible in considerations of LRE—emphasizing the subordinate nature of LRE within their relation (Bartlett, 1993). Huefner (1994) distinguished the *Roncker* standard from the later frameworks by suggesting that, before *Daniel R.R.*, the portability standard was used in cases concerning the provision of special education classrooms or facilities in neighborhood schools for a child, rather than in determining instruction in a regular classroom.

This distinction clarifies the consideration of cost only if a continuum of placements is made available.

Although the burden of proof in placement cases generally rests with a school seeking to place a child in a separate setting, this expectation can also be less than clear. The court in *Clyde K v. Puyallup* (1994) challenged the side opposing the hearing officer to provide one more scintilla of proof, yet in *Oberti v. Board of Education of Clementon School District* (1993), the court placed the burden on the school when a parent requests a regular setting for the child because of the Act's strong presumption in favor of mainstreaming (Pitasky, 1996).

In 1994, the school district involved in *Sacramento City Unified School District v. Rachel H* (1994), filed a petition asking the U.S. Supreme Court for a review. The issues raised in this case reflect the lack of unanimity across circuits. They raise some nagging questions and address others that recent local decisions have clarified:

> a. When education professionals determine that a student with disabilities has not achieved, and *cannot* achieve, measurable academic progress in the regular education environment, can educators place the student in less than a full-time mainstreaming program?
>
> b. If not, does a school have to subject a student with disabilities to repeated failure in a full-time mainstreaming environment in order to have a record of full-time placement before it can place the student in a program that involves less than a full-time mainstream placement?
>
> c. With respect to the Ninth Circuit Court's rejection of the *Daniel R.R.* test, should the student's mainstreaming rights depend on the circuit in which the child resides?
>
> d. IDEA requires that placement decisions be made by knowledgeable persons, based on assessment data. Does this regulation represent an educational philosophy that is inconsistent with the mainstreaming preference? (Yell, 1995b, p. 399)

Yell (1995b) observed that the Supreme Court denied the petition to review these questions. Bateman (personal communication, April, 1996) suggested that perhaps the court is waiting for the field of special education to sort out these issues in subsequent litigation and directives. Some recent decisions and dicta seem to provide increased clarity to the first two questions.

Trends in LRE Case Law and Federal Directives

Case Law. In summarizing the outcomes of LRE-related case law, the following themes emerge.

1. The focus is on the needs of the individual child, with some indication that "the particular characteristics associated with different types of disabilities can directly affect the success, or failure, of inclusion" (Pitasky, 1996, p. 27).

2. There is no federal mandate requiring placement in a neighborhood school.

3. There is no federal requirement that a district attempt a regular setting with a child before deciding on a separate setting.

4. Although academic and social benefits are important factors in determining LRE, these can only be balanced with regard to an individual child.

5. There is some indication that age is a factor in regular class placement, with more elementary students than middle school or secondary students placed in regular classrooms for instruction.

6. Courts attend to the effect of disruptive students on peers and adults, often requiring behavior management plans in regular classes or separate placements.

7. Courts consider health threats (e.g., classroom safety would be considered if a student with a disability had a contagious condition with a realistic chance of transmittal to others, and environments that provide necessary medical support would be the LRE for medically fragile students).

8. For students with low-incidence disabilities, scarcity of limited resources and the advantages of pooling them may provide justification for a student's placement in a more restrictive instructional setting (Pitasky, 1996).

Federal Direction. A statement was released through U.S. Secretary of Education Richard W. Riley in December, 1993, regarding the inclusion of special-needs students in regular classrooms: "We do not advocate a 'one size fits all' approach in making decisions about how students should be educated. Educational placement...should be based on individual student needs and address the issue of adequate resources for both students and teachers" (Riley, 1993). Similarly, in February, 1994, in a memo to the Chief State School Officers, Thomas Hehir, Director of OSEP, wrote that recent judicial decisions reaffirm "the important principle of implementing Part B's FAPE and LRE requirements by making placement determinations based on the unique needs of the individual student." As recently as October, 1996, OSEP clarified that LRE determinations are to focus on individual needs in reply to an inquiry as to whether changing demographics in a geographic area could be held as a reason to reduce the number of separate classes and separate schools for the purposes of LRE (*Letter to Anonymous,* 1996).

In summarizing the legal issues surrounding LRE, Arnold and Dodge (1994) wrote that "the law doesn't prohibit separate classes and separate schools; it merely requires they be filled on the basis of student need—not administrative convenience" (p. 23). Champagne (1992) observed that

> the trend is for the monopoly on wisdom and effectiveness that may have been the province of the segregated institutions to be broken up and disbursed to even the most ordinary of educational settings. But it is an uneven trend, and a contentious one. Simple LRE rules, therefore, are understandably elusive. (p. 16)

WHAT LIES AHEAD

Maloney and Schenker (1995) predict that future placement concerns will center on court moves to strengthen the disciplinary authority of schools regarding special education students. They see the basis in recent LRE frameworks, which have allowed for the consideration of a student's effect on the rest of the class. For a child with serious behavior problems, this is particularly apt. Changes in the 1997 amendments of IDEA that added stringent prohibitions against bringing weapons to school are an additional move toward allowing local schools more discretion in the removal of a special education student from a regular school setting. Other predictions for legal action related to LRE involve the inclusion into regular classrooms of young students with cognitive disorders, increased flexibility in the funding of special education programs, and increased emphasis on formal mediation in the resolution of conflicts between parents and school districts.

In reflecting on case law, Maloney and Shenker (1995) suggested that the courts, between 1980 and 1988, employed "curriculum standards to determine the least restrictive environment for students with disabilities, considering in large part the academic benefit the student might receive" (p. 2). Since 1989, however, inclusion of exceptional learners into regular classrooms "has come to be considered a civil right, not just an educational standard" (p. 2). Does the acceptance of the regular class as the starting point for any consideration of student placement, as indicated in *Holland* (1994), reflect a current confidence in regular education's strategies and commitment to address functional exclusion, to break the association of difference with deficiency, or to meet the requirements of FAPE for an individual child? Does this consideration stem from the embrace of social integration? Or is it really the current formulation of an old point of contention between educators and legal advocates in the development of Section 1412(5)(B) concerning removal from general education—tension between the requirement that the child be removed only when progress "cannot be achieved satisfactorily" on the one hand and the expectation, on the other, that placement will be first with nondisabled children "to the maximum extent appropriate"?

An examination of the legal foundations underpinning LRE, and the decisions of case law and federal directives over time, reinforce Turnbull's (1990) conceptualization of LRE as both an educational strategy and a legal principle in which "needs sometimes do prevail over the presumptive right to regular education placement and programming" (p. 161). Examining LRE through a legal lens reveals that defining the standard of *appropriate* has been, and continues to be, central to this discourse. In addition, determining when progress cannot be achieved satisfactorily has produced analytic frameworks that address the inherent tensions between civil rights and educational needs.

Close inspection further suggests that the law and its regulations speak to several levels of decision makers—those concerned with the practicable exigencies of their school system's ability to provide an integrated education for their students with disabilities and those IEP committee members obliged to recommend an appropriate program for an individual child. Decisions regarding the interpretation of FAPE in the LRE are also confounded by the confusion of federal guidelines coming from the EAHCA/IDEA with state regulations that are frequently more prescriptive. Courts have held that states may not offer less than the federal standard, but they may offer more. This decision has had an impact on instructional placements for exceptional learners in varying localities with regard to the definition of the appropriateness standard as well as the utilization of delivery systems that have developed in response to state funding formulae. The economics of funding special education and the consequent impact on placements in the LRE are clearly related to the provision of what the EAHCA/IDEA calls "a full educational opportunity." Deeper consideration of this important issue, however, exceeds the boundaries of our current discussion, but perhaps it is timely to raise here the question of just what is considered offering less than the federal standard, not more. In the case of LRE, does restricting separate placements through state distribution formulae increase or reduce both civil rights and educational opportunity? Compliance with federal legislation requires that implementation be guided by the particular needs of a particular child in a particular set of circumstances. Although the 1997 amendments to the IDEA call for states to employ placement-neutral funding formulae, the question remains: Is there really such a thing as revenue-neutral placement?

Clearly, equitable provision of FAPE in the LRE depends on both constitutional protections and appropriate instruction. It relies on a legal and an educational détente: "The focus of LRE implementation must remain in the creation of less restrictive alternatives, rather than on the reduction of unduly restrictive choices" (Turnbull, 1981). In creating social policy regarding LRE, the courts have only been willing to go so far, displaying reluctance to exceed the policy choices of legislatures, professionals, and parents themselves. Perhaps legal reasoning, replete with its discretionary tool kit, "reflects an understanding that courts are far from preeminent actors in the system of democratic deliberation.... In a well-functioning democracy, the most important social commitments emerge not from courtrooms, but from the reflective judgments of a nation's citizenry" (Sunstein, 1996, pp. 195–196).

5

The Viewpoint of Educators: Environment and Learning

Some years ago the mathematician-philosopher Jacob Bronowski explained the profundity of cutting stone blocks for building as opposed to molding clay. As an achievement in what Bronowski called the "ascent of man," this simple act of splitting stone was unparalleled, because it compelled analysis and impelled us to examine, somewhat simultaneously, the nature of the stone, the nature of our tools, and the principles that dictated how the two would interact. This focused examination, as you might guess, is what became science.

I always think of the description of similarities between disabled and nondisabled students as the subordinate clause used to support the main ideas about how they are different. This, I believe, leads us to examine the nature of the individual students, the nature of our tools, and the principles that dictate how the two might interact. This examination we might call "special education."—M. Gerber, personal communication, January 8, 1997

In this chapter we explain and interpret the concept of LRE from an educational perspective in order to determine whether underlying assumptions about LRE in relation to FAPE have changed, and if so, whether the concept remains an ethical educational strategy. We examine the implementation of LRE in theory and in practice: first, as a theory of facilitative educational environments; second, as a set of research findings on American placement practices. Our content analysis of the abstracts of professional placement literature from the 1960s through the mid-1990s organizes in a chronological and conceptual framework a description of the restrictiveness of educational environments. Analyses of historical trends in the literature reflect changes in educational attitudes and practices. We provide summary statements of quantitative and qualitative research that empirically assesses the effects of inclusive versus separate instructional settings and addresses the relation between student learning outcomes and instructional environments for students with various disabilities and learning needs. Crockett obtained further information in interviews with contemporary educational theorists who hold contrasting perspectives on the concept of LRE and the provision of special education.

123

ENVIRONMENT AND LEARNING

In January, 1977, Crockett assumed the responsibility for teaching 66 Long Island kindergartners—33 children in the 2 ½-hour morning session and another 33 for the same amount of time after lunch. She had no assistance from another adult, but benefits included a classroom of generous size and a wise principal who encouraged the use of the classroom walls as a teaching tool. The principal counseled that most of the general education students would learn incidentally from stimulating charts that served as more than decoration and from numerous hands-on learning centers around the room. This would free the teacher, Crockett, to pay particular attention to children whose needs required more specific instruction—as best as could be done in such an overcrowded situation. Crockett and other teachers worried about who among the 66 might miss out altogether on meaningful instruction in this school district, which annually voted down its school budget.

Just one month earlier, in December, 1976, the National Center for Law and the Handicapped in Indiana submitted comments from the field to the BEH on the third draft of the consolidated concept paper under Part B of PL 94-142. Concerned with the imprecision of the language under the section titled *Least Restrictive Environment*, the Center took issue with the phrase "…that education in regular classes with the use of supplementary aids and services cannot be achieved satisfactorily," asking, "to whose satisfaction is the provision addressed?" (National Center for Law and the Handicapped, 1976, p. 3). Stating that the educational interests of the exceptional learner are of foremost concern, the Center suggested that the following wording be substituted:

> that special classes, separate schooling, or other removal of handicapped children from the regular educational environment occurs only when the nature or severity of the handicap is such that education in regular classes with the use of supplementary aids and services is for that person significantly educationally inferior to and less productive than a placement outside the regular educational environment. (National Center for Law and the Handicapped, 1976, p. 4, italics in the original).

This recommendation was not incorporated into the federal regulations, but this early attempt to qualify the educational experience a child might receive is important to preserve. Within this language is implicit reference to a range of educational services and the possibility that success for a particular student might not be provided in a general education setting. The standard of satisfactory progress in the regular class, combined as it is in law with the standard of appropriate schooling with nondisabled students, provides a conceptualization of meaningful educational opportunity with a multiple focus on the educational benefit received, the characteristics of the student receiving it, and the circumstances surrounding its provision. Sarason and Doris (1979) suggested that if PL 94-142 wanted to eliminate segregation practices in the spirit of the *Brown* (1954) decision, then the term *least restrictive alternative* would never have been used. "What this item boils down to is that when a school district can show that the use of a regular educational environment accompanied by supplementary aids and services is not adequate to give the child what he or she needs, educational segregation is permissible" (p. 369). The writers of the law knew of the opposition to racial integration and mainstreaming; they knew this was a radical bill (J.J. Gallagher, personal communication, November 22, 1996; F.J. Weintraub, personal communication, January 7, 1997). Writing the law at a time influenced by racial segregation, the developers needed a mechanism that embodied an emancipatory spirit but maneuvered politically, aware of an institutional environment resistant to change: "*What the law intends is that the number of segregated individuals should be reduced somewhat...* Public Law 94-142 intends a modest quantitative change and, in that respect it is miles apart from the 1954 decision which ruled segregation unconstitutional" (Sarason & Doris, 1979, p. 369, italics in original).

The Meaning of Place

> A sense of physical place—location in space, where things are and where things happen—is basic to much of human thought.... One can hardly imagine an existence without being somewhere, and the where of being is nearly always a partial determinant of the quality of being.... What is said to be possible, probable, desirable, or permissible in certain places may change, either based on empirical findings or because social values change, or both. (Kauffman & Lloyd, 1995, p. 5)

Kauffman and Lloyd (1995) observed that instructional settings provide social ecologies that are critical for academic learning and socialization. In the wake of *Brown v. The Board of Education of Topeka* (1954), the issue of how students should be grouped for instruction needs sophisticated scrutiny both within special education and in general education policies of choice such as magnet and charter schools. Kauffman and Lloyd raised the following questions: To whom does the *Brown* decision apply in grouping students for instruction? Does it consider disability as well as race, or characteristics such as age, gender, interests, or academic performance? Does *Brown* apply only to placement in school districts, or does it apply to school buildings and individual classrooms? Does *Brown* prohibit voluntary segregation of students or separation from the regular class when sanctioned by due process protections?

"Granted that legal racial segregation of public facilities, including public schools, is despicable, hyperextension of the notion that it is inherently inequitable to separate students on any basis brings us recursively to the issues of fairness" (Kauffman & Lloyd, 1995, p. 11). With regard to educating exceptional learners, Gallagher (1994) suggested that we define fairness more appropriately: "fairness does not consist of educating all children in the same place at the same time (and with the same curriculum?) but in ensuring that the student has basic needs met and is traveling a well thought-out road to a career and a satisfying life style" (p. 528).

The central question in defining place for educational purposes rests with what we are trying to accomplish with a particular student as that road is traversed. Kauffman (1995) observed that "educational placement is defined by more than the physical space students occupy. It also involves the methods, materials, and equipment used in instruction, the particular students being taught, the teacher or teachers who provide instruction, and the tasks students are asked to perform" (p. 230). In his consideration of instructional environments, Kauffman noted that "all environments are inherently restrictive. The significance of an environment is not that it is restrictive in a general sense but that it is restrictive of specific things" (p. 226). Many years earlier, Cruickshank (1977) had raised a good point with a brief question: "least restrictive of what?"

Effective Educational Environments

To an educator, the idea of a learning environment is less an issue of liberty than of practical instructional potential that can either facilitate or impede the task of learning basic knowledge and skills "necessary for survival in the modern world" (Stockard & Mayberry, 1992, p. x). In their summary of the literature related to educational environments, Stockard and Mayberry (1992) reviewed research on different aspects of general educational environments. The list of literature is absent studies investigating issues of student placement for exceptional learners but examines group learning outcomes in regular settings for such social and psychological variables as the composition of educational groups and the effect on students of school and classroom climates. Other literature examines the practical aspects of learning environments, considering "how school facilities and expenditures, teachers' qualifications, and school and classroom size affect students' achievement" (p. xiii). Circling beyond this realm, to draw on Bronfenbrenner's (1979) image, are studies that examine how the community environment influences the group achievement of students. Stockard and Mayberry noted that this general educational literature has not featured the influence of the social context or environment on an individual's behavior.

The Student and the Environment

The Interface of Child and School. Jones (1995) referred to the child–school interface and considered specifically the interactions between an individual learner and the particular ecological variables that circumscribe his or her social context. Emphasizing students with emotional and behavioral problems, Jones noted that various professionals within the field of education have vastly different perspectives with regard to their perceptions of this child–school connection:

> Despite the evident overlap in the subject matter of child psychiatry, educational psychology and sociology of education, there is a crucial difference between disaffection as investigated by sociologists (who emphasize social implications of truancy, disruptiveness, or evasion of academic tasks), and problems which require clinical attention (and might involve truancy, etc.). Clinicians are interested in problems which transcend the educational setting in which the problem comes to light; educationalists are concerned with the impact of pupils' problems in the educational settings. Obvious as it is, the qualitative difference between problems imported into child/school transactions and school-endemic problems needs stating.... A popular sociological thesis is that the school, representing middle-class values, favours children of a middle-class background. Regarding "unconventional" home styles (e.g., single parenthood) as detrimental or as just different is a matter of opinion; emotional deprivation due to parental neglect cannot be dismissed as a case of parents' and teachers' differing ideologies. (p. 248)

Jones (1995) explicitly stated that professional educators view individual characteristics, educational benefit, and student placement from varying foci and are not necessarily discussing the same issues at all. Before assuming that special needs can be met in the ordinary classroom, we need a better understanding of a child's particular needs within the school environment and beyond.

Individualized Instruction. Throughout the history of education tensions have existed between ideal and mass education and between the role of personalization in defining the ends and providing the means of instruction. Quintilian, an educator in the 1st century A.D., remarked "let him that is skilled in teaching ascertain first of all, when a boy is entrusted to him, his ability and disposition.... Let him next consider how the mind of this pupil has to be managed" (Quintilian, as quoted in Osin & Lesgold, 1996, p. 621). As a Roman teacher, Quintilian's challenge lay in adapting individual instruction within a class of diverse students, unlike his Grecian counterparts whose more aristocratic methodology was tutorial Socratic dialogue (Osin & Lesgold, 1996). Osin and Lesgold (1996) observed that, "except for the last two centuries (a relatively short period in historical terms), schools provided students with individualized instruction. The fact that students were together, even in the same room, did not mean that they studied the same materials" (p. 630). Nor were there great expectations for their success.

Several factors have inhibited the growth of individualized instruction in American schools, including the adoption of European grade-level models of pedagogy, the cult of industrial efficiency, which sought to provide cost-effective instruction by dividing students into classes of presumed equal proficiency, and the technological insufficiency in the 1960s and 1970s to support popular and more differentiated instructional models such as multiaged grouping, adapted education, and nongraded schools (Osin & Lesgold, 1996). As early as 1890, C. W. Eliot, then president of Harvard, decried the practice of educational mass-production, claiming that the

> "grouping together of children whose capacities are widely different" was not only "flying in the face of nature" but also the "worst feature of the American school." Returning to the same theme two years later, Eliot proposed a solution. To fulfill their democratic mission, schools should take the "utmost possible account of individual instruction"; should grade "according to capacity," and should promote pupils not "by battalions," but by the most "irregular and individual way possible." (Hamilton, 1989, p. 132)

The emphasis on educational mass production, however, continued well after Eliot's denouncement, persisting years beyond the 1925 yearbook of the National Society for the Study of Education dedicated to adapting the schools to individual differences. It remained barely affected by the progressivism of Dewey, whose pedagogy took firmer root in private rather than public schools (Osin & Lesgold, 1996). Osin and Lesgold (1997) suggested that such standardized education belies a lost recognition of intellectual diversity:

> the explicit messages of equality of the American ("all men are created equal") and French ("liberte, egalite, and fraternite") revolutions have been taken too literally by many groups in society, and instead of being understood in their true meaning of equality of rights, they have been transformed into a false ideal of uniformity. (p. 652)

Nicholas J. Anastasiow observed from his perspective as former Director of the Institute for Child Study at Indiana University from 1968 to 1978 that those years held no curriculum for exceptional children—just watered-down mainline material. There was a lack of agreement among regular educators on a child-centered philosophy of education, and teaching and assessment practices proceeded based on group norms. Most schools continued to employ whole-group instruction dominated by drill and practice, memorization, and graded texts:

> There wasn't a regular classroom I visited in which I would place a child with special needs, let alone my own child. There was little allowance for individual differences, let alone extra individual differences. What I'm saying is that the LRE's mainstreaming policy is flawed in that it is based on assumptions of educational practice that do not widely exist in the schools. (Anastasiow, personal communication, November, 1996)

Education and Exceptionality

Although Anastasiow saw the concept of LRE as perched precariously upon the faulty foundation of general education, Dunn (1968) faulted special education for enabling its counterpart (general education) to ignore the need to shore up its base by taking responsibility for its cast-offs from the regular class. The solution lies at the foundational level of education and exceptionality, observed Bateman (1994), who suggested that even if individualization were the goal for all students, disabled or nondisabled, "even if one had unlimited resources, it is possible that the means of individualization that are effective for special education students might not be the same means as those for regular education students" (p. 517). Gallagher (1990) observed that "it is not merely bias against handicapped children that causes educators puzzlement; it is concern about what integration means in this context and about engineering effective education for everyone given these impressive differences" (p. 35). Gerber (1996) observed that "historically, special educational programming emerges as the unavoidable consequence of the immutable fact of human differences in conflict with the ambition to build systems of universal mass education" (p. 157). In this sense, Gerber viewed special education as embodying elements subversive to the delivery of universal public education: "special education's focus and priorities challenge schools to produce a radical form of social justice: equality of educational opportunity for students who are sometimes characterized by extreme individual differences" (p. 156).

The Interface of General and Special Education

Special education has dual roots in both idealism and pragmatism. Semmel et al. (1994) recalled that, as a result, "reformist zeal and vision constituted a substantial part of the historical traditions of special education as a field of practice" (p. 40). Although early visionaries sought to find a niche for special students in public education and "to minimize the handicapping consequences of significant differences while supporting the effectiveness of regular classroom teaching" (p. 41), special education was also the creation of administrators who were hampered by insufficient resources yet challenged by complex operations and multiple goals. By the late 1960s, and largely influenced by civil rights legislation, the field became very sensitive to issues of equity and appropriateness in its procedures. "A scholarly field used to thinking that appropriate schools could be built up around knowledge of individual differences now faced a world in which the behavior of schools in compliance to policy determined what would be considered individual differences" (Semmel et al., 1994, p. 47). The focus of thought in special education shifted from issues of identification and curriculum, with a view to long-term outcomes, to efficient and fair management of service. It followed that "a different type of scholarship was needed, one that could embrace the compensatory, reciprocal relationship between real individual differences, on one hand, and schools, and school policy, on the other" (Semmel et al., 1994, p. 47).

Meredith and Underwood (1995) noted that the movement that drove the development of federal special education legislation was spawned from the failure of the general education system to respond even minimally to the instructional needs of exceptional learners. They described the general education system as fragmented and diverse, with local power sources providing directions that vary greatly from one school district to another and across states. A faithful representation, in their view, shows general education as focused on the provision of group teaching and learning, with keen political concern for costs, muted responsiveness to particular parental concerns, and accountability that is political rather than legal.

In contrast, Meredith and Underwood (1995) characterized special education as having a "semi-official constitution" in the EAHCA/IDEA—one without a general education counterpart. The premises embodied in law require sensitization of teachers and administrators to the provision of individualized instruction based on carefully documented need and achievement and substantive parental decision making while operating "under the bright light of judicial oversight" (p. 202). These authors used the example of student disciplinary issues to illustrate the inherent tension associated with educating exceptional learners in regular education settings:

> To those operating from the regular education paradigm, it seems irrational to allow students to operate in the same classroom and be governed by completely different rules and norms, particularly when the offending child's actions are perceived to be outside any concept of acceptable classroom behavior. To those operating from the

special education perspective, such a result is not only mandated by the IDEA, but is completely consistent with a more individualized remedial theory of constructing orderly behavior. We do not believe one paradigm is inherently superior; however, it seems very difficult to employ two different models in one classroom. (Meredith & Underwood, 1995, p. 223)

In their view, both political and pedagogical conflicts have affected positive service delivery because "unfortunately, the framers of the IDEA did not fully consider the thorny issues surrounding implementation of a new model through traditional regular education institutions" (p. 199).

Meredith and Underwood developed a model for contrasting the underlying premises of special and regular education. Because their analysis combined political, legal, and pedagogical considerations, it offers a foundation from which to continue the discussion of instructional settings for exceptional learners. They viewed special education as focused on individual student goals and achievement with educational programs being individually negotiated. In counterpoint, they described regular education as focused on group instruction with the size of the group determined by the "political winners". Special education features parental empowerment, whereas regular education relies on community empowerment, complete with political decision making and taxpayer power. Legal accountability guides special education, with costs being secondary to outcomes. Parents are given significant ability to enforce their rights and those of their children in court. Political accountability guides regular education, and costs are as important as educational outcome. In contrast to special education, there is limited judicial review of regular education. Special education has a federal focus and locus of control; regular education has a state and local focus and center of control (Meredith & Underwood, 1995, p. 198).

Some special educators find fault with what they call a dual system of service delivery, seeming to seek reproachment with general education by blaming "the well-established flaws of the special education status quo" (Gallagher, 1990, p. 34) —an uncertain classification system of identifying children for services, low expectations for student achievement, lack of program effectiveness data, and the potentially negative effects of separating children from regular programs. These theorists argue that a merger of special and general education and the development of a unitary system of service delivery is the solution to improve both equity and excellence.

Meredith and Underwood (1995), in defining the different values and missions of special and regular educators, did not espouse any particular form of assimilation. Rather, they probed the foundational premises that support instructional practices. They called for difficult work at the interface of both fields that threatens to make the optimistic calls for a unitary system sound overly facile and fatuous. Clearly acknowledging that each strand of education was developed to address unique problems, Meredith and Underwood called for modifications of both general and special education in response to current issues of cost, educational standards, and school safety that are raising questions of the adequacy of either.

Service Delivery Goals

Gallagher (1990) saw the important dilemma of "how to integrate and diversify at the same time" (p. 35) as integral to a synthesis of the concepts of integration and educational excellence. Turnbull (1990) argued for the concept of LRE to be "infused with a sense of liberation, not of restriction" (p. 188), offering expansive and rich educational alternatives for exceptional learners when their presumed instruction in the regular classroom is rebutted by their particular circumstances. In reviewing environments and learning, we need to examine the goals and objectives that have driven the provision of an appropriate education for exceptional learners.

EDUCATIONAL FOUNDATIONS OF LRE

The Language of Educational Placement

Precision in the language used to examine the foundations of LRE is no less important to educators than to lawyers, with some educational terminology reflecting a more place-bound or a more service-oriented conceptualization of service delivery. The term *least restrictive alternative* (LRA), first applied to special education placement, seems to imply that an instructional setting is an alternative to some other place. *Least restrictive environment* (LRE) seems to imply an environment in which something occurs. Tucker (1989) attributed the switch in terminology to a desire of policy makers to expand the emphasis of the concept from location to what actually occurs in a particular instructional setting. This service-oriented conceptualization has been slow in coming he observes and has not been facilitated by the change in terminology:

> Virtually everyone would agree that the word environment means more than location. Yet when paired with the term "least restrictive" in the application of services for students who are handicapped, the term has remained almost exclusively a term of literal placement without reference to conditions or circumstances that exist in that location. As generally used, LRE represents an issue of the availability of facilities, and/or an issue of advocacy

pressure to be physically located in a given place, rather than an issue of the program effectiveness of the conditions existing in that place. Physical placement as an end in itself cannot represent LRE fully. But it does represent a simple concept and therefore requires less energy to implement than would a more service-oriented application of LRE. A more comprehensive concept of LRE is one that starts by identifying a student's specific needs and then asking what are the most normal conditions under which those needs can be provided. (pp. 456–457)

Different orientations, definitions, and interpretations pepper the professional placement literature and are illustrated in some of the following descriptions.

Definitions of LRE

Salem and Fell (1988) reported a dizzying variety of state-level interpretations of LRE from 40 educators of the deaf across the United States. Samples of local policies recorded in their own words consider LRE to mean the following: "placement in public schools," "mainstreaming," "the place where parents think the child will be best educated," "placement in public school programs—frequently—very small, newly established programs, with a wide range of ages and learning abilities, and levels of hearing" (pp. 69–70). One administrator claimed that "most LEA's think that, first, LRE must be satisfied, and second, education is discussed. Mainstreaming has become the goal not the process for education" (Salem & Fell, 1988, p. 69).

Gross and Vance (1975) provided a rich description of the early confusion surrounding instructional settings for exceptional learners:

> a number of catch phrases and slogans have been associated with or used interchangeably with the term mainstreaming. For example, mainstreaming has been interpreted as an attempt to provide services to special education students in the "least restrictive program alternative." The least restrictive alternative has been defined as the delivery of special education services under the highest possible degree of "normalization." "Normalization" has been referred to as an attempt to organize special education services in a way that allows maximum opportunities for "integration". Finally, "integration" is said to be an attempt to provide programs and services to handicapped students in the "mainstream"!!! Special education has obviously gone full circle with its mainstream related jargon and as a result definitions for each of these terms have become blurred. (pp. 106–107)

Heron and Skinner (1981) defined LRE as "that educational setting which maximizes . . . the student's opportunity to respond and achieve, permits the regular education teacher to interact proportionally with the students in the classroom, and fosters acceptable social relations between nonhandicapped and [handicapped] students" (p. 116). Burgdorf (1980) saw the LRE as a means of breaking practices that epitomized

> "the child must fit the program" attitude common among old-line educators; if a child is out of step with academic or behavioral expectations, the child is to be booted out. The concept of least restrictive environment, on the other hand, mandates that efforts be made to adapt the program to the special needs of the child so that the child can be educated, if possible, in the regular setting, and, if not, in an environment as close to the regular classroom situation as can be made educationally appropriate. (p. 283)

Burgdorf (1980) described mainstreaming as "an educational term analogous to the legal concept of the least restrictive alternative" (p. 292) but pointed out little consistency or precision in the use of terminology. Osborne and DiMattia (1994) similarly distinguished between the terms *least restrictive environment* and *mainstreaming*, suggesting that the terms should not be used interchangeably:

> LRE refers to the legal principle that students with disabilities are to be educated as close as possible to the general education environment. Mainstreaming is an educational term that refers to the practice of placing students with disabilities in general education classes with appropriate instructional support. Mainstreaming is one means of meeting the LRE requirement; but the IDEA does not require mainstreaming in all cases. (p. 8)

Brown, Nietupski, and Hamre-Nietupski (as cited in Nietupski, 1995) offered a concept of LRE for students with severe disabilities in 1976 calling for placement "in self contained classes in regular schools and to have ongoing interaction with nondisabled peers" (p. 41). In the 1980s, Biklen (1985) described four LRE components of physical integration, functional integration, social integration, and societal integration. More recently but in the same tradition, Salisbury and Smith (1991) suggested that LRE has both a conceptual and a legal definition. To these authors, "the law . . . presumes that services will be delivered in the classroom the child would attend were he or she not handicapped" (p. 25). Conceptually, however, they defined the term LRE to mean "educating a child with a disability in a way 'that least limits or restricts that child's opportunities to be near and interact with other typical children'" (p. 25); see also Taylor, Biklen, Lehr, and Searle, 1987.

Taylor (1988) was explicit in stating that he analyzes LRE not as a legal prescription but as a policy directive. He constructed a definition of LRE broad enough to include

> positions that reject institutions, special schools, and other segregated settings...as well as those that envision a continued role for these environments.... The principles of LRE for residential, educational, vocational, and other services may be defined as follows: Services for people with developmental disabilities should be designed according to a range of program options varying in terms of restrictiveness, normalization, independence, and integration, with a presumption in favor of environments that are least restrictive and most normalized, independent, and integrated (p. 45).

This conceptualization, which specifically addresses services for people with developmental disabilities, does not clearly define the policy arena that it intends to address. Although the normalized characteristics of placements are emphasized, there is no mention of the different purposes inherent in community living, educational benefit, or vocational training. Taylor's conceptual definition of LRE is problematic in its attempt to encompass both community services and the provision of education without distinguishing the roles of children and adults. Taylor is lauded by Lipsky and Gartner (1997) for his vilifications of the LRE, but his working definition of LRE is not conceptually aligned with the procedures of special education law.

Taylor (1988) self-destructed his broadly worded conceptualization of LRE with criticisms apparently based upon practice with developmentally disabled adults. He assailed the continuum of alternative placements for emphasizing location over service, for legitimizing environments restrictive of integration, and for confusing segregation and integration with a diminution of intensity of services. His rebukes claiming that LRE exalts professional opinion and impinges on individual rights while ignoring personal wants speak more to a patronizing protectiveness that affronts adults with disabilities in the community. It is misplaced, however, in its application to students in educational settings, ignoring the developmental nature of childhood and the legally mandated focus on parental involvement in special education planning.

Taylor aptly criticized corrupt use of the continuum, suggesting that too often movement is made only when space is needed or new venues become available. He did not consider, however, the possible appropriateness of the continuum as a readiness model for some students, nor for individuals other than those with developmental disabilities. Finally, he applied affective dimensions associated with residential living to school life, suggesting that changing settings "can destroy any sense of home and may disrupt relationships with roommates, neighbors, and friends" (p. 48).

Taylor's conceptualization of LRE, and its subsequent repudiation, is confounded by the mixture of people (i.e., children and adults), purposes (i.e., community living and education), and places (i.e., home and school) that he so broadly included. His sociological perspective recalls Jones' (1995) observation that when it comes to student placement, sometimes it cannot be assumed that professionals are even discussing the same issues.

Korinek, McLaughlin, and Walther-Thomas (1995), in contrast, confined their remarks to the appropriate education of exceptional learners in schools and relied on the legal definition of LRE for the provision of services:

> IDEA is grounded in the belief that professionals and families, each representing a different perspective, should work together to ensure that appropriate decisions are made regarding students with disabilities . . . LRE and the corollary requirement that each student be provided a free appropriate public education (FAPE) based on his or her unique educational needs rather than on a disability category are designed to protect the civil rights of students with disabilites. (p. 10)

These authors provided a service-oriented framework offering a useful dyad of LRE and collaboration. They suggested that both play critical roles in the development and delivery of effective programs for exceptional learners: "LRE is focused on the protection of fundamental educational rights of students with disabilities, whereas collaboration is focused on the responsibilities of adults to develop programs and provide services for those students" (Korinek et al., 1995, p. 9).

Gottlieb et al. (1991) viewed LRE as "that environment which imposes the fewest restrictions on a child's cognitive, emotional, and/or social development, regardless of the physical location of that environment" (p. 97). For them, individual assessment of the student and instructional placement are closely intertwined. Before a placement determination can be made, a minimum of information should be collected on the ecology of the general education classroom into which the child is scheduled to be placed.

Morsink and Lenk (1992) also considered the selection of the LRE as a match between the learner's needs and the characteristics of the environment and stated that determination of the LRE should be based on three issues. First, decisions should be made on an individual basis based on the student's unique educational needs. Second, factors that can make an environment that appears to be less restrictive for a student actually more restrictive should be considered. These factors include a range of student variability and class size that stretch a classroom's limited tolerance for diversity, teacher attitudes and training, and impact on other students in the classroom. Third, educators should identify factors of effective instruction that categorize any environment within the continuum of placements.

The Continuum of Alternative Placements

The legal concept of LRE in special education has been put into practice as a continuum of educational placements ranging from those considered most to least restrictive. The frameworks of the continuum described by Reynolds (1962) and the cascade of services depicted by Deno (1970) served as the bases for identifying possible instructional settings for exceptional learners. Implicit in Reynolds' continuum model and in Deno's cascade is the idea that if the regular class is not designated as the LRE, an important objective of instruction is to prepare the student for transitions to settings considered more inclusive of children with and without disabilities.

Weintraub (personal communication, January 7, 1997) remembered the earlier rendering of Deno's cascade and the effect of legal disputes such as the PARC case on its depiction:

> If you look back at the original model of the triangle, there was another triangle underneath that was for the kids who were uneducable. Well, while we were fighting for right-to-education, we started fighting that one. We said, "Can't have that," so we wiped it out, made it one triangle.

Using the Continuum. "The U.S. Department of Education Annual Reports to Congress (1981, 1982) reported efforts by state and school districts to increase the movement of handicapped students to less restrictive environments" (Yoshida, 1986, p. 14). Yoshida noted that it follows that the continuum and cascade models not only identify alternative settings to the regular class but also have been interpreted to indicate that those termed less restrictive are more desirable than those considered more restrictive—regardless of their effects on individual students. The goal of mainstreaming derived from these models becomes "the transitioning of students to less restrictive placements and their continued maintenance in those settings" (Yoshida, 1986, p. 14). Such implementation of placement in the LRE directs educators to focus on placements and not on program goals. As a result, too often transitions occur without support, clear goals for the student, or subsequent monitoring of achievement. Yoshida cautioned that "focusing on placements may prove so satisfying to school district personnel that determining goals for the instructional program and the students themselves may become secondary or of no importance" (p. 14). In an early illustration of this problem, Yoshida referred to the insufficient attention paid to the instructional outcomes for students following California's efforts to address the overclassification of minorities for special education in response to the *Larry P. v. Riles* litigation:

> Although district personnel were most concerned about complying with the *Larry P.* consent decree and orders by the State Department of Education to decertify and transition students to regular class, personnel at neither the district nor building level knew whether the decertified students were achieving or adjusting socially in their new classrooms. Very few were given any transitional help; rarely were any instructional or social goals stated for these students. School district personnel were aware of student status only if the students were referred again for special class. Apparently, district personnel were satisfied that these students were succeeding if they merely remained in regular class. (p. 14)

Yoshida noted that transition to a less restrictive environment is only the first step and that program goals, such as academic achievement and social growth, should be clearly stated. In an early conceptualization of integrated services, Kaufman et al. (1975) offerred an alternative to a unidimensional perspective by determining that mainstreaming refers to the

> temporal, instructional and social integration of eligible exceptional children with normal peers. It is based on an ongoing, individually determined educational needs assessment requiring classification of responsibility for coordinated planning and programming by regular and special education administrative, instructional, and support personnel. (Kaufman et al., 1975, pp. 40–41).

This definition, which has been criticized for attempting to achieve the ideal (MacMillan & Semmel, 1977; Semmel, Gottlieb, & Robinson, 1979), is consistent with the provision of an appropriate education in the LRE as prescribed by federal law. It also advances the law's imperatives for collaboration among professionals and individual placement decisions based on a student's unique educational needs.

Transenvironmental Programming. Most studies of mainstreaming and inclusion have explored the effects on students once they are in the regular classroom setting. There is little information about how best to help students move from one setting to another and how to sustain their success after the transition (Fuchs, Roberts, Fuchs, & Bowers, 1996). The challenge to provide effective programming across educational environments was picked up by

Anderson-Inman (1981) and extended by the recent work of D. and L. Fuchs and their colleagues. This approach, known as *transenvironmental programming*, focuses on "the acquisition of skills deemed critical for success in less restrictive settings and the transfer of these skills from *training* to *target* environments" (Fuchs, Fuchs, Fernstrom, & Hohn, 1991, p. 134, italics in original). This reintegration process provides students who have mild disabilities (i.e., LD, BD, S/L) four levels of support: an assessment of the behavioral and academic expectations in the receiving environment, instruction by a special educator in skills needed in the new environment, practice and use of these skills in the new setting, and evaluation in the mainstream to determine academic and social adjustment (Anderson-Inman, 1981; Fuchs et al., 1991).

Fuchs (personal communication, December 9, 1996) noted that these studies have been heroic in effort. There was much collaboration between special and general educators as well as numerous hours of support from project staff in developing instructional interventions in the mainstream. All teachers involved were volunteers, and special educators were given the incentive of a small stipend. Even with all these facilitating factors, students with disabilities demonstrated no gains in the regular class, although they had made steady gains in the self-contained setting prior to transition. It is disturbing that in this and subsequent studies of transenvironmental programming experimental students with mild disabilities generally did not demonstrate academic gains once placed in regular education for instruction (Fuchs et al., 1996).

Individual Students and Classroom Environments

Zigler (1996) framed the difficult issue of instructional settings for exceptional learners positively, asking, "What kind of transactions do we want to see in classrooms and how may disabilities affect these transactions?" (p. x). Keogh and Speece (1996) suggested looking inward and examining environmental variables, or the ecologies of classrooms, because schooling is both an influence on and a contributor to the risk status of all students and to long-term outcomes for students with LD. They contended that "educational status is, in part at least, a function of 'goodness of fit' between child attributes and schooling demands, noting that for some children 'educational risk' changes relative to setting and to time" (p. 5). Various scales have been developed for use with students that attempt to match their individual attributes with characteristics of learning environments (Epstein, Quinn, & Cumblad, 1994; Greenwood, 1996; Vaughn & Schumm, 1996).

The Restrictiveness of Educational Environments. Epstein, Quinn, and Cumblad (1994) observed that although the LRE concept "was widely accepted by special educators, the meaning of the term 'restrictive' has been difficult to define" (p. 108). Working from a list of instructional settings, including the continuum and cascade conceptualizations of Reynolds (1962) and Deno (1970), they suggested that an educational environment can be made restrictive in and of itself by the physical facility's accessibility or its proximity to a student's home, the rules and requirements in its governance that control activity, free movement, or personal choices; or the level of normalization available to a student through association with peers, curriculum, and instructional materials.

These authors acknowledge that their working definition of the restrictiveness of instructional settings is limited by the absence of such environmental characteristics as "staff tolerance for behavioral heterogeneity, extent to which instruction and management strategies are individually based on student's needs or sensitivity to the social status and needs of students with internalizing and/or externalizing behavioral disorders" (Epstein et al., 1994, p. 117). Their words ring true that "teachers and students in regular classrooms are often very unaccepting of behaviors that are characteristic of students with EBD and there is nothing unrestrictive about social rejection" (p. 117).

In keeping with the LRE requirements of federal law to individualize placement decisions, an analysis of the restrictiveness of educational settings must be partnered with a comprehensive evaluation of the student's behavioral and academic functioning, family status, residential restrictiveness, and the use of community services (Epstein et al., 1994). These authors emphasized the contextual power of the particular embodied in the concept of LRE and underscored the centrality of the notion of appropriate as centered on the child.

Many educators of the deaf support this approach. In 1988, another conceptual rendering of placement options and LRE was advanced by the Commission on the Education of the Deaf. This model is circular and negates the concept of hierarchy in moving students toward integrated settings. "The point is that the ordering of least restrictive environments from greatest to least is completely dependent on the individual child. In the abstract, the placements themselves are equivalent" (Underwood & Mead, 1995).

Keogh and Speece (1996) underscored the importance of ecobehavioral programming by suggesting that children, especially those with learning disabilities, "are especially vulnerable to schooling effects, including changes in instructional and curricular demands and to teachers' expectations for performance" (p. 5). These authors encouraged continued research into classroom ecologies focusing on the quality of student-to-student and student–teacher interactions, issues of curriculum and instruction, and organization and management.

CONTEMPORARY CLASSROOM ENVIRONMENTS

In order to determine whether general education settings have become more instructionally facilitative since the passage of PL 94-142 in 1975, recent studies in both elementary and secondary schools were examined to better understand the status of special education for exceptional learners in the context of more inclusive programming. The following descriptions of classroom ecologies provide contemporary snapshots of students and teachers, curriculum and instruction, and the organization and management of resources.

Students and Teachers

Characteristics of Students. Exceptional learners are a diverse group compared to the general population and also vary greatly from one to another. The exceptionalities that interfere with their classroom learning may involve "sensory, physical, cognitive, emotional, or communication abilities or any combination of these.... Exceptionalities may vary greatly in cause, degree, and effect on educational progress, and the effects may vary greatly depending on the individual's age, sex, and life circumstances" (Hallahan & Kauffman, 1997, p. 8).

Hallahan and Kauffman (1997) presented an educational definition of exceptionality that argues for the acknowledgment of differences and the relevance of specialized instruction:

> For purposes of their education, exceptional children and youths are those who require special education and related services if they are to realize their full human potential. They require special education because they are markedly different from most children in one or more of the following ways: They may have mental retardation, learning disabilities, emotional or behavioral disorders, physical disabilities, disorders of communication, autism traumatic brain injury, impaired hearing, impaired sight, or special gifts or talents.... Two concepts are important to our educational definition of exceptional children and youths: (1) diversity of characteristics and (2) need for special education. The concept of diversity is inherent in the definition of exceptionality, the need for special education is inherent in an educational definition. (p. 7)

Hallahan and Kauffman pointed out that exceptional learners and their classmates share many similarities but caution that often the most typical students receiving special education, those with learning disabilities, appear to have no obvious differences from other students with learning problems. Kavale, Fuchs, and Scruggs (1994) argued that students with learning disabilities have more severe academic deficits than do their low-achieving peers. Furthermore, according to Rieth and Polsgrove (1994), these students have well-documented problems in the classroom, including severe deficits in basic literacy and numeracy skills; generalized failure and below-average performance in content areas such as science and social studies; inadequate student-survival skills such as study and test-taking skills, listening well, and taking notes; pervasive lack of motivation and passive learning behaviors; and inadequate interpersonal skills.

Characteristics of Teachers. The American teaching corps also represents a diverse demographic profile. In the United States, special education teachers are considerably younger than their general education counterparts. Almost half are younger than 40 years old, whereas only 35% of regular educators are in this age range. Approximately 90% of elementary general and special educators are female, but the secondary level shows a considerable gender difference between special and general educators. Women comprise 77% of secondary special educators but only 53% of secondary general educators. The ethnic comparison of special and general educators is similar, but representation of African American teachers is 25% higher in special education. A greater percentage of special educators hold a graduate degree, but their colleagues in general education have more years of teaching experience (Cook & Boe, 1995).

Teachers' Perceptions of Mainstreaming or Inclusion. There is general agreement that for students with disabilities to be served well in inclusive settings the regular education teacher must be supportive of both the principles and challenges of teaching them. Scruggs and Mastropieri (1996) reviewed 27 survey reports in which 9,772 teachers were asked about their attitudes toward mainstreaming children with disabilities. These reports spanned the years 1958 to 1995 and included teachers from Canada, the United States, and Australia. Regardless of geography or chronology, the willingness of these educators was inversely related to the degree of additional classroom assistance such students might require. Only about one fourth agreed that mainstreaming most students with disabilities was desirable. About the same number said they thought they had sufficient time, training, and resources to implement it successfully. Most responded that they lacked the skills or training in modifying instruction as well as the time and resources. Most wanted reduced class size, greater material and personnel support, and more time for planning and implementing instruction and collaborating with support staff. Full-time inclusion in the regular classroom met with strong negative response in two 1994 studies, with 80% of respondents in one report saying they felt coerced into full inclusion. The authors noted that responses were surprisingly stable from the earliest to the most recent reports. No systematic relation appeared between teachers' attitudes and publication date, lending support to the idea that "teachers regard students with disabilities in the context of procedural classroom concerns (which have improved little if any in recent decades), rather than in the context of social prejudice and attitudes toward social integration (which appear to have improved somewhat in recent decades)" (p. 71).

Instructional Interventions for Exceptional Learners

Teaching Conditions. In addition to larger classes, teachers are currently responding to a wide range of instructional levels within general education, with estimates indicating that more than five grade levels are represented per classroom in some schools (Fuchs, Fuchs, Hamlett, Phillips, & Bentz, 1994). Given current fiscal restraints, teachers are not often supported when special education students are integrated. "In addition, this greater responsibility is not always accompanied with more intensive preparation of teachers and administrators, increased educational support, more manageable class sizes, or state of the art technology" (Roberts & Mather, 1995, p. 50). Lieberman (1996) referred to increased demands on classroom teachers and questioned not the ideals but the strategy of full inclusion: "We are testing more, not less. We are locking teachers into constrained curricula and syllabi more, not less.... The flexibility demanded by full inclusion is rarely encountered" (p. 17).

Roberts and Mather (1995) observed that "regular educators are not trained to provide diversified instructional methods or to cope with the needs of diverse learners" (p. 50). Similarly commenting on the infrequency with which general educators employ pre-referral intervention strategies, Gottlieb et al. (1994) found that other than knowing that these children needed one-to-one instruction, almost two thirds of the 206 referring classroom teachers could not indicate what resources they would need. Only 16% indicated they could be trained with the necessary skills to retain these children in their classes, and only 10% presented activities that could reasonably be described as curriculum adaptation.

There is evidence that students are not typically receiving needed support from general educators, who are more often concerned with conformity than accommodations for individual students in the regular class (Bos & Vaughn, 1994; Lieberman, 1996; Roberts & Mather, 1995). For example, in studying interventions that elementary and secondary teachers would be willing to use, Johnson and Pugach (1990) and Ellet (1993), respectively, found that classroom teachers at both levels highly ranked general and nonspecific strategies such as encouraging and supporting attempts at academic improvement, emphasizing the good qualities of behavior, demonstrating difficult tasks, and establishing specific consequences for appropriate behavior. In a study of 775 general educators, K–12, Schumm and Vaughn (1992) reported that teachers are likely to make adaptations on the spot during instruction rather than to plan for their use ahead of time. Information sources used for planning and adapting instruction most frequently come from interactions with other teachers, with parents, or directly with the student; resources outside the classroom, such as other agencies or textual data from IEPs or psychological reports, are rarely used.

Teaching Practices. Effective teachers in general and special classes have been found to use a variety of elements of instruction, including teacher-directed instruction with individual feedback; student opportunities for active academic responses; high rates of contingent reinforcement; adaptive teaching strategies to accommodate individual differences; a high rate of interaction among students, teachers, and peers; instruction at a brisk pace and in small steps; progressive goals to 100% mastery; structured lessons; strategy instruction; and computer-assisted instruction (Ellet, 1993; Fuchs & Fuchs, 1995a; Morsink & Lenk, 1992). Most of these practices have been validated using 1:1 or small group instruction in special education settings but not in inclusive ones. Others, such as team teaching, consultant teachers, and cooperative learning have yet to be validated for exceptional learners in a regular class setting (Fuchs & Fuchs, 1995a).

In general, teachers are more likely to use practical strategies that are easy to implement, effective, and conducive to their classroom routine and teaching style. Gajria, Salend, and Hemrick (1994) used the term *teacher acceptability*, suggesting that it "refers to the extent to which teachers view a strategy as easy to use, effective, reasonable, fair, consistent with their teaching style and philosophy, and appropriate for their setting" (p. 236).

Some general educators rate accommodations as more desirable than feasible. Schumm and Vaughn (1991) reported that 93 teachers (i.e., 25 elementary, 23 middle school, and 45 high school) identified as feasible those requiring no instructional or curricular changes and could be done with relative ease. Similarly, these teachers identified as desirable adaptations that require them to reinforce and encourage students, establish personal rapport with them, respect mainstreamed students as individuals and involve them in whole class activities, establish appropriate routines, and adapt classroom management strategies. Adaptations considered least desirable and feasible included adapting long-range plans, modifying the physical environment, adapting regular materials, using alternative materials, adapting grading criteria, and providing individualized instruction. Vaughn and Schumm (1996) concluded that "teachers are willing to make accommodations that demonstrate acceptance of the student . . . but less willing to make adaptations that require planning, instructional, or environmental adaptations" (p. 109).

As a result of their extensive work in elementary and secondary classrooms with hundreds of teachers and students, Vaughn and Schumm have added a critical element to their fundamental research question. In addition to seeking the most effective practices for exceptional learners in the general education classroom, they now ask which ones are feasible to implement, likely to be used by teachers over time, and will positively influence the performance of all learners in the classroom, including average and high-achieving students. "We have reframed the question because we have learned that teachers' beliefs about instruction focus on meeting the needs of the class as a whole and not on implementing specific instructional practices that will meet the needs of target students" (Vaughn & Schumm, 1996, p. 110).

Curricular Organization and Management

Appropriateness of the General Education Curriculum.   Three beliefs underlie the assumption that the general education curriculum is appropriate for exceptional learners: this curriculum can be modified to meet the diverse needs and learning styles of all students; teachers are able to assess students' needs and modify the curriculum accordingly; and teacher training and inservice programs help teachers acquire the skills necessary to teach a diverse group of students (Roberts & Mather, 1995).

These assumptions beg critical questions: Can the curriculum be modified to meet the needs of all students? Can professional training positively affect teaching practice? Are teachers providing specialized instruction for individual students with disabilities as they attempt to offer an improved, personalized, and accommodating educational experience for all students? Such questions have practical merit. If an accommodating general education provides academic and social benefit to a student with a disability so that he or she makes progress from grade to grade, then conceivably more students could be disenfranchised from mandated services and more districts released from costly obligations (Zigmond, 1995).

The formal curriculum of a school .denotes the plans made to guide learning, including the structures and practices to implement what is to be taught and learned (Pugach & Warger, 1993). Instructional practices flow from curricular imperatives dictating policies of class grouping, grade levels, grading practices, grade retention, and academic content. "Teaching to the middle" is a practice that may be appropriate only in classes of homogeneous students. "Many students do not have the ability to keep pace with the curriculum the way it is structured within the general education classroom and thus may experience a different kind of segregation—the exclusion from the basic right to learn" (Schumm et al., 1995, p. 335).

Content Coverage.   Classroom life is frequently dominated by concerns about covering the curriculum. Even the practices of elementary and secondary teachers considered to be effective with exceptional learners in their classrooms reflect priorities such as planning for content coverage and classroom activities, not individual needs. At the secondary levels, students with learning disabilities are expected to cover the same content and at the same pace as other students, although modifications are more likely to be made at the elementary level. Monitoring of students occurs largely by checking on what they are doing with little systematic monitoring of understanding, and success of lessons and time to introduce new content is based on the performance of the class as a whole and the amount of content coverage demanded by the curriculum. "The class moved on, whether the students understood the material or not" (Schumm et al., 1995).

Extensive conversations with teachers suggest less concern with students' knowledge acquisition or with the need for additional help or explanation than with whether students demonstrate interest, create discipline problems, and enjoy the lessons. Many elementary teachers reflect a classroom ecology more supportive of social acceptance and self-esteem than of academic learning. Middle school teachers seem more concerned with content coverage and discipline problems. High school teachers refer to issues of fairness and express concern that to identify or accommodate a handicap would make a student stand out and thus would not prepare him or her for the real world (Vaughn & Schumm, 1996).

Demands to cover the curriculum facing content area teachers in inclusive settings may serve as a barrier to full and effective implementation of strategy instruction beneficial to some students (Scanlon, Deschler, & Schumaker, 1996). This becomes an administrative issue, and "teachers need assurances from supervisors that when there are several special needs students in their classrooms they will not be held accountable for covering the full content of the curriculum. The first priority must be to ensure that the students succeed in learning the content that is covered" (Bos & Vaughn, 1994, p. 445.)

Goal Setting. The general education curriculum is not often individualized, nor are instructional decisions based on assessment data. There is also little evidence of a relation between IEP goals and subsequent instruction (Roberts & Mather, 1995). Disturbing results of interviews conducted over 8 to 10 years by Gottlieb et al. (1991) indicate that fewer than 10% of general educators who had exceptional learners in their classes had more than perfunctory knowledge of the children's IEPs. None had participated in a formal multidisciplinary conference regarding the child's progress. The majority of teachers had never seen the IEP, and a substantial percentage did not know what an IEP was. Gottlieb et al. asked, "How can we seriously maintain that a regular class placement is appropriate when the child study teams know little about the general education class, and the general education teacher knows little about the mainstreamed special education pupil?" (p. 101).

In special education settings, however, there is concern that too often the IEP becomes the only instructional guide, and instead of adapting the general curriculum for the student, many special educators only address individualized goals (Pugach & Warger, 1993; Sands, Adams & Stout, 1995). There are few reported systematic investigations of how these goals are set for students' performance at the class, school, district, or state levels. Whether in a separate setting or a regular classroom, little is known about how special educators make decisions for their students' short- or long-term academic goals, and empirically guided methods of identifying appropriate goals are not available (Rieth & Polsgrove, 1994). In addition, these goals are often set in spring, months before final grades document the efficacy of the current program. This practice makes it difficult to set goals that are both attainable and ambitious. Fuchs, Fuchs, and Hamlett (1989) observed that goal standards often underestimate student performance and that special educators need prompting to raise them to realistic levels. In this way, "existing professional practices that lead to the establishment of underestimated performance goals for disabled students may be contributing inadvertently to the students' lack of academic progress" (Rieth & Polsgrove, 1994, p. 122).

Behavior Management. Positive and effective management of students' social behavior is a highly significant problem in both general and special education. Safe and effective instructional environments depend on carefully designed and implemented school-wide behavior management plans (Walker, Colvin, & Ramsey, 1995) However, most schools do not create and implement effective, proactive school-wide discipline plans, and the consequence is extraordinary difficulty in managing behavior at the classroom and individual level. Many students with disabilities, particularly those with emotional or behavioral disorders, present complex and highly demanding behavior management problems, and these problems may be impossible to resolve in the context of the typical general education environment (Brigham & Kauffman, in press).

Management of Student Diversity in Inclusive Settings

To attempt to manage engaging and effective instruction, collaborative and consultative staffing models have been developed, and several instructional models including cooperative learning, peer tutoring, and curriculum-based management have been transplanted from special settings to regular classrooms. Most studies validating these practices for exceptional learners have been conducted in special education settings, suggesting limited assumptions for their success in regular classroom environments (Fuchs & Fuchs,1995b; Schrag, 1994). For example, controversy surrounds the generalizability of cooperative learning research because many of the studies were conducted in special experimental classrooms. The studies bode optimistically for social benefits, but the academic progress for students with disabilities is not so clearly indicated (Shrag, 1994).

Room for Improvement in Service Delivery. These descriptions indicate that practices in general education settings are not uniformly conducive to the specialized instruction associated with effective practice. They also suggest the need for a deeper professional understanding of required services for exceptional learners if general education teachers are to provide specially designed instruction. Bateman (1992) predicted that special education in the 1990s would focus on the all-important issues of curriculum. She stressed the need for schools to specify performance standards and to adopt instructional approaches and curricular materials that have been effective. "As long as we are content for children to engage in certain activities or processes, without regard to outcome, we will continue to have large numbers of children failing" (p. 34).

Research Issues and LRE

Current evidence from inclusive classroom ecologies suggests that individualized instruction for students with disabilities is infrequent and often provides more to accommodate teachers than learners. To protect children from "well-intentioned experimentation," Martin (1995a) wrote that policymakers should not, as a scientific matter, use the general enthusiasm for inclusion and its adoption elsewhere as criteria for decision making. He called for a study of student outcomes and an answer to the question, "Will inclusive programs provide more effective programming?" (p. 193).

Martin encouraged "careful, systematic measurements on the child," including both achievement scores and specific measurement in areas of difficulty, as well as "sophisticated measures of self-concept and socialization" (p. 194). Jenkins et al. (1994) observed that although "'experiments in schooling' are on the increase, rarely are they accompanied by the kind of outcome-oriented research that is required for us to make progress in teaching and learning" (p. 357). For example, in at least one state, academic outcome data such as grades, grade retentions, and dropout rates that could be used to monitor the impact of increased inclusive programming were not being collected systematically and summarized on a school or district basis for students with LD. Enabling outcome indicators—social acceptance in the regular class, satisfaction with class placement, attitude toward learning, and parental satisfaction—were the more frequently used measures (Houck & Rogers, 1994).

In an era of educational reform focused on improving and measuring results, decision makers struggle with a number of questions. Can the same outcomes be defined for all students, regardless of level of functioning? Should outcomes be looked at on a system-wide basis, an individual basis, or both? Should outcomes for special education rest on different assessment systems from general education (Bruininks, Thurlow, & Ysseldyke, 1992)?

Research Designs. "Numerous studies of the effects of service delivery models have been done, but most of them have been so seriously flawed that the results are not reliable" (Hallahan, Kauffman & Lloyd, 1996, p. 452). Marston (1987-1988) held that outcome studies have been compromised by the means with which gains have been measured. For example, against whom should the student with disabilities be compared, and how should progress be assessed? Early studies on the effectiveness of regular class placement simply evaluated whether the experimental mainstreaming program yielded better academic achievement, social adjustment, or classroom behavior than the control resource room or self-contained class. In short, they measured the outcomes for students who were socially and academically stronger from the beginning with lower performing students in special education settings (Fuchs & Fuchs,1995a).

Another oversimplification occurs when the results of program research are reported collectively as effective for all students rather than as the separate effects for students of different ability levels or disability classification (Hallahan et al., 1996). The often quoted meta-analysis of Carlberg and Kavale (1980) is frequently truncated and summarized by reporting the collective results of regular versus special class placement for students who are mentally retarded, emotionally and behaviorally disordered, and learning disabled. As a result, proponents of full inclusion cite Carlberg and Kavale as evidence that education in the regular class is more beneficial to students with disabilities than education in special settings. A closer analysis of the separate results reveals something else. For students with MR, regular class placement was superior. However, "the average BD/ED or LD student in special class placement was better off than 61% of his/her counterparts in regular class" (Carlberg & Kavale, 1980, pp. 301–302).

In designing studies of educational programs in the mainstream, Gottlieb et al. (1991) posed two research questions essential to service delivery: Do the mainstreamed children function within a range of proficiency that the classroom teacher believes acceptable for the child to progress adequately and remain in the class? and Would similar outcomes emerge if the control group in the separate class setting received the bulk of attention and resources? The challenge then becomes, "Can we construct self-contained placements that are superior to integrated placements on a set of redefined dimensions? If we can, are mainstreamed environments still the preferred placement?" (p. 104).

Odom et al. (1996) suggested that no single methodological approach can adequately provide the knowledge with which to address all types of research questions. Attributing their distinctions to Habermas, they described three types of constituent interests—technical, practical, and emancipatory—and matched to these interests different research approaches best suited to provide the relevant information. Applied to instructional settings for exceptional learners, technical interests require a focus on how variables relate to or are caused by others. This need is best met by traditional research designs and experimental studies that consider the effects of inclusive practices on some aspect of student performance. Practical interests address questions that are best answered through an understanding of process. For example, qualitative methods such as observation and interviews could be used to investigate the process of including exceptional students in general education settings. Process interests can also be served by a combination of quantitative and qualitative methodology. Emancipatory interests center on knowledge derived from innovation in which the participants have been actively engaged in developing a practical model, implementing it, and systematically judging its effects. Examples of such participatory research include what these authors term "market-driven research," in which "the researcher's questions are aligned with the identified needs of a program or participants"; "action research," in which "teachers are directly involved in developing and conducting research in their classrooms"; and "fourth generation program evaluation" in which "stakeholders . . . play a primary role in evaluating the process and outcomes of educational programs" (Odom et al., 1996, pp. 24–25). This model has useful application in identifying which methodological approach offers insight into research questions posed by varying constituent interests, whether in reading research on student placement or engaging in it.

Carnine (1994a) suggested that educational decision makers responsible for service delivery evaluate studies according to the manageability of the interventions, the elements of their effectiveness, principles of accountability, clarity for replication, equity, and cost benefits. Unfortunately, results are not frequently published in a way that facilitates such analysis. The key is for researchers to report their results in a manner that fosters this practical use.

In considering research on instructional settings for exceptional learners, MacMillan et al. (1996) offered the reminder that anecdotal case reports are illustrative only and "cannot confirm theories concerning universals. Nevertheless, they can challenge universals" (p. 149). When applied to student placement, "it does not, however, constitute confirmation for the position that all children with disabilities can benefit from inclusive placements. To paraphrase Lieberman, the fact that Stevie Wonder is a talented musician cannot be taken as supporting a position that therefore all blind individuals are talented musicians" (MacMillan et al., 1996, p. 149).

MacMillan et al. (1996) applied an empirical standard on data to support the practice of full inclusion and called for more research that captures "the variability between types of disabilities, among students with the same disabilites, regular class teachers and classrooms, the availability of resources and services, parent attitudes and preferences, and measures of child outcomes (p. 156). They claimed that polarization within education has occurred because of a lack of agreement over the dependent variable. In short, what should we measure? Is it student performance, or is it the degree of integration? The former approach, aligned with those whom Fuchs and Fuchs (1991) termed the conservationists, considers inclusion to be the independent variable and seeks to determine the effect of inclusive settings on academic and social achievement. The latter approach, aligned with abolitionists who would eliminate the continuum of placements, considers inclusion as the dependent variable. In other words, they measure how much integration, or inclusion, is facilitated by various factors such as teacher attitudes and parent beliefs. Successful inclusion then becomes more a question of how much, rather than what's happening. In this event, "the lessons of history have not been learned, as the exclusive emphasis on setting ignores the fact that settings are merely contextual variables in which the interactions of importance occur" (MacMillan et al., 1996, p. 146).

CONCEPTUAL THEMES AND HISTORICAL TRENDS

The following content analysis organizes in a chronological and conceptual framework how the restrictiveness of educational environments has been studied and portrayed in the professional literature from the 1960s to the mid-1990s. Historical trends are analyzed, addressing how the literature reflects changes in educational emphasis over 30 years. Assisting in this analysis was a colleague with a master's degree in special education and 17 years of experience teaching exceptional learners.

Although the placement of students has long been a critical issue in special education, few reviews have organized the themes of the literature from a historical perspective. Hallahan and Cruickshank (1973) presented the trends in the professional literature within the field of learning disabilities from 1936 to 1970, and Richardson (1980) followed the trends of the special and regular education relation in educating students considered educably mentally retarded from 1940 to 1976. Hays (1993) analyzed the historical content of publications in gifted education journals, and Dunlap and Childs (1996) followed trends in intervention research in emotional and behavioral disorders from 1980 to 1993. There are topical bibliographies on various aspects of student placement, such as mainstreaming and inclusion, but we could find none that viewed the topical data historically.

Method of Literature Search

The professional literature on the topic of student placement is vast and represents much activity through each 10-year period. As early as 1980, Winschel noted that "the tide of literature on mainstreaming threatens to engulf us" (p. 493). Considering the quantity of material written subsequently on the topic, he would not have overstated the case by repeating the fateful words, "apres moi le deluge."

Research results and discussions of topics related to student placement in the LRE can be found in state and national reports, books and chapters, and professional journals in both special and general education. For example, the ERIC electronic databases for 1966–1996 list 607 selections by keyword search of "least restrictive environment," but only 143 of these were in professional journals. Similarly, the entry "mainstreaming and student placement" for the same three decades generated 768 selections, with 327 in journals. We addressed our analysis to published professional literature because journals serve as ready references for practitioners seeking guidance and reflect issues of current interest to readers in different years.

In scanning the literature for emergent attitudes and practices regarding instructional settings for exceptional learners, we focused on the period of 1966–1996. These years represent a range across which to observe historical trends from the emergence of the federal presence in education in the mid-1960s to issues leading up to the passage of federal special education legislation, its subsequent enactment, and its troubled implementation in subsequent years.

In identifying and classifying the topics of articles related to student placement over 30 years, our goal was to derive a sampling of placement literature over time large enough from which to see themes and historical trends that reflect attitudes and practice. In order to amass the amount of data required to show these general directions, it was necessary to consider the contents of article abstracts. We searched the ERIC system and PscyhLit data bases for terms used most frequently in describing instructional settings for exceptional learners, such as LRE, mainstreaming, and inclusion.

Search terms included the following from the PsychLit Database, 1974–1996: *least restrictive environment*; *educational placement and funding*; *educational placement and mainstreaming* combined with the terms *preschool, early childhood, elementary*, and *secondary*; *educational placement and inclusion* similarly combined *with early childhood, elementary*, and *high school*, as well as *special education*; *inclusion* combined with *education* and *studies*; *inclusion and outcomes*; and *mainstreaming and outcomes*.

The ERIC Database, 1966–1996, required the use of slightly different search terms including *least restrictive environment; mainstreaming and student placement*; *mainstreaming and outcomes of education*; *inclusion and student placement*; and *inclusion and education,* combined with *preschool, elementary*, and *secondary*.

It is interesting to note some early descriptive terms used in one 1977 topical bibliography on mainstreaming (Council for Exceptional Children, 1977): *handicapped children, aurally handicapped, hard of hearing, exceptional child, special classes*, and another, *grouping (instructional purposes)*, which parenthetically explains itself. The most commonly used referent in this bibliography is *regular class placement*.

The term *inclusion* was not evident in searches related to student placement before 1982. For searching databases, the keyword term *inclusion* is not as useful as *mainstreaming* or *student placement* because it frequently picks up references to the developmental thought process of class inclusion for young children or simply identifies the keyword of *inclusion* in a journal's abstract.

Our intent was not to be exhaustive in our search but to derive a large enough sample of articles on topics related to student placement from which to observe general trends. We made the decision not to restrict our analysis to articles published in selected journals; instead, we wanted to see the wide range of professional journals publishing guidance on placement from 1966 through 1996 so that future analysis might address the themes emphasized by particular publications. For example, of future interest but exceeding the boundaries of this analysis is a study of trends within those journals that have a primarily general education readership to assess how and how frequently issues of instructional settings for exceptional learners appear.

Coding the Abstracts

Individual abstracts were classified initially into categories broad enough to be relevant for historical analysis yet having a definition sufficiently general so that articles could be assigned on the basis of information contained in brief summaries. As classification proceeded, categories were added or eliminated. By the end of this process the articles had grouped themselves into seven major content divisions: foundations, preparation for integration, placement trends and issues, instructional issues, outcomes for students, parental involvement, and school reform.

Although the last two categories might be considered as fundamental to special education, parental concerns about placement and the relation between special and general education implicit in school reform were significant enough in their own right not to be subsumed in this analysis as subcategories of the foundations division. Additionally, each of the seven categories was divided into professional commentary literature or research studies. The latter were further analyzed as being either experimental or nonexperimental in nature.

Foundations. Articles within the foundations division fell into three categories essential to the notion of LRE, including definitions of the term, legal issues in its provision, and policy commentary on the relation of general to special education.

Preparation for Integration. This division represented articles addressing not only professional and paraprofessional training but also preparing exceptional learners as well as nondisabled peers for their instruction in general education settings. Typically, this process literature concerned topics such as developing positive attitudes and behaviors and employing reintegration scales and ecobehavioral assessments to facilitate student placement.

Placement Trends and Issues. Articles that fell within this division represented the largest cluster and included articles on general concerns and data trends in finance, use of IEPs, use of the continuum of placements, placement decisions, qualitative indicators of school-wide environments, and program evaluation issues.

Instructional Issues. Articles in this category addressed instructional arrangements such as classroom organization and management, curricular design, and instructional practices to meet the needs of exceptional learners in mainstream or inclusive settings.

Parental Involvement. This division represented literature addressing informational needs of parents and articles reflecting parental perspectives or levels of participation in their child's education.

Outcomes for Students. Articles dealt with such issues as the benefits of special education, how these benefits ought to be measured, student assessment, transitions from school to work, or postsecondary education.

School Reform. This division included articles that addressed restructuring of schools to better blend the instruction of exceptional learners with nondisabled peers. Separate from general policy commentary, these articles specifically addressed mainstreaming or inclusion as school reform strategies.

Results of the Abstract Analysis

Our search yielded a total of 736 articles published in professional journals on the topic of student placement for exceptional learners dating from 1966 to 1996 (see Fig. 5.1).

Frequency of Literature Themes Over Time. Our search revealed a paucity of literature from 1966 to 1976, with only a meager four articles across the time span. One article was categorized as foundations, one as instructional service delivery, one as parental involvement, and one was a study in student outcomes.

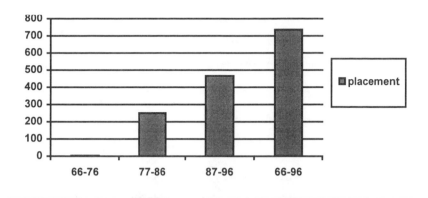

Figure 5.1. Frequency of professional placement literature from 1966 to 1996.

From 1977 to 1986, the number increased to 251 articles, with 188 (75%) professional commentary, and 63 (25%) research studies. The placement trends and issues division ranks first with 84 articles: 66 commentary and 18 studies. Preparation ranks second with 64 articles: 36 commentary and 28 studies. The foundations division ranks third with 40 pieces of professional commentary. In fourth place are instructional issues with 38 articles distributed between 34 commentary and 4 studies. Fifth place is occupied by the section on student outcomes, with 16 articles: 7 commentary and 9 studies. Only 9 articles addressed parent issues, with 5 pieces of commentary and 4 studies. No articles addressed school reform.

From 1987 to 1996, the numbers sharply increased to 481 articles, or a 92% increase over the previous decade. Commentaries amounted to 336 articles (70%), and there were 145 research studies (30% of the total). Placement trends continued to dominate with a total of 148 articles in this period, including 109 pieces of commentary and 39 studies. Preparation remained second with 110 articles: 68 commentary and 42 studies. Foundations remained third with 73 pieces of professional commentary. Instructional issues remained fourth, representing 69 articles. Commentary literature accounted for 48, and studies for 21. Student outcomes retained its fifth place standing with 44 articles: 11 commentary and 33 research studies. Articles on parents issues accounted for 22 articles: 12 commentary and 10 studies. School reform issues emerged and accounted for 15 pieces of professional commentary.

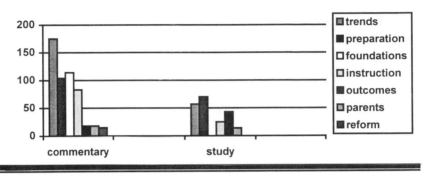

Figure 5.2. Number of commentaries in contrast to number of studies.

Frequency of Themes and Types of Literature. We were interested to know how many of the 736 articles represented research studies and how many could be considered professional commentary (see Fig. 5.2). We found that the preponderance of articles (527, or 72%) represented professional commentary. The remaining 209 (28% of the total) qualified as research studies.

Research Literature

Type of Study. Of the 209 research studies, 172 (82%) employed nonexperimental qualitative methodologies or survey approaches. The remaining 37 (18%) utilized experimental designs and quantified data.

Population and Setting Characteristics. Only rarely were specific population and setting data presented in the abstract, but greater specificity regarding the details of disability, age of subjects, grade levels, and sample size appeared in the decade from 1987 to 1996.

Themes in the Professional Literature

General Placement Trends and Issues. This category of service delivery represented the largest division, with 232 articles appearing in our search from 1966 to 1996, with 175 representing professional commentary and 57 research studies (see Fig. 5.3). Qualitative methods or surveys were used in 53 and quantitative methodology in only 4. From 1966 to 1976, no articles fell into this category. From 1977 to 1986, there were 84, with 66 commentaries and 18

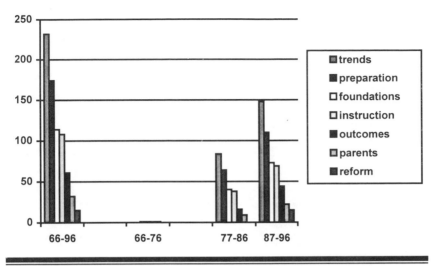

Figure 5.3. Number of articles in each theme over 30 years and by decades.

research studies. In the years from 1987 to 1996, there was an increase of 76%, to 148 articles, including 109 pieces of professional commentary, and 39 studies.

Preparation for Integration. This division included a total of 174 articles from 1966 to 1996, including 104 pieces of commentary and 70 research studies. Of these studies, 63 used qualitative methods or surveys; only 6 used quantitative methods or experimental design. From 1966 to 1976, there were no articles in this category. From 1977 to 1986, we found 64 articles—36 were professional commentary, and 28 were research studies. In the span from 1987 to 1996, the number increased by 72% to a total of 110 articles—68 commentaries and 42 studies.

Foundations. The foundations division included a total of 114 selections of professional literature from 1966 to 1996. There were no research studies under this heading. This division broke down into three subdivisions: policy commentary on the relation between general and special education (52), legal issues (34), and definitions of LRE (28). From 1966 to 1976, only 1 article appeared, dealing with legal issues. From 1977 to 1986, 40 articles appeared, with 6 addressing policy, 17 legal issues, and 17 defining LRE. From 1987 to 1996, the number increased to 73 articles, an increase of 83%, with 46 addressing policy, 16 legal issues, and 11 defining LRE.

Instructional Issues. This category of service delivery included a total of 108 articles. Commentary accounted for 83 and research studies for 25. From 1966 to 1976, only 1 article was found, and it was professional commentary. From 1977 to 1986, the number increased to 38 articles, with 34 commentaries and 4 studies. From 1987 to 1996, this number increased to 69 articles, an increase of 82%, with 48 commentaries and 21 studies.

Outcomes for Students. In this division, we found 61 articles. Professional commentaries accounted for 18, and research studies represented 43. Quantitative data and experimental data were more prevalent in this section, with 26 studies utilizing this methodology and 17 utilizing qualitative or survey methods. From 1966 to 1976, only 1 study and no pieces of professional commentary were found. From 1977 to 1986, 16 articles included 7 pieces of professional commentary and 9 studies. In the span from 1987 to 1996, the number of articles increased to 44, an increase of 175%, with 11 commentaries and 33 research studies.

Parental Involvement. Only 32 articles addressing parental issues in student placement appeared from 1966 to 1996 under the terms used in our search. Of these, 18 were professional commentaries. All 14 research studies in this section used qualitative methods or surveys. Only 1 commentary appeared from 1966 to 1976. From 1977 to 1986 the number of articles increased to 9, with 5 professional commentaries and 4 research studies. From 1987 to 1996, the number increased to 22, an increase of 144%, with 12 commentaries and 10 studies.

School Reform. This category clearly is more of a contemporary one and represents efforts since the mid-1980s. There were 15 articles that addressed this issue, with all 15 published between 1987 and 1996. None were research studies.

Summary

Although much has been written on student placement in 30 years, the literature in this study reveals less emphasis on instructional service delivery than on administrative delivery trends. Results suggest that over this time span, efforts have addressed the amount of integration. The research emphasis on practical and emancipatory interests and qualitative and survey methodologies suggests more efforts to describe the processes involved than to determine the effects of inclusive practices. Although more recent articles address student outcomes and parent involvement along with issues of school reform, technical research that evaluates effects of instructional practices for exceptional learners is needed in greater supply to substantively guide practice.

COMMENTARY FROM CONTEMPORARY THEORISTS

As part of this study, Crockett spoke with educational leaders influential in writing about the difficult issues of LRE within the professional literature. Each respondent was sent an outline of the study and the questions that would guide the interview. Sixty-minute interviews were given by Laurence Lieberman and Douglas Fuchs; Dorothy Lipsky sent her responses by letter. Maynard Reynolds and Crockett spoke for 3 hours over a 2-day time span. Rather than a structured interview, the conversation covered the topics less formally, and a summary of some of the main points is presented below.

Maynard C. Reynolds

Maynard Reynolds, Professor Emeritus of Educational Psychology at the University of Minnesota and former President of the Council for Exceptional Children, began his post-doctoral academic career in 1950. His special concerns are in the classification and eligibility of students to receive special services. Writing in 1976, Reynolds noted that

> schools are there, not to make grand predictions about youngsters, but to make a difference in their lives. What the teacher does in school must make a difference. The problem is to attend to children and to arrange environments so that we make a constructive difference in the lives of children. I think we've only begun to realize how complex that is. (Reynolds, 1976, p. 48)

Reynolds finds the measurement work of Cronbach and Snow—indicating, for example, that the treatment differences and the individual difference variables that produce interactions must be considered in making plans for exceptional students. He finds of interest current work by many others such as Stanovich and Palinscar, as well as approaches to addressing diversity in classrooms such as those posed in 1990 by Carnine and Kameenui. Much of the conversation addressed the provision of LRE in the administrative sense.

Q: Has your opinion of the usefulness or suitability of the LRE concept as an educational strategy changed over time? Reynolds, who published the first model of the continuum of alternative placements in 1962, before the notion of LRE appeared in federal law, views student placement now, as then, as part the progressive move toward inclusion. In his view, the concept of LRE is best summed up by considering that if the government (public agency) is going to involve itself in the life of a citizen, it should do so as unobtrusively as possible. Hence, it should instruct children with disabilities in regular school environments whenever possible, paying close attention to program efficiencies and moving ahead "with all deliberate speed" to do so. This is consistent with his former thinking. Reynolds "rejects rigidly total ideas about mainstreaming or inclusiveness."

According to Reynolds, this progressive inclusion, which LRE addresses, is inevitable. In his thinking, the most significant elements of the EAHCA/IDEA legislation, "the matters that must be carefully protected and preserved," are universal access, or the right to an education, and parental involvement in educational decisions. These moral concepts have the most significance in moving greater numbers of children to regular class settings. Reynolds was not fully supportive of some of the draft legislation such as Senate Bill 6 (S6), which became PL 94-142, and testified with his colleague, Bruce Balow, in Congressional hearings cautioning against its passage without closer examination. His concerns then were with categorical funding, the apparent bounty it placed on the heads of children in order for them to receive services, and the bill's neglect of early childhood education.

> I came into working with children in the psychoeducational clinic not as a special educator. There really was hardly anybody who was coming into that work as a special educator because, at that time, in the early 1950s, few universities offered training in that field. So, I think there was not that kind of identity, the boundaries, the categories for the children. Much of that thinking (about categories) seemed simplistic, confining, and misleading. The challenge was to achieve an understanding of each child who was having difficulties learning and to find ways to be helpful to each of them.

Q: Upon what did you think its success would hinge? Successful implementation, for Reynolds, depends upon addressing a student's needs and not on what he considers to be the field's negative overreliance on labels and categories, particularly in making placement decisions. A main theme of his work before and after the law has been a deep aversion to "doubtful classification of students," unless there is a clear and distinct reason to do so (such as blindness or deafness). In providing services, he argues for emphasis on the measurement and importance of the rate of a student's learning.

Q: How would you size up the effects of the LRE concept? Reynolds argues that the IDEA continues to revolve around categorical funding and the consequent emphasis on classifications, and what he terms "child labeling." He thinks the law quickly fostered a litigious response to conflict resolution. Much of his conversation focused on efficiency and economy, funding formulae, and fiscal incentives or disincentives for implementing the LRE principle. Reynolds is concerned that great harm will come to special education if the costs of services are disregarded. He supports the idea of a per district cap, set at the state level, within which districts would have to set priorities for service delivery. Reynolds supports more research to determine areas that truly are taxonomic—or, to quote a friend of his, "nature carved at its joints"—and the development of interventions to support them rather than classifications made up for convenience. Reynolds makes a distinction between classes and taxons (cf. Reynolds, 1989).

Q: Would you suggest the LRE principles be refined or replaced? Reynolds acknowledges that the following statement sums up his thesis: funding systems should not totally neutralize placement decisions but should introduce bias toward placement in the least restrictive environment (LRE), meaning the general school setting. He intends this to represent the continuous forward movement of progressive inclusion, which began with special class placement in the early 1900s and is still moving forward toward unity. He supports an evolving continuum—thinking that the time has come to close special schools and provide an in-school continuum, "with outside clustering options for students with a demonstrated need for a particular aptitude-treatment intervention," such as for students who are deaf. Reynolds believes that "it is not appropriate to force absolute total enrollment of seriously disabled children in regular classes. A continuum of arrangements should be maintained in 'regular' schools but with as much mainstreamed placement as feasible."

Crockett suggested, in her conversation with Reynolds, that school district leaders must make LRE options possible so that the placement committee meeting on behalf of a student can make LRE decisions that are individually appropriate. Distinct roles and responsibilities of district policy leaders and placement decision makers are not often separated and their differing agendas are not made explicit. This entanglement can send a confusing message to placement committees to provide LRE to the greatest degree possible when they are obliged to ensure LRE as part of an appropriate education to a particular child. The power to provide district-wide services (i.e., to make buildings accessible, to distribute resources) and the responsibility to ensure them directly to an individual (i.e., determining programming and placement based upon the quality of services provided by the district) do not reside at the same level. Reynolds agrees with the conceptualization of a different focus for decision making regarding instructional settings for exceptional learners, one at the district level and another at the level of the individual child: "District policy leaders and administrators have responsibility for moving resources to mainstream settings and to provide necessary training and support systems."

Dorothy Kerzner Lipsky

Dorothy Lipsky responded briefly in her letter to the questions. Lipsky began her studies in education as an undergraduate. The birth of her son, Daniel, with spina bifida, powerfully redirected her focus to special education. In addition to her current role as the director of the National Center on Educational Restructuring and Inclusion, Lipsky has served as a school superintendent as well as chief administrator in the Division of Special Education of the New York City public schools. Among those whose work she particularly respects are Asch, Biklen, P. and D. Ferguson, Gartner, Giangreco, Hahn, Minnow, W. and S. Stainback, Taylor, Thousand, Villa, and Walberg.

Q: Has your opinion of the usefulness or suitability of the LRE concept as an educational strategy changed over time? "I believe that the federal legislation, especially regarding LRE, has had an important and positive impact," wrote Lipsky, who also noted that the limitations on it have been twofold: the conceptual limits as described in Taylor's (1988) analysis and the fact that "legislation has to be implemented to make a difference in fact."

Q: Upon what did you think its success would hinge? Despite what she and Taylor see as conceptual problems with the concept of LRE and its continuum of placements, Lipsky concluded that "without the legislative direction (indeed, mandate), it is doubtful that the progress that has been made concerning the non-segregation (no less inclusion) of students with disabilities would have occurred."

Q: How would you size up the effects of the LRE concept?

> The guiding principle is the appropriateness of the education for the individual student, i.e., FAPE. LRE is, in effect, a subset of FAPE. Increasingly, I have come to believe that for all students the appropriate education is in the general education setting, with the necessary supplemental aids and support services. (Such a formulation overcomes the limits that Taylor identified with the LRE concept.)

Q: Would you suggest the LRE principles be refined or replaced? "While this formulation suggests that only an inclusive placement with the necessary supports meets the standard of appropriateness, nonetheless, given the present climate I would favor continuation of both the FAPE and LRE requirements."

Laurence M. Lieberman

Laurence Lieberman received his doctorate in special education from Teacher's College, Columbia University, in 1972 and taught in the New York City public schools. In addition, Lieberman served with the Bureau of Education for the Handicapped and chaired the Special Education Doctoral Program at Boston College for five years before becoming a school system consultant. He had much to say about what he sees as the role of special educators "now and for the foreseeable future" but prefaced his answers to the questions by addressing who should be served within special education:

> In terms of LRE, we need to define who is a candidate for special education, and why we do special education. Once those questions are answered, LRE becomes much clearer. In 1990, PL 94-142, the Education for the Handicapped Act, became PL 101-476, the Individuals with Disabilities Education Act. It was a very important conceptual shift, not just semantics. The distinction between disability and handicap helps us understand who special education is for and why we do it.
>
> A disability is an objective condition. It exists in people. It is measurable. It is observable. Some people have missing limbs. Some cannot see or hear. Others have measurable and observable cognitive impairments, chronic emotional disturbance, or genuine dyslexia. These are conditions in human beings. A child with autism is autistic even when no one is looking. It is within. It is part of who that person is. It is objective.
>
> A handicap is a subjective phenomenon. A handicap is a quality of life issue that has to do with limitation of choice. If you are handicapped, your choices in life may be limited. Can you be disabled and not be handicapped? Yes. Jim Abbott, a pitcher for the California Angels baseball team has one arm. He is disabled, but not necessarily handicapped. Two people may be blind from birth. Both are disabled. Yet, both, or one, or none of the two, may be significantly handicapped. It depends on the choices they might want to make that their disability prevents and consequently alters the quality of their lives.
>
> Special education is for people with disabilities who are in danger of becoming handicapped if they do not receive special services. Why do specialists provide orientation and mobility training for blind children, sometimes in special settings? Because they are trying to prevent the handicap of not being able to move in space from developing in a disabled person. Why do we pull students with learning disabilities out of class and provide special instruction? We are trying to prevent the handicap of not being able to read from developing in a disabled child. That is why we

do special education. We are trying to prevent handicaps from developing in students with disabilities.... Why can't any child failing in school be a candidate for special education? If we do not say that a child needs a disability up front, it gives the school system the license to write the curriculum in blood. It says to the school system, in effect, that curriculum failures are acceptable and, therefore, students may be eliminated by placing them in a program outside the responsibility of the regular classroom. Special education is not for regular education curriculum failures. Special education is for individuals with disabilities.

Q: Has your opinion of the usefulness or suitability of the LRE concept as an educational strategy changed over time?

My opinion of the usefulness of it has not really changed. LRE is useful in the sense that special education has been too separate and too segregated. A friend in Ohio defines inclusion as nothing more than least restrictive environment taken seriously. You have to respond to what the law says and the law says students with disabilities should be in a regular classroom when appropriate.

I do not think people really understand that the bigger issue is curriculum.... The curriculum of preventing handicaps from developing in disabled children cannot always be found in the regular classroom.

Q: Upon what did you think its success would hinge? "You need to have a continuum of services . . . and success hinges upon whether or not we keep students from becoming handicapped.... We need flexibility. That's the key. LRE provides the kind of flexibility we need."

Q: How would you size up the effects of the LRE concept? "The effects are very profound. I think prior to something like Deno's cascade model, many people never really thought that children could be effectively served in the classroom . . . that they could succeed."

Q: Would you suggest the LRE principles be refined or replaced?

I do not think there is anything wrong with the principles. I hear people say the law is bad. It creates all kinds of problems. We were better off before. I disagree. Before PL 94-142, I was working with blind students declared uneducable, therefore deemed unworthy of having an educational opportunity. It is a good law. Just because something is abused and not implemented well does not mean that

the thing itself is bad.... I think LRE is a very powerful concept and
I think it's going to last many, many years. It makes sense.

Douglas Fuchs

Douglas Fuchs, Professor of Special Education at George Peabody College,
Vanderbilt University, has written widely on issues related to instructional
assessment for students with learning disabilities, student placement, and
educational policy. He received his doctorate in Educational Psychology from
the University of Minnesota in 1978 and was a student of Stanley Deno, Frank
Wood, James Ysseldyke, and Robert Bruininks. Before working as a staff
psychologist in a special education preschool program in Minneapolis, Fuchs
served as a first-grade assistant teacher in a Baltimore school for children with
emotional and behavior problems and as a fourth-grade classroom teacher in
Philadelphia. His thinking on issues related to LRE has been influenced by
many, including Stanley Deno, Jay Gottlieb, Charles Greenwood, Dixie
Huefner, Joseph Jenkins, James Kauffman, and Naomi Zigmond.

*Q: Has your opinion of the usefulness or suitability of the LRE concept as
an educational strategy changed over time?*

It has. It has considerably. When I went through the University of
Minnesota, people who influenced my thinking at the time were
people like Maynard Reynolds, and Bruce Balow—a very bright
guy who was my advisor and very staunch advocate of
mainstreaming at the time. LRE was, well, the mainstreaming
movement. There was no inclusion movement back in the 1830s!
So I came out of that thinking that most students, virtually all
students, belonged in the mainstream. Over time my thinking about
that changed, I think, quite a bit as a function of increased
experience in the mainstream. To make a long story short, the more
I worked in the mainstream, the more skeptical I became of claims
that it could essentially be all things for all people. I became more
convinced that *it,* the mainstream, could not change—not that *we*
could not change practice in the mainstream. I think we can and we
should, but there are very definite limits to what we can reasonably
expect of *it.* So as my conception of the mainstream changed, my
feeling grew that alternate placements were important. So my
opinion has changed in that fashion. I was a product, if you will, of
the University of Minnesota and the state of Minnesota, and liberal
thinking, progressive thinking.

I have tried to become an articulate and forceful spokesperson
for the importance of the continuum of services, but in the process
I found it to be frustrating because the truth is, no one's got a

corner on the truth. The least restrictive environment is such a very important, pivotal, complex and interesting issue. The more that I found myself defending the continuum, the more I realized that I did not want my work to be seen as little more than defending the status quo because I knew the status quo to be very, very unsatisfactory in many places—not all places, but in many places. Special education was and is broken in a lot of places, including a number of large cities, and to be helpful to the field, and children, and parents, I felt like I needed to almost play two sides against the middle. I felt like I had to try to point out the wrong-headedness of the extremists for the inclusion movement, while on the other hand try to light a fire under those who, for whatever reason, were way too complacent about the way things were.

Q: Upon what did you think its success would hinge?

I do not feel we know how to implement LRE successfully.... I really think that as a field we do not know how to responsibly move kids across settings. I don't think we know how to do it, and the two most prevalent options or alternatives are, I think, fundamentally flawed—the case-by-case, which is the more traditional, conservative approach that flows from much that is in the federal regulations on the continuum, on the one hand, and inclusion on the other.

Q: How would you size up the effects of the LRE concept?

I think that, for the most part, the principle is ignored. The problem in talking about this is that we are talking about a very, very decentralized phenomenon. There are over 15,000 school systems in the United States and there are 15,000 different stories, and nobody has their finger on the pulse of the 15,000. So, whatever we say, whatever anyone says, irrespective of how knowledgeable and thoughtful, there are going to be lots and lots of exceptions or contradictions out there. I think that in many school districts, LRE is a very poorly understood concept, and rarely observed. I think there are very few, precious few, special education teachers who, when they receive a child, be it in the resource room or self-contained room or anywhere, understand that their success or failure will depend in part, not totally but in part, on whether they are capable of moving that child up. I would bet that, conservatively put, a majority of special education teachers do not understand that that is their responsibility. This is not to denigrate them. It is because the lines of authority are unclear. Relationships between special and general education, oftentimes, are confused, complicated, non-existent. Role definitions are broad enough to incorporate things like making sure that Johnny has a smooth landing in a general education setting, but there is no follow-up. There are no data to indicate whether in fact he is learning three months after re-integration. There is nothing coming from the top, from the director of special education, or the superintendent of schools. I think what is happening now is that there is an alternate way of explaining LRE. It is an interpretation of LRE as inclusion—as the buzzword. It is more than just a buzz word. It is an operating principle in many school districts. We probably have more students in general education classes full-time now than ever before. But is that LRE? I would argue strenuously that it is not LRE.

Q: Would you suggest the LRE principles be refined or replaced?

There are two criteria for LRE as far as I am concerned. One is the child is placed in a setting that puts him or her as close as possible to age-appropriate non-disabled peers, and, two, that the setting is one in which the child can derive educational benefit. The instruction in that setting has to benefit the child academically. That is the second criterion, so when we are talking about students with severe learning problems, here is where my skepticism is about just how accommodating general education can be.

I remain to be persuaded that the general education classroom is the best place for such a student full-time if we care at all about the student learning fundamentals and basic skills as well as higher cognitive functioning. Part of my skepticism is based on the frequent observation that non-disabled, normal achieving kids, scads of them, are failing because the classroom teacher cannot provide for them. If those kids are failing how are the learning disabled kids going to do? The other side will say, well, because inclusion means bringing not just the student into the regular classroom but resources that heretofore were not brought to bear. Well, I have tried to look carefully at what those resources are and how they play out, and it is not impressive. I have read very carefully Naomi Zigmond's and Jan Baker's observational studies of so-called exemplary inclusive schools across the country and what happens when we have team teaching or co-teaching going on and what we do not have in virtually every instance is individualized, intensive, systematic, data-based instruction. It just does not happen, and without that, many kids who have severe learning problems are not going to learn.

I think that my efforts, and the efforts of a number of my colleagues, were not hit or miss efforts, or one-handed efforts, but a kind of heroic effort. That has taught me that there are certain things that we can and should expect of general education. Changes can be made, should be made, but it is just wildly romantic, delusional, to expect that general education can serve all students in accordance with FAPE and LRE and, moreover, can do justice to gifted children being brought back from gifted programs, do justice to bilingual children coming out of ESL programs, that literally all kids can be . . . the more I think about it, the more persuaded I am that the full inclusionists do not even believe their rhetoric and that they say these things not because they really believe them, but because it puts the bar at the highest level encouraging people to jump much higher than they would jump if the bar were at a less high level.

PRINCIPLES FOR EDUCATIONAL LEADERS

LRE is an associative concept. It addresses at once special and general educational concerns. LRE requires that committee members decide on a placement for an exceptional learner only after thoughtful consideration of student and setting—and then only temporarily; these decisions must be revisited at least annually. Each contemporary theorist spoke directly to this interplay. At the end of the conversation, Fuchs suggested three principles for educational leaders, emphasizing the direct relation between effective special education and effective general education: high expectations for all students, valid accountability systems, and implementation of best instructional practices. These principles serve well to wrap up the issues of environment and learning. As Fuchs (personal communication, December 9, 1996) noted:

> The first principle is to really, truly believe in higher expectations for all students. All students can learn to higher levels, which is not at all the same thing as saying that all students can learn to the same very, very high standards. That is ridiculous, but all kids, literally all kids, can learn to much higher levels, and leaders should expect and demand that everybody in a school system act on that belief, whether they truly believe it or not.
>
> The second important principle is that some valid accountability system be in place so that everybody knows whether or not students are moving in that direction, and if they are not moving in that direction, that things will change in an effort to turn it around for those students.
>
> The third principle, related to the first two, has to do with best practices: that there would be an expectation that teachers, and others involved in the instruction of students, use best practices; that they understand what best practices are; that either they, or with the help of others, can distinguish between fraud and

hucksterism, on the one hand, and programs that have gone through rigorous validation on the other; and that in choosing the valid practice or program it is incumbent on the teachers to use it in the manner prescribed. If we can expect surgeons to follow well-accepted practices and procedures and routines as they do brain surgery, we sure can expect teachers to follow accepted, validated procedures and routines as they teach various subject matter.

6

The Viewpoint of Parents:
Environment and Full Participation

> We must not let an awareness of difference keep us from trying with
> everything that we have to eliminate it or ameliorate its
> unpleasantness. But in our desire to rid ourselves of the frustration of
> such a staggering responsibility, we must not forget that some of the
> different differ—differ so much that they need protection.... Only
> the brave dare look upon the gray—upon the things which cannot be
> explained easily, upon the things which often engender mistakes,
> upon the things whose cause cannot be understood, upon the things
> we must accept and live with. And therefore only the brave dare look
> upon difference without flinching. —Hungerford, 1950, p. 417

Our intent in this chapter is to portray the power and inclination of parental
politics to determine whether assumptions have changed and cultural values
have redefined for parents the purpose of schooling, the status of their
exceptional children in schools and society, and the desirability of the LRE
principles. We draw on personal reflections and perspectives more directly than
in previous chapters. What emerges is not simply a discussion of the parental
issues surrounding student placement but a brief history of parental influence on
special education practice during the last half of the 20th century. The evidence
points to the continual need for parents' participation in both their children's
education and the political process. Their participation is necessary to protect
the best interests of their children and to focus educational interventions on
equity and effective instruction.

BACKGROUND

Until 1991, New York State used a two-phased approach to IEP construction. In
the spring, committees on special education met with teachers and parents to
develop the Phase 1 IEP, which consisted of administrative information
regarding the child's classification, present levels of performance, and annual
goals in academic, social, and physical skills. From these, management
requirements were determined—how this student could be supported in an
instructional setting. The student's current placement was continued, or, if

changes in functioning appeared to indicate a change in need for instructional management, evaluations were done to determine whether the increase or decrease in student performance suggested new goals that might require a different setting for implementation. Within 30 days after the opening of school in the fall, teachers and parents met once again. This time, short-term objectives based on the student's classroom performance in the first month of instruction were developed to address the annual goals established the previous spring. This Phase 2 IEP then guided subsequent instruction and related service delivery for the school year.

This format, which was not without its problems, was popular with many parents and professionals who enjoyed the immediacy of developing objectives based on the student's actual functioning in the current class. After the state's revised regulations required that these two phases be merged into one IEP to guide instruction better, school personnel kept the substantive autumn meetings with parents, but with a new agenda. No longer were conversations confined to the production of short-term educational objectives; they were expanded into more processes-oriented explorations of parental and professional expectations for the child. When suitable, school personnel included the child in the meeting. At Henry Viscardi School, the resources of the school were brought to bear in this effort, and each teacher and parent met with a related service provider most clearly related to that child's need for educational support—either an occupational, physical, or speech therapist; a psychologist; or a social worker. Each person came to the meeting with questions and concerns, prepared to share information and discuss priorities for the year that included moving toward independence, emotional life and social skills, use of academic learning, and preparation for future work. Although school personnel and parents collaboratively crafted these topics, Bigge's (1991) model for identifying meaningful activities across the settings of home, school, and community was an implicit guide. Professional and parental planning, in this manner, was not superficial or routinized but personal and productive.

PARENTAL CONCERNS AND CHOICES

Weintraub (1976) contended that public policy is evolutionary. Changes in the organization of services and the pedagogical practices of educating exceptional learners certainly bear out his point. The meetings held at Henry Viscardi School represent a collaborative partnership required by law but supported by strong results for students. They are also a far cry from many contemporary professional and parental encounters and from the early association of parents who, along with professionals, advocated not only for their child's access to the schoolhouse but for the development of the very field of special education itself.

The Development of Parental Involvement

Parent and community involvement are essential ingredients—perhaps the most crucial components—of building stronger schools," Secretary of Education Richard W. Riley told reporters at a news conference at which new PTA standards for parental involvement were released (Jacobson,1997). Twenty-two years before, however, the link between teachers and parents of children with disabilities was legally forged in the EAHCA/IDEA requirements for parental participation in program development and for procedural safeguards requiring parental notification to ensure that school professionals do not act unilaterally on behalf of a child (Kotler, 1994).

Early policymakers considered parental involvement essential to the prevention of educational abuse:

> The value of individualized planning depends on including an effective advocate for the child in the planning process and enforcing the child's plan. Policymakers recognized the potentially adversary relationship between the school and the child so they empowered parents to act in the child's interest. Parents would represent the child in the IEP meeting. an impartial hearing would resolve disagreements between school officials and the parents. Parents could request an independent education evaluation. The parent's advocate role follows traditional conceptions of parental authority, and policy makers presumed that parents would be effective advocates. (Tweedie, 1983, p. 61)

Potential conflict resolution was not the only motivation for parental involvement. E.W. Martin (personal communication, November 12, 1996), a key developer of federal special education policy and former Director of the Bureau of Education for the Handicapped, referred to his own early experiences as a speech clinician in shaping his views toward parental participation:

> An early influence for me both in terms of content and philosophy, was the director of the speech and hearing program at the University of Alabama. This was an absolutely brilliant woman by the name of Ollie Backus. Backus had been well educated at Wisconsin with Lee Travis, one of the pioneers of the field. She came out of a doctoral program which at that time was highly medical in orientation. (The doctoral programs were limited, I think, for the most part to Big Ten universities. They were strong academic programs.) In her course of development, she became persuaded that the appropriate context for speech therapy, as we called it then, was in the interpersonal relationships that the child was having, including the relationships with parents and with other children. So we moved

away from the strictly biological, what might be called, although not meant to be pejorative, somewhat mechanical approaches to training with speech—the tongue and the jaws and so forth—into trying to understand the psychological foundations of speech. We wanted to understand what psychological factors there might be that would either influence a child's development in a speech program (for example the effects of organic disabilities like cerebral palsy and cleft palate), or could create an environment that would foster the therapeutic process.

All that was very important to me and to my later input into policy as the head of the Bureau of Education for the Handicapped because it tended to really focus on individuals as individuals. It tended to be concerned about their feelings as well as whatever mechanical problems they might have. It tended to lead us into the use of psychotherapeutic tools to understand the difference in children, to understand, in a sense, how to help them set free the creative process in them that could lead to speech change. It also brought us into contact with their parents, developing a great compassion for these parents, and also developing parent counseling kinds of approaches that would help them, in turn, with issues like discipline, and sharing feelings with their children, and a number of areas that have become pretty much a standard in the development of family-centered programming. (Martin, 1996)

In 1986, Congress passed Public Law 99-457, The Education of the Handicapped Act Amendments, which mandated that by the 1990-1991 school year, all states receiving special education funding expand these services to children 3 to 5 years old. These amendments stress the family–professional relationship and require the development and utilization of an Individual Family Service Plan containing a statement of the family's strengths and needs that might affect a child's development. Before the passage of these amendments, some states, such as New Jersey specified (even for school aged children)

counseling and/or training for parents relative to the education of a pupil as a related service, reflecting the federal definition of related services as "such developmental, corrective, and other supportive services...As may be required to assist a handicapped child to benefit from special education." (Margolis & Tewel, 1990, p. 290)

When the EAHCA was reauthorized as the Individuals with Disabilities Education Act (IDEA) in 1990, social work was established officially as a related service. In 1991, services were expanded to participating states under Part H of the IDEA, stressing early intervention for infants and toddlers from birth through 2 years. This Infants and Toddlers program, as it is commonly called, extends the commitment to families and to the early and continual support of their exceptional children.

Such legislation has its roots in much earlier events. Winzer (1993) suggested that civilian war efforts during the 1940s contributed toward the enhanced public perceptions of adults with disabilities: "By October 1942 it was estimated that 3 million disabled men and women were engaged in the war industry throughout the country" (p. 372). As veterans returned injured or maimed, medicine and rehabilitation services responded with vaccines and inventions that spurred hope in the idea that life could be meaningful despite disability. Through this period of increasing support for adults with disabilities, parents of exceptional children became more willing to admit to the presence of their children's disabilities. Conn (1996), in a recent biography of the Nobel Prize-winning author Pearl Buck, wrote that

> In 1950, Buck published a book called *The Child Who Never Grew*, a story about her retarded daughter, Carol. The book was a landmark. Specifically, it encouraged Rose Kennedy [mother of President John F. Kennedy] to talk publicly about her retarded child, Rosemary. More generally, it helped to change American attitudes toward mental illness. (p. xv).

Pearl Buck acknowledged directly, "I wrote this little book especially for parents of retarded children" (Conn, 1996, p. 441). It was written as a fundraiser, and all the royalties Buck received went to the Vineland Training School, a special school in Vineland, New Jersey, for individuals with mental retardation.

Even before World War II, parents of children with disabilities had become more aggressive about acquiring the means to address their children's special needs. In the early 1930s, a few parents' groups began to form nationwide, the first group being the Cuyahoga County Ohio Council for the Retarded Child, established in 1933. "Throughout the 1940s, parents almost spontaneously began uniting to form strong, local, state, and national organizations. By 1954, for example, more than 30,000 people were actively involved in groups for retarded children" (Winzer, 1993, p. 374).

D. Stedman (pesonal communication, November 22, 1996) credited the outreach of young professionals and the hiring of full-time leadership staff for these parental associations in the 1950s with furthering parental advocacy on behalf of exceptional learners:

> Two things happened after the second war. One is that the veil came down between the professionals and the parents. They weren't relating to one another anymore as customer and vendor because younger professionals and the advocates for education or psychology

began to go over barricades with parents. They would have been ostracized from their guild in the past for doing that. But they became famous, and . . . they did kind of demythologize the professions a little bit for the parents and they became more emboldened. The second feature is parents began to organize and hire full-time executive directors. Gunnar Dybwad was the first full-time national executive director. I mean, they never had any full-time people. The directors acted almost like union organizers. They would say, "You do this," and "You do that." They were better fund raisers and they formed a fabric of state associations.

Not always on easy terms, professionals and parents of exceptional learners blended scholarly and political forces to advocate for legislative support. In 1953, the National Association for Retarded Children produced a position paper entitled *Educational Bill of Rights for the Retarded Child*, proclaiming the right of every retarded child to "a program of education and training suited to his particular needs" (Zigler, Hodapp, & Edison, 1990, p. 4). "The combined parental and professional groups became a potent force. They developed considerable local, state, and national prestige and added their voices to the call for carrying out fundamental mandates" (Winzer, 1993, p. 373).

Maynard Reynolds, now retired from his professorship at the University of Minnesota, received his doctoral degree in Educational Psychology from that institution in 1950, and one year later was asked to return as the director of the University's psychoeducational clinic, where he had worked as a graduate assistant. He recalls this experience as the foundation for much of his thinking about special education and parental participation. His recollections also spin a history that joins the establishment of university training programs in special education with the mutual development of parental advocacy groups during the 1950s:

I ended up majoring in educational psychology with a minor in psychology, and I started working in a clinic. It was called a psychoeducational clinic, and it was a place where children were referred always jointly by their parents and by the school staff, and I was quite interested in that. It was dealing with kids who weren't learning to read or kids who were misbehaving—where there was a lot of concern about these kids in the schools. We required that the parents and the school jointly refer them, give us information, and then we would study the children and make recommendations. A lot of the kids we saw in that clinic would today be labeled learning disabled, but the leadership within the university came more out of the department of curriculum and instruction, the people who taught the ordinary courses in remedial reading and so on. We used to see lots of kids and we trained students, students who were in remedial reading or in counseling, and gradually we started building up the program in special education and school psychology. We didn't really think so much about special ed in categorical terms. That came later. But our clinic was the place at the University where kids who were exceptional would come and where related program developments were initiated.

After I finished the Ph.D., I took a job for one year in California with the California State University at Long Beach. Then they asked me to come back to be the director of that clinic. That was in 1951. I should say there wasn't very much special ed at the University at that time. There was a well-established program in speech pathology and audiology, and there was a fairly well-defined program in remedial reading, but that was all. It was about that same time that special ed was coming alive. I think it was just about that same time that Sam Kirk, who had been in Milwaukee, was asked to go to the University of Illinois to head a special institute that would be strongly oriented toward research concerning exceptional children. I think that was the first move in a graduate school to establish a special education program that would be heavily invested in research. There was kind of a long-standing program in vision at Columbia University's Teachers College. You could spot narrowly-framed things that were going on in various universities, but that movement at Illinois was big.

Now, it happens that the National Association for Retarded Children became big and very powerful, politically powerful, and really caused a lot of legislative efforts in various states and at the national level. That group was formed in Minneapolis in 1950, preceding by a year my coming to the University of Minnesota Clinic. As I worked in that clinic, I developed contacts, as you would expect, with all the people that were the leaders of that ARC movement. Parent groups were forming in other categorical areas as well. Many of the active parents in these groups became my good friends and colleagues. At the University we began a set of meetings involving, for instance, the Crippled Children's Society, and the Association for Retarded Children. In the spring of '52, the Dean of the College of Education and I called a meeting and we had responses from 35 agencies and parents representing local cerebral palsy parent groups, parents of retarded children, small groups concerned with vision problems, and so on. We formed what we called the Minnesota Council on Special Education and in 1955 we achieved the legislative provision that called for what they termed an Interim Commission. The legislature only met every two years and they established in '55 this special group to study programs for special ed. The group included a future governor and a member who later became a very prominent Congressman. In '57, the Interim Commission came out with their report. I worked very closely with that commission, almost like a staff person. It changed radically the provision of the schools for special ed, and it also gave a special appropriation for the University to start its special ed department. At that point, I shifted from the psycho-educational clinic, although I stayed very close by and started the special ed department. Bruce Balow became director of the clinic. That was 1957. (M. Reynolds, personal communication, November 9, 1996.)

This interconnected genesis brings understanding to Anastasiow's observation about that period: "I believe parents mainly wanted their kids to be able to go to school and trusted the teachers, but mainly the therapists, to know what to do" (personal communication, November 12, 1996). Gallagher (personal communication, November 22, 1996) suggested that parents, accustomed to relying on professionals, were surprised by their political power:

I think what the parents discovered more or less by accident was how much political clout they really had. The reason why they had political clout is that there isn't a politician alive that wants to stand up and say "I'm four square against support for handicapped children." I remember sitting in a hotel room in Chicago where the Illinois Parent Association representative was talking to the head of the appropriations committee for the state legislature. He said, "Look, on this bill we're pushing at the state legislature, we are going to have one of our members, or more, down at these hearings every day. We're going to take names of the people who are supporting this and those that are against it. We are going into the district of those that are opposed to it and we're going to fight." And he said, "We may not beat you but it will cost you twice or three times as much to get elected." And he said to me, "I just want you to know where we're coming from. We're very serious about this." And I said, "Yeah, okay, I understand."

Once you get into a situation where people say, "Here's a politician who is such a rotten person that he's against helping handicapped children"—well, that's a devastating kind of charge to make, and no politician wanted to be on that end. As a matter of fact, they loved to be on your side. They would then come up and say, "Look, I am for these special people and I am going provide help for them."

In a lively conversation, Gallagher noted that state parents' associations were very strong for a period of time, but Stedman suggested that "their flame burned out when they thought they had arrived." Gallagher concurred: "They were successful. They got what they wanted, and success is what ruined them." Said Stedman: "They became sort of ecumenical, and that took the juice out of the various tribes."

Borthwick-Duffy, Palmer, and Lane (1996) noted that parents of children with cognitive impairments were united in their push for educational access for their children in cases like *PARC v. Commonwealth of Pennsylvania* (1972). This was a relatively homogenous group of stakeholders, unlike the widely divergent group of contemporary constituents affected by the full-inclusion movement. Palmer (as cited in Borthwick-Duffy et al., 1996) concluded from his 1995 survey of 460 parents of children with severe disabilities—a group that full-inclusion advocates present as solidly supportive of such programming—that these parents were not united in their opinions about the efficacy of full inclusion. "Over half (54%) were opposed to the idea of full-inclusion for their children. Among the 15% of parents who were enthusiastic about inclusion for their child, only a subgroup would likely be willing to confront the schools and demand inclusive placements" (Borthwick-Duffy et al., 1996, p. 312). Commenting on the current status of parent advocacy, these authors observed that parents who are satisfied with the traditional provision of special education for their children have had little cause to express their views. As a result, those parents who support the preservation of the continuum of placements have received minimal, if any, media exposure: "Contented citizens make tedious human interest stories" (p. 312).

Parental Projects

Jane DeWeerd, now retired from the Office of Special Education Programs at the U.S. Department of Education, worked for Drs. Gallagher and Martin at the Bureau of Education for the Handicapped. She, too, cautioned parents not to become complacent about the gains won for their children and to be vigilant on behalf of their exceptional needs. Her perspective on parental involvement in early childhood education is informed by her experiences as the coordinator of the initial 24 federal First Chance projects supported by Congressional enactment of the *Handicapped Children's Early Education Assistance Act* in 1968. These, and the subsequently funded projects, represented a wide array of programs for preschool youngsters with various exceptionalities across the country. Some projects relied on an inclusive model, others on separate classes. Exemplary programs were selected for dissemination and replication through the National Diffusion Network (1980).

DeWeerd's tasks in the 1960s and 1970s were to direct the selection of creative yet viable projects that were demonstrably effective, to monitor their continued effectiveness, to disseminate information about their success, and to assist in their replication in other locations. In this capacity, she and her staff linked parental and professional project directors across the country, many of whom augmented either their child-find efforts or their service delivery incentives with basic but successful techniques. To involve families with young children in new programs, some project directors enlisted clergy to advertise from the pulpit. One director, Louise Phillips of Arkansas, anxious to find children with Down Syndrome for a newly formed program, asked postal workers to look for children who looked different, and to scan the windows of houses as they delivered the mail, in case a child were peering from behind a curtain. The message was to look for children who might have been mentally retarded and kept at home during the day, excluded from schools. Coupons for free pantyhose were offered by one Wisconsin program to mothers whose children had made progress in between sessions because of their teaching.

"It really is hard to imagine how hungry parents were for support in the early days," said DeWeerd (personal communication, December 16, 1996) who remembered one mother from Texas walking 12 miles, against her husband's wishes, to attend parent training. "It was touching," she recalled,

> the first year that all of the project directors, many of them parents, came together in Washington with the National Early Childhood Technical Assistance team. Sam Kirk was the Chair, and Nick Anastasiow was on the Board, and we strung a clothesline across the meeting room and the project directors hung samples of new curriculum and information about their programs on it. The first hospitality gathering wouldn't end on schedule! The hotel was upset, but these parents and professionals were so glad to talk to others involved in early childhood special education.

DeWeerd is a positive advocate for parental involvement with advice for policymakers: "I guess I believe in the power of people—parents and professionals. Have confidence in them; give them a chance; and get familiar with real situations both at home and in the school environment."

Parents and Student Placement

According to Kotler (1994), "although some professional special educators joined the coalition pushing for the adoption of the [Individuals with Disabilities Education] Act, there has never been a commonality of purpose or viewpoint between parents and special educators" (p. 363). Kotler, a Pennsylvania law professor and the father of a son with autism, has written thoughtfully about placement issues with a keen insight born of both experiences. He asked to what extent courts should defer to the professional expertise of the special education establishment:

> If parents could truly be given greater power to influence decisions, would this accomplish the substantive goals of the Act more

efficiently than preserving the status quo or even returning to the status quo ante? After all, the goal of equalizing the power of parents and special educators was an instrumental one. It was to be a means of accomplishing certain goals, not an independent goal in itself.... Can we realistically expect special educators to promote those goals and protect the child's and society's best interest as defined in terms of those goals? On the other hand, in view of limited resources and a need to achieve measurable results, is it workable to place the decision-making power in the hands of parents? (p. 367)

Present Practice.   Autism, Kotler argued, pushes the concepts of both appropriateness and integration. He uses data based on the Lovaas method to support the necessity of early intensive behavioral intervention to maximize the realistic possibility for "recovery" of normal function by school age. This methodology is similarly endorsed by Donna Cattell-Gordon, who with other parents in Charlottesville, Virginia, founded the Virginia Institute for Autism in the fall of 1996, in response to what they considered to be poor public programming for children with autism in the Central Virginia region. Both Kotler and Cattell-Gordon emphasized the conundrums posed by autism, which is misunderstood, underdiagnosed, variable in its manifestations, and only recently demonstrated to be responsive to specific treatment in very young children (Cattell-Gordon, personal communication, March 11, 1997; Kotler, 1994). Cattell-Gordon explained that the Lovaas approach requires intensity and repetition provided in individual sessions that often amount to 35–40 hours per week in environments that offer little sensory distraction to the child. To her, the payoff is in the rate of recovery for the children. She observed that so much is counterintuitive in the treatment of autism that her son Daniel's general education teachers often hinder rather than help him learn to cope with his classroom environment. (We are aware of the controversy surrounding the Lovaas approach to the treatment of autism, but this controversy does not negate these or other parents' perspectives on LRE; see Gresham and MacMillan, 1997a, 1997b, and Smith and Lovaas, 1997, for discussion of the controversy.)

These elements pose a challenge to providers of early intervention services to ensure that staff professionals stay abreast of new approaches and to consider the cost effectiveness of the interventions they provide. Kotler (1994) expressed additional concerns with "institutional inertia, lack of professional input into program selection, and lack of legislation requiring that programs be reviewed for effectiveness" (p. 370). More significant, he suggested, are low professional expectations for significant student progress.

Several placement issues collide in the issues raised by Kotler (1994) and Cattell-Gordon (1997): Can appropriateness of programming be separated from effective methodologies? When do methodological approaches based on solid research become dismissable by districts as options that are not offered? How does classroom ecology affect the faithful application of a particular methodological approach?

Cattell-Gordon (personal communication, March 11, 1997) noted that for parents of young children with autism there is a steep learning curve and the clock is ticking against the time when neurological responsiveness to treatment will wane. Kotler (1994) proposed several corrections to address what he termed "the devastating problems of delay" that are exacerbated by education agencies with the ability to further delay the provision of services. Among his suggestions is the arguable position that appropriateness of programming be defined by its potential to enable integration into general education settings. Less controversial is his proposition that school districts be obliged to provide parents with full disclosure about the effectiveness of programming options for their children. Kotler made the troubling point that because parents and professionals have never shared a real commonality of purpose, "the net result has been a law which clearly embodies a principle of parental participation, but that principle has met with pervasive opposition by members of the special education establishment" (p. 363).

Past Practices.   In 1960, Betsy Balsdon similarly rebelled at the professional stance taken by educators of her daughter: "This is all we can do." Balsdon (personal communication, March 22, 1997) remembered being told to institutionalize her daughter, Holly, who was born in 1958 with cerebral palsy and severe mental retardation. Her decision not to do so is one that she does not regret, but she acknowledged that it has had a significant effect on her family.

Instead of removing Holly from home, resources were mustered. Betsy's mother traveled 40 minutes across Long Island by bus to help daily in her care. To access services through the Easter Seals Association, the family, which included two other young children, relocated to Florida. After 2 years of unsuccessful treatment, the family moved back to Long Island where, eventually, Holly was enrolled at age 7 in a day program run by the local Association for Retarded Children (ARC). The school closed following the passage of the EAHCA in 1975, but the ARC converted the building into a residence and established a vocational education center to serve students like Holly over the age of 18 years. Holly lived at home until she was 25 years old, when she became a resident of a community group home in upstate New York.

Holly was born too early to benefit from PL 94-142 and the provisions of a free appropriate education in the LRE. Balsdon said, "If it hadn't been for the private agencies, Holly would have had nothing." She encouraged young parents now facing similar frustrations to secure early intervention for their children and to participate in community activities that enhance the quality of life for both parents and children. Balsdon noted that unconventional goals and unconventional solutions are essential commodities. Rigid school placement options eliminate the flexibility necessary to respond to such complex personal and practical circumstances.

Parental Advocacy: A Case in Point

The following example illustrates effective parental advocacy on behalf of the preservation of the traditional concept of LRE in the provision of a FAPE. In June, 1993, the New York State Education Department (SED) issued a statement of preliminary policy considerations for educating students with disabilities in the LRE. The Draft Policy Statement on Least Restrictive Environment (New York State Education Department, 1993) advanced a philosophy of full inclusion into general education settings by suggesting six principles:

- All students with disabilities are entitled to special education services within a unified education system based on their individual needs.

- Inclusion is the ultimate goal for all students with disabilities regardless of their disabilities or current placement.

- A continuum of specialized separate programs will continue to be available. Placement in such programs will be made only after a comprehensive, nonbiased assessment of a student's needs. In addition, the Committee on Special Education/ Committee on Preschool Special Education must document that the benefits of educating the student in a specialized program clearly outweigh the benefits of inclusion within the general education program with appropriate support for the student and the teacher.

- Overrepresentation of children of color in special education will be systematically addressed and eliminated.

- Funding for special education programs and services should be based on student need, not student placement. Flexibility should be built into a revised funding scheme to support and promote inclusive programs for students with disabilities.

- Preservice and in-service programs should be redesigned to prepare professionals for their respective roles in developing and implementing inclusive programs to prepare them for their role in developing and implementing such programs. Parents should likewise have access to comprehensive programs to prepare them to fully participate in these processes. (New York State Education Department, 1993, p. 5)

Regional discussions were scheduled across the state for the following autumn, but the topic became so heated that regional representatives of the SED passed out opinion questionnaires rather than receive oral or written testimony. "We were told that acceptance is the hardest part of this," said Karen Silver (personal communication, November 12, 1996). "Parents on both sides of the issue were frustrated because they had come ready to speak on behalf of their children. The state rep said, 'Don't yell at me, I'm nobody!'" Along with her husband, Richard V. Silver, Karen Silver prepared her testimony to be presented to the New York State Education Department Public Hearing on Least Restrictive Environment in September, 1993. Silver, a special educator by training, spoke from her perspective as both a professional and a parent. Her daughter, Alison, was diagnosed at age 8 months as having cerebral palsy and cortical blindness. Said Silver (1993),

> These conditions have left her, at the age of six, unable to sit up unsupported, unable to stand, with virtually no prospect of walking, with limited use of her left arm and nonfunctional use of her right arm with speech that is impaired but intelligible, and with severely limited vision. And yet despite all of these disabilities she is functioning intellectually at grade level. She recognizes all upper case letters of the alphabet and knows the corresponding sounds. She can count to 100. She speaks in complex sentences with a vocabulary that is advanced for her age. She understands basic concepts of addition and subtraction and designs word problems to try to stump her eleven year old brother. There is simply no way that this could have occurred without the specialized programs that have been available to us since she was an infant.

Silver argued that her daughter's school represents a specialized, not a segregated, environment in which children with physical disabilities can both learn and mature. Excerpts from her testimony follow.

> The draft states that there should be a full continuum of services and that a general education setting is not the least restrictive environment if it "prevents the child from receiving an appropriate education to meet his or her cognitive, social, physical, linguistic and/or communicative needs." However, the draft also states that *inclusion* is the ultimate goal for *all* students with disabilities *regardless* of their disabilities or current placement. These statements are contradictory, and the latter is frightening. There is clearly a heavy bias towards full inclusion regardless of what is best for the child—and as the parent of a disabled child that scares me.
>   I fear that if this bias is not removed, those charged with administering this policy will necessarily conclude that the best

place for Alison and children like her is a general education classroom. Indeed, I fear that eventually, full inclusion may well be the only option that will be available to us as parents. To be sure, the draft speaks of parental involvement in the decision-making process. But what meaningful involvement can parents have if their choices are restricted and the placement of every child is predetermined by *policy* before a CSE meeting ever takes place? Not all children who require special education are the same. The diversity of programs which exist today came about because parents and educators fought for them, recognizing that there was no single setting which could possibly meet the wide-ranging needs of the disabled school-age population.

As a result, I must oppose the unduly narrow definition of "least restrictive environment" that results from the draft's emphasis on inclusion. Inclusion is not a legal mandate. It is a yet-unproved placement policy. Indeed, there is not adequate empirical evidence that children with low incidence disabilities can be successfully or cost-effectively—and here the emphasis must be on *effectively*—educated in inclusionary settings. I submit to you that your guidepost for determining what is the least restrictive environment for each child must be that which most *enables* the child to learn. That environment is one in which a child can be a full participant.

Ladies and gentlemen, I say to you as a parent that it is simply unacceptable that those who know nothing about our child and others like her should set policy which could have the effect of depriving her of her legal right to a full continuum of placement options.... Make no mistake, I am not saying that there is anything inherently wrong with inclusion in individual situations. As a special education teacher, I have experienced the sense of accomplishment and satisfaction of helping a student progress to a more inclusive setting. What I object to, however, is a policy that establishes a presumption that inclusion is the goal for *every child.*

I suggest that we recognize that all disabled children are not the same, that placement decisions are highly individualized and must be made on a case-by-case basis, and that the goal of such decisions should not be a particular setting, but an environment which produces the best results and facilitates the disabled child's education.

Silver, like other parents, sent her testimony directly to the state capital in Albany. The tension between the SED's intended policy statement targeting full inclusion as the goal for all students with disabilities and the mixed reactions of parents across New York, resulted in the Regents' decision to retain and enrich the continuum of placements, to address placement-neutral rather than inclusion-oriented funding, and to retain a focus in teacher preparation programs on unique student needs.

Thomas Neveldine, co-author of the state draft policy on inclusion, reported that because of the large number of letters and expressions of concern from parents, the policy would be significantly altered. In June, 1994, Mr. Neveldine disseminated the *Least Restrictive Environment Implementation Policy Paper* (New York State Education Department, 1994). This document reflects a positive amalgamation of parental and professional perspectives. Although it is visionary, it does not abandon the focus on individuality implicit in the relation between FAPE and LRE:

> The Board of Regents' approval follows extensive discussion over several years throughout New York State with advocates for children and families, teacher organizations, school administrators and others interested in students with disabilities. The policy supports a continuum of alternative placements being available for students with disabilites based on their individual needs, while focusing attention on the need to establish more opportunities for students with disabilities to participate in general education programs with the availability of appropriate supports and supplementary aids. In addition, it lays out a plan for increasing technical assistance to educators and families to help them meet the needs of students with their community schools.

The policy statement identifies a general goal of moving toward an educational system that accommodates the needs of all students, and it specifies eight goals and eight principles to support them. These are presented below in wording taken from the 1994 document. In each instance, the goal is presented first, followed by the principle (in italics and enclosed in parentheses):

- **Strengthening and Expanding General Education Services**—Support services must be enhanced to maintain students who are experiencing learning difficulties in general education. (Principle: *Services and programs will be made available to students based on their individual needs, without regard to classification.*)
- **Funding Reform**—The Regents will propose State Aid formulae for special education which will be fiscally neutral and will adequately support all options with the continuum of alternative placements. (Principle: *A continuum of alternative placements will be available to meet the needs of students with disabilities.*)
- **Supporting a Continuum of Alternative Placements**—The State will ensure and support the provision of a continuum of

alternative placement...in all regions of the State to meet the diverse needs of students with disabilities. Inclusion is an option within the continuum of alternative placement for students with disabilities. (Principle: *All students with disabilities will have equal access to a high quality program based on their individual needs and abilities and designed to enable them to achieve desired learning results established for all students. Educational placement decisions for students will be determined by a process which first considers a general education environment in the school the student would attend if he/she did not have a disability.)*

- **Promoting Statewide Equity and Access**—Placement in separate programs will be made only after a comprehensive, nonbiased assessment of a student's needs. (Principle: *The removal of a student with a disability from the general educational environment occurs only when the needs of the student are such that, even with the use of supplementary aids and services, his/her needs cannot be met. However, consideration must be given to the impact of a student with a disability on the education of other students in the general or special education class when making placement decisions.)*

- **Increasing General Education Opportunities**—Full implementation of the existing continuum of alternative placements will be achieved by increasing options for placement of students with disabilities in general education. (Principle: *Efforts will be made to access and coordinate with other available services within a local school district, BOCES or agency program before a student fails in his or her current educational placement.)*

- **Strengthening the Role of Parents and Guardians**—The State will support parents and guardians of students with disabilities in becoming equal partners with school personnel to assist...in understanding the abilities of their children and developing the IEP. (Principle: *The responsibility for all students is shared among all staff of the school. Parents and guardians will have an opportunity for meaningful participation in the development of the Individualized Education Program (IEP) as equal partners with school personnel.)*

- **Focusing on Results**—Students with disabilities will have equal access to a high quality program, based on their individual needs and abilities, in order to achieve desired learning goals established for all students. The expected benefits to the student in the placement option selected will be indicated according to the full range of the student's needs and abilities (academic, social, physical, management needs). General goals, such as preparation for employment or postsecondary education and independent living, should be pursued for all students with disabilities. specific curricular goals will be included, as determined appropriate, through the IEP process. (Principle: *Students with disabilities will be full participants in all aspects of the school program, including extra-curricular activities, to the maximum extend appropriate to their needs.*)

- **Transitioning Students Back to General Education**—When appropriate, students with disabilities in separate special education placements will be transitioned back, to the maximum extent appropriate, into general education. (Principle: *Students with disabilities in segregated placements will transition to general education, when appropriate.*)

FOCUS ON INSTRUCTION & ASSESSMENT OF STUDENT PROGRESS

The historical and contemporary perspectives offered by both professionals and parents suggest that full participation for exceptional learners in the educational life of American schools can only be sustained by the full participation of parents and professionals in the political process. The meaning of LRE seems to have survived over time but with a greater shift toward instruction in the general education setting. Consequently, further work is indicated for advocates to press for an increased focus on instruction and assessment of student progress. A good way to begin is to pay long overdue heed, and fiscal support, to the IDEA's requirement for states to provide a comprehensive system for personnel development, which supports the provision of FAPE in the LRE by ensuring that professionals are trained in and use instructional practices found effective for exceptional learners. Another is to operationalize the meaning of appropriate in order to clarify the role of LRE.

Martin (1995a) found neither a change in the philosophy nor the goals of including persons with disabilities necessary. He called for improved, specialized instruction and services with "an acceptance of the obligation to measure what we do in terms that are important and significant to the total lives of our students: Do our programs meet the test of assisting students to attain postschool success and positive self-regard?" (p.199). The key is in demonstrating what is meant by "appropriate." "Where we've gone wrong in special education is that we haven't followed how kids have done. We have not interpreted 'appropriate' as empirically derived by student outcomes. We have used argument instead of data in making placement decisions" (E.W. Martin, personal communication, April, 1996). By proceeding without data, the field has been susceptible to what Martin called "the myth of mildness," that these students are not so tough to teach or so different in their educational needs. "Without data," he said, "all we have are assumptions."

7

Implications
and Future Directions

> If we are correct . . . that larger social forces are at work in the
> shaping of education policy, then what are those forces this time?
> Clearly, there is concern for equity in education.... Fairness and
> equity are the key concepts (Gallagher,1994, p. 528).

Our intent in this chapter is to inform placement decisions by providing
information about how schools might proceed to fairly provide exceptional
learners with educational benefits alongside their nondisabled peers *to the
maximum extent appropriate*. We focus primarily on the interrelations among
instructional settings, legal prescriptions, and social values in providing
meaningful educational opportunities to children with disabilities. We draw
together conceptual and historical elements to underscore the importance of the
strategies required to achieve such opportunities. These strategies include the
careful definition of equity required for LRE to be a vehicle for full educational
opportunity, the effective instructional practices and personnel preparation
required for LRE to be a viable educational strategy, and the powerful parental
participation required to secure the best interests of exceptional learners and to
focus efforts on their effective and equitable instruction.

In many ways, the Individuals with Disabilities Education Act can be
viewed as classic liberal legalism, focusing on the individual rights of a citizen
and then employing procedures to enforce and protect those rights (Kotler,
1994). Specifically, the IDEA establishes interrelated goals: Children with
disabilities have a right to a free appropriate public education, and such
education be provided in the least restrictive environment appropriate to that
child. Kotler (1994) established the philosophical basis for this approach in both
rights theory and utilitarian theory:

> A rights theory requires the provision of education as an
> acknowledgment of the disabled person's dignity as a human being.
> A utilitarian model . . . requires the reduction of disability because of
> the long-term cost effectiveness of such reduction, and reflects the
> prevalence of an economic model of law which is itself based on a
> utilitarian philosophical and political foundation. (p. 339)

Aside from issues of rights and utility, however, the passage of federal special education law also shifts the power relation between a minority group within society and the citizenry at large, two groups whose interests and values are often significantly different. Despite the procedural protections embedded in the Act, professionals and parents have criticized how, in practice, the law functions. Procedural protections have been frequently reduced to empty ritual, and "ambiguity and disagreement regarding what constitutes a substantively 'appropriate' program are commonplace. The formalistic procedures to protect parental rights have not served to level the playing fields between parents and educators" (Kotler, 1994, p. 341).

Once the protective efficacy of the law is questioned, there are two responses to a legalistic solution—one that views law as only another form of oppression pitting the relatively powerless against a monolithic bureaucracy and another that attempts to probe the underlying assumptions of the law to find the fault lines (Kotler, 1994). The conceptual and historical underpinnings of LRE that we review in this book flow from this second response. In many ways, the IDEA and its predecessor, the EAHCA of 1975, are thoughtful laws, embued with a flexible mechanism in the LRE requirement, which establishes a dynamic relation between a student's unique educational needs and the circumstances under which those needs are met. This mechanism does not obfuscate but facilitates the law's primary object of providing FAPE, and it does so in a fashion that transcends the limitations of any one setting as well as the limitations imposed by the temporal vicissitudes of any era's social interests or public concerns.

Kotler (1994) acknowledged the grave threat of the contemporary public's distrust of its schools and social programs, and he saw another threat in the lack of consensus among stakeholders regarding the possibility for increased achievement in the academic or social functioning of exceptional learners:

> Low expectations lead to ineffective programming. Poor programming yields poor results. Poor results are then interpreted by many as proof of the original misperception that education for the disabled child is a well-meaning but ultimately futile gesture. If this misperception continues to exist and the goals of the Act [IDEA] are not perceived as being within the realm of possibility, the briefly formed consensus which prevailed when the Act was passed will evaporate, particularly in the face of scarce resources. As a result, the Act will become largely superfluous in the day-to-day realities of the provision of special education. (p. 342)

We agree with Kotler's (1994) observation that, regardless of the shortcomings of either the legislation or its implementation, "of even greater importance to the success of the Act is the existence of an underlying social consensus in favor of educating the handicapped. In the absence of such a consensus and broad-based willingness to be bound by the Act, failure is inevitable" (p. 342). Kotler held an underlying assumption that educational success for exceptional learners is, indeed, possible, and "that it can break the cycle of low expectation and failure which currently drives the system" (p. 342). This book has been written from the same assumption and similarly contends that "once the fundamental underlying commitment to special education is reestablished, interpretation and amendment of the existing legislation to realize that commitment is entirely possible" (p. 343).

INSTRUCTIONAL SETTINGS AND CONCERNS FOR EQUITY

As educators concerned about instructional benefits for exceptional learners, we could only take heed when reading Halpern's (1995) critique of the invidious consequences of integration policies on educational pedagogy for African American students following Title VI of the 1964 Civil Rights Act. Halpern noted that other disenfranchised groups, including students with disabilities, gained from the provisions of Title VI, but their participation shifted the emphasis to a more generic civil rights stance, diminishing the salient aspects of racial discrimination in providing an equal education to Black children. Instead, this legalized inclusiveness shifted the emphasis from meaningful educational opportunities for African American children to a mindless integration that counted their heads in racially mixed schools but discounted their instructional needs related to long-term educational disadvantage. Halpern's reflections underscore the danger in abandoning the central meaning of providing students with educational access— that education has to mean something to the students who receive it.

> The struggle in the twentieth century to combat racial discrimination in schools grew out of deliberate attempts by whites to limit the educational opportunities provided to blacks. Hence, in its origins, the constitutional assault on racial discrimination in schools in this century concentrated on the inadequate quality of education provided to African Americans. That legal battle was part of a larger political struggle, dating back to the end of the eighteenth century, to provide greater educational opportunities to African Americans. Both the courts and civil rights litigators lost sight of the focus on educational opportunity and quality in enforcing the two greatest legal victories in that struggle—that is, *Brown v. Board* and Title VI. Instead, in working to implement those legal landmarks, both courts and litigators assumed that merely eliminating the barriers that segregated students in schools would equalize educational opportunity. That proved to be a simpleminded and fatally flawed assumption. (p. 311, see footnote 2)

The racial integration of students in the public schools was to serve not only a communitarian purpose of social acceptance but as an opportunity for full participation in instruction directed toward individual achievement, an education with purpose as set forth eloquently in *Brown v. Board* (1954). The assumption was that leveling the educational playing field was different from simply providing access; the implicit emphasis was on equity, not simply equality. Halpern (1995) noted:

> Unequal treatment in schools was qualitatively different from unequal treatment or segregation in transportation, movie theaters, restaurants, restrooms, and other public facilities. Denying blacks access to education was more pivotal in perpetuating their subordination. In *Brown v. Board* and the major cases that preceded it, equal opportunity for an education was the objective that blacks sought and that the Supreme Court required. The Court recognized that equal access to educational opportunities, irrespective of race, was important because of the contribution that public education made to the collective life of the nation and because of its impact on the life opportunities of individuals. Therefore, *Brown v. Board* and the pre-Brown cases stressed not segregation, but the injury resulting from being denied an opportunity to receive an equal education. (p. 314, see footnote 2)

This concept that the state must equalize opportunities for its citizens has a long American tradition and spurred the move toward free, tax-supported public schools in the early 19th century (Urban & Wagoner, 1996). *Brown v. Board* (1954) added a new dimension in declaring that essential to the provision of educational equality was the dissolution of a second system of schooling for Blacks. The Court in *Brown v. Board* for the first time declared that separate educational facilities were "inherently unequal." According to this reasoning, for equal educational opportunity to be achieved, segregation must end. "This new proposition changed the course and direction of future legal action, both in constitutional litigation and in the enforcement of Title VI. It produced a new word, *desegregation,* a word not used in the pre-*Brown* cases" (Halpern, 1995, p. 315, italics in original, see footnote 2).

Grappling with the difficulties of implementing *Brown*, judges, civil rights lawyers, and those enforcing Title VI sought means that were objective and easy to measure in overcoming resistance to and evaluating progress toward integration. The guidelines developed and approved by the courts served to alter educational policy profoundly. Halpern (1995) wrote:

> After the Guidelines and the cases confirming their approach, there was no longer much concern in the legal process for the quality or

character of the education provided to blacks?... Instead, the focus
was on the need to mix students in the schools on the basis of their
skin color. Realizing the vision of *Brown v. Board* became defined,
almost exclusively, as the achievement of integrated student bodies
in schools . . . and the elimination of the administrative structures
that, before Brown, had kept students segregated. Achieving the
appropriate black-to-white student ratio became the ultimate—and
really the *only*—objective under the Constitution and Title VI. Equal
educational opportunity for black children—a meaningful chance to
obtain the skills, training, and preparation that schools supposedly
offered—was no longer the objective or the legal right to be realized,
and was seldom even discussed. (p. 315, italics in original, see
footnote 2)

There is a similar danger in conceiving of the placement of students with
disabilities in instructional settings as being only an issue of integration—a basic
right to educational access to the same schoolhouse as the neighbor's child. This
thinking presumes that the local school has the will and the capacity to respond
to a range of student diversity and learner characteristics. Halpern (1995)
reminded us that American civil rights legislation compels our society to do that
which it lacks the political will to accomplish:

The weakness of the political base supporting the enforcement of the
legal right in Title VI is directly related to the need, in the first place,
to resort to the law to establish the right and then to the need to
litigate relentlessly about its implementation. (p. 320, see footnote 2)

In situations requiring majority acquiescence to a minority demand, Bell's
(1980) theory of interest-convergence seems relevant. Using political history as
legal precedent, this theory emphasizes that "significant progress for African
Americans is achieved only when the goals of Blacks are consistent with the
needs of Whites" (Tate, 1997, p. 214). Applied to issues of exceptionality, the
theory raises questions. What about the threats to the majority posed by the
special educational needs of students with disabilities: hefty financial expenses
of aids and services, disruptive behaviors of some students that interrupt
classroom learning, overly aggressive behaviors of others that threaten safety,
lower test scores and, consequently, depressed school profiles that threaten
administrator's jobs and lower local real estate values? The threats of a
contemporary backlash to policies of earlier public concern are real, upping the
ante for sensing where the interests converge (Tate, 1997).

Bell (1980) made the point that White society had much to gain
economically and politically in abandoning segregated schooling in the 1950s,
at a historical moment when the West was competing with Communism for the

affections of the Third World nations emerging from their own colonialism. Equally pragmatic in their views, Stedman (personal communication, November 22, 1996) and Gallagher (personal communication, November 22, 1996) noted that members of Congress had much to gain economically and politically from supporting PL 94-142, pressed as they were by state legislatures fiscally strapped from right-to-education cases and hounded by parent groups advocating on behalf of their disabled children. Gallagher made the point that politically, no elected official in the era of the Great Society wanted to be connected with insensitivity to the needs of "handicapped children." Weintraub (personal communication, January 7, 1997) suggested that interests, then, did not converge around providing funds for students who were merely having some difficulty learning. Twenty-five years ago it was necessary to capitalize on "the handicapped" as having minority status by virtue of categories with which the public was familiar: blind, retarded, deaf, emotionally disturbed, and so on. Sentiment ran strong for protecting the disenfranchised and unfortunate, but state interests converged over capturing the funds to pay their legal debts.

The EAHCA/IDEA legislation, in considering the provision of FAPE in the LRE uses the phrase *full educational opportunity*. At the turn of the century, we ponder questions about what would happen without the protections of this flexible if ambiguous legislation and without politically pandering to what has traditionally been a soft spot in the American heart. First, do we have a sufficient number of individuals in our society whose interests converge around the education of those who are different—who acknowledge both the nature of disability embodied in the concept of LRE and the desire for those who are different for greater normalcy—to claim what is needed for success? Second, do we have professionals in our schools "with the bravery to confront exceptionality for what it is: difference that demands an extraordinary response" (Kauffman, 1997a, p. 130)?

Will the concept of educational equity for exceptional learners be overlooked in the current business and financial climate? Will the shift "from fiscal equality to adequacy . . . that is moving attention away from traditionally underserved students toward a discourse on high standards for all students" (Tate, 1997, p. 216) have a negative effect on the equitable provision of FAPE in the LRE? Where is the interest convergence? Said Halpern (1995), the amount we spend on educating children, and the quality of the education we provide, "are fundamentally not questions of legal rights. They are issues of public philosophy and public policy, perhaps even public morality, not readily reducible to or controllable by litigation or notions of legal rights" (p. 321, see footnote 2). If we are to rely on law to settle these accounts for children with disabilities, we may lose our vigilance in preserving the discourse concerning the quality and character of the educational opportunities we provide.

INSTRUCTIONAL SETTINGS AND DYNAMIC SYSTEMS

Issues of equity for students in instructional settings, from early childhood programs through 12th grade, are rife with polarities and far from a concern limited to special educators. Durden (1995) referred to "a pervasive set of educational either/ors—ability grouping vs. cooperative learning, phonics vs. whole language, 'exclusion' vs. full inclusion, and homogeneous grouping vs. heterogeneous grouping" (p. 48). He noted that teachers and administrators are often compelled to choose between these dualities, one of which has been politicized into a societal ideology that makes its opposite politically incorrect even if pedagogically sound. When examined philosophically, these grouping strategies in each case, reflect different conceptions of

> where meaning originates in education and what criteria are brought to bear in judging appropriate instructional format—either upon the most discrete, most differentiated unit determined by individual difference or upon the most comprehensive entity, where the needs of the whole community prevail. (p. 48)

The politicization that establishes these poles as either conservative, favoring a focus on the child, or liberal, focusing on the social contract, is exacerbated by professional literature, which emotionally challenges one's Americanness or democratic principles, depending on one's starting point. Durden (1995) quoted a school principal writing in a journal for educational administrators: "The ability grouping of educational opportunity in a democratic society is ethically unacceptable.... We need not justify this with research for it is a statement of principles, not of science" (p. 48). When there are no faces of particular children to attach to these principles, these words arouse a patriotic zeal that stirs the communal spirit and rekindles the advocate's heart, but teachers and administrators who work daily in the schoolhouse know intimately that the debate is not between principles and science. In fact, it is not a debate at all. It is a dynamic swirl of pupils and principles and pedagogies—all the particulars called for in cultivating meaningful and productive learning. Durden argued that

> precollegiate educators need to re-establish with confi-dence the assessment of each child's academic strengths and weaknesses and the matching of those results with a variety of educational services inside and outside of school. Educators must reassert the value of individual differences in a community setting and reclaim for their profession a commonplace: that people learn at different rates, in different styles, and at different levels. And the "system" must embrace this dynamic organizationally and attitudinally. (p. 38)

Bronfenbrenner's (1979) ecological model of human development comes to mind with its rendering of reciprocal interactions among the subsystems negotiated between individuals and social settings. Applying it, in general, to issues of student placement honors the complexity that stark dualities between sociological and educational perspectives deny. The concept of LRE, in its application to exceptional learners and instructional settings, provides a similar dynamic reciprocity, one that Durden suggested is missing when an either–or approach to student placement holds sway.

Kirp (1995) imagined competing equities that challenge schools, like no other institution, to be "non-racist, non-sexist, nonclassist, open places; palaces of learning, enclaves of joy which respond equally well to a range of children's talents and desires which would fill a modern-day Noah's Ark" (p. 110). He remarked that

> in day-to-day school life . . . equity has more to do with paying attention to the broad array of claims—some based on need and others on effort or performance—that students advance. It also entails attending to the concrete choices that teachers and administrators make on a day-to-day basis; what deserves attention, in the name of equity, is the content of teachers' exchanges with students, teachers' conversations with one another and with parents after school, and professional dialogue as well.... This view of the equities—as significant, particularized, in conflict, and in flux—is consistent with the larger aims of contemporary educational reform. It is a conception that confirms both the protean nature and the breadth of aspiration that the idea of educational equity entails. (p. 110)

INSTRUCTIONAL SETTINGS AND SOCIAL JUSTICE

Philosopher Kenneth Howe frames the issues of educational equity somewhat differently, subsuming them within the requirement of justice, what he concludes to be the sine qua non of social institutions. Howe's (1996[3]) complex analysis similarly involves the reciprocity between the individual and the society, between personal interests and public concerns: "Justice can only be achieved under arrangements that take the broader community into account and prevent partiality from running amuck" (p. 60). Howe was quick to note that a polarity, or a forced choice, between "the view from nowhere" and "the view

---

[3] *Note.* From Educational ethics, social justice and children with disabilities by K.R. Howe. In C. Christensen & F. Rizvi (eds.), *Disability and the dilemmas of education and justice* (pp. 46-62), 1996, Philadelphia: Open University Press. Copyright 1996 by Open University Press. Reprinted with permission.

from here" in making ethical determinations should not exist. Howe's analysis reflects numerous elements addressed in earlier chapters of this examination of LRE. His descriptions of the various ethical positions resonate with the struggles surrounding the preservation or repudiation of the requirement for the continuum of placements.

Howe explained that *the view from nowhere* was coined by Nagel (1986) to represent the abstract principles of equality and impartiality. Decisions made from this view assume that everyone's interests are counted the same; there is no acknowledgment of personal interest. In contrast, *the view from here*, drawn from the communitarian notions of Aristotelian ethics and contemporary care theory, eschews deliberations made from abstractions, preferring those based in traditions, communities, and concrete relationships.

It is easy to imagine conflicts of student placement arising from these polar positions, but Howe, like Durden (1995) and Kirp (1995), maintained that not all ethical deliberations need to be arbitrated from the stance of either–or. There is wisdom in accommodating one to the other rather than relying on a singular approach to serve the demands of justice: "What needs to be recognized is that there is no solution to the problem of the tension that exists between these two moral perspectives, that there is no comfortable 'moral harmony' to be had" (p. 51, See footnote 3). Howe drew examples from special education's history to illustrate both views. The right-to-education cases and subsequent federal legislation were a principled view-from-nowhere response when exceptional learners were denied access to public education. In this instance,

> reliance on the view from here—on local communities and concrete relationships—proved woefully inadequate.... The principle of equality of educational opportunity . . . was taken to supersede community values, and was mandated in the face of marked resistance from local school districts. (p. 50, see footnote 3)

In most instances of special education decision making, there is now—and has been—a continuum of responses and perspectives ranging from one view to the other, with the players cast in certain roles and deliberating in different ways vis-à-vis the view from here and the view from nowhere (Howe, 1996). Referring to *Hendrick Hudson District Board of Education v. Rowley* (1982), "Amy Rowley's parents are expected to adopt the view from here, for instance, whereas Supreme Court justices are expected to adopt a view, if not from nowhere, at least from much farther away" (p. 51, see footnote 3). This thinking is reminiscent of Sunstein's (1996) description of another continuum used to settle social conflicts—the range from rules to untrammeled discretion employed in judicial decisions.

Howe offered some examples familiar to teachers and administrators of the ways in which both principled and particularized views operate within school systems, imagining a regular educator versus a special educator versus a principal versus a superintendent, all working in the same district yet having different perspectives as well as degrees of influence. Each has a different set of "role-related obligations . . . I offer the general observation that how effectively conflicting perspectives and roles can be accommodated depends in no small way on the degree to which the context in which they must be negotiated exemplifies justice" (Howe, 1996, p. 51, See footnote 3). The fundamental question is how to ensure that a fair share of education, in terms of the principle of equality of educational opportunity, is had by all students in American schools:

> The extent to which citizens and educators can (should) forgo what they identify as their personal and community interests depends on the extent to which they can be confident that the burdens and benefits of doing so will be fairly applied to all. If they cannot be assured they will not be made worse off than others similarly situated by giving up something in the name of justice, why should they not scramble for all they can get? This observation helps to ground John Rawls's (1971) basic premise: "Justice is the first virtue of social institutions." (p. 51, see footnote 3).

Placing social justice center stage, Howe contended that it is not identical with the principle of equal educational opportunity, which in its strict definition only requires the removal of formal barriers to access and, more progressively, requires equalizing resources at least to some basic floor. This formal definition falls considerably short of the mark in providing equity of opportunity. Howe illustrated his point by drawing on the opportunities offered in an English-only classroom to monolingual Chinese-speaking children:

> It is often insensitive to the profound influence that social factors can have on educational opportunities, even when formal barriers are absent and resources such as funding are equalized.... And this is precisely what the Supreme Court decided in the celebrated *Lau v. Nichols* (1974) case when it declared that the educational opportunities provided to Chinese children under these circumstances were not "meaningful." In order, then, for educational opportunities to be meaningful—to be worth wanting—they cannot be construed in terms of the formal features of educational institutions alone. Instead, they must be construed in terms of the interaction between these features and the characteristics that individuals bring to educational institutions. (p. 53)

Compensatory notions of equity are sensitive to this interaction and attempt to address productive learning by compensating for characteristics of individuals that put them at a disadvantage in schools. This approach, underlying most federal educational law and its application to special education, differs little from its application in other respects: "children with disabilities are to have their disadvantages mitigated as far as possible in order to have a fair chance of attaining the educational criteria deemed worthwhile" (Howe, 1996, p. 56, see footnote 3). The compensatory strategy has become a target from various political quarters. It has been excoriated for extinguishing individual initiative and promoting centrist intervention. It has been charged as neglectful of social class, race, and gender serving to enshrine the status quo. Perhaps the strongest indictment against the compensatory approach, "is that it takes the traditional goals of schooling for granted and, compensating as deemed necessary, applies them indifferently to all children" (Howe, 1996, p. 57, see footnote 3).

Howe (1996) offered the democratic definition of equity as an alternative to abandonment of the principles of equal educational opportunity under the assumption that it is not legitimate. In contrast to either the formal or compensatory definitions of equal educational opportunity, this interpretation takes into greater account the wishes of a disadvantaged group to reject compensation because the cost to their identity is too high. It also embodies the notion of an egalitarian distribution of resources when compensation is provided, which Howe described as linking "a fair share of education to participatory democracy" (p. 56, See footnote 3). In this approach, "the key concept . . . is a democratic threshold, or the type and amount of educational achievement required for citizens to be able to participate as equals in the democratic process" (p. 55, see footnote 3).

Howe (1996) remarked that such distribution is overlooked in what, in the terms of political theory, is a libertarian approach. Such an approach identifies equality "with respecting individuals' autonomy to the greatest degree possible, and justice with intervening to the least degree possible in the kinds of social and economic arrangements to which autonomous individuals freely agree" (p. 47, see footnote 3). Fair distribution is similarly ignored by a utilitarian view, which "identifies equality with treating all individuals the same in calculating the benefits associated with social and economic arrangement, and justice with social and economic arrangements that maximize benefits" (p. 47, see footnote 3).

With regard to special education, Howe supports the democratic definition of equal educational opportunity with its notion of resource distribution, combined with a liberal egalitarian philosophy that respects personal autonomy but "sanctions more pervasive intervention in social and economic arrangements to mitigate the effects of the natural and social 'lotteries'—whether one is disabled and who one's parents happen to be, for instance—to help ensure 'fair equality of opportunity'" (Howe, 1996, p. 47, see footnote 3). This compound approach further expands the equity discourse by encouraging an expression of diverse identities in the design of institutions such as schools and the distribution of supports to reach intended goals. Howe explained it further:

> Education remains an enabling good, but in order to be morally defensible as well as effective, it must afford recognition of the diversity of background and life circumstances of the children it seeks to educate. By "recognition" I mean something more than mere tolerance, more than merely putting up with those who are different. I mean including others on their own terms. Now, although this democratic interpretation requires the inclusion of a much wider spectrum of voices in negotiating the goals, curricula, and practices of schooling than has historically been the case, it does not require abandoning wholesale the idea that some educational goals, curricula and practices should be shared. (p. 55, see footnote 3)

Howe (1996) argued that the formation of democratic character is the primary obligation of public schools and that allowing for recognition and being recognized are reciprocal and essential to fostering this character in students: "There is no surer way of doing this than by providing face-to-face practice in deliberating with those who have different values, interests, talents and life circumstances" (p. 57, see footnote 3). This degree of participation is a necessary condition for equity, but inclusion is not sufficient to provide for equality of educational opportunity: "Mere inclusion, for instance, physically including children with disabilities in regular classrooms but otherwise excluding them from meaningful participation, can do little to promote equality of educational opportunity. Even when done right, however, inclusion still may not be sufficient" (p. 57, see footnote 3).

This analysis reaches toward the view from here to inform the principled view from nowhere embodied in the concept of equality of opportunity. Howe forwarded the notion of belonging as an enabling ingredient in democratic education, of equivalent value to the principle of equal educational opportunity and for some students the key to their productive learning:

> This response squares with the considerations adduced by care theorists and communitarians and it also supports inclusion. I think it is basically correct, but I attach one important proviso: that it not be construed so as to reintroduce the forced choice between the view from nowhere and the view from here—between principles, social justice and equality of educational opportunity on the one hand, and caring, community and belonging, on the other.
>
> Social justice is not identical with equality of educational opportunity. When equality of educational opportunity cannot be attained [in the case of significantly limited cognitive capacity] social

> justice still makes demands, including educational ones. In this vein,
> the democratic interpretation has as one of its requirements that *all*
> persons be afforded recognition and have their self-respect secured, a
> requirement that can be met here. Rather than being goals separate
> from social justice, or actually at odds with it, fostering caring,
> community and a sense of belonging are its prerequisites. Thus, an
> emphasis on caring, community and a sense of belonging should not
> be seen as *alternative* to an emphasis on social justice. (p. 58, italics
> in original, see footnote 3)

Howe's (1996) analysis conjures up for us a dynamic system that imagines the often dichotomously conceived notions of social reform and student performance, endemic to LRE conflicts, as interconnected to each other and linked with the centerpiece of social justice. LRE becomes a dynamic mechanism that connects the view from nowhere (i.e., the principled notions of both normalization and student performance) with the view from here (i.e., how such normalization will affect the performance of this particular child under these particular circumstances). In making placement decisions we are doing more than simply determining whether a setting is inclusive of nondisabled peers. We are addressing the issues of what, for this student, comprises a full educational opportunity. We need to guide our thinking from a conceptualization that has at its center a just and fair ground that supports equally the opportunities for achievement of either an academic or social threshold to participate in the nation's citizenry. For some students, the emphasis in effort will be on achieving what is more readily understandable as equal educational opportunity; for others it will be on equality of participation in community membership. Even without the legal principle of LRE, the view from nowhere and the view from here are not mutually exclusive in an environment of mutual concern, but their effective combination on behalf of exceptional learners without the law is unachievable in the absence of social justice.

Sarason and Doris (1979) argued that mainstreaming is a moral issue, deeply related to the notions of social justice:

> It raises age old questions: How do we want to live with each other?
> On what basis should we give priority to one value over another?
> How far does the majority want to go in accommodating the needs of
> the minority? (p. 392)

If, as Howe (1996) suggested, we are to proceed toward productive learning for students that results in democratic character appropriate to the capacity of each citizen, then it follows that we need to facilitate the relation between a student's specific learning needs and the ecological elements of learning environments required to address those needs. This purposeful approach to student placement joins personal interest—in this case a student's meaningful education—with the public concern for equity and justice.

In 1903, Martin Barr, Chief Physician at the Pennsylvania School for Feebleminded Children, sought to encourage in his general education colleagues an appreciation for an equitable education that takes into account the principled notion of standards tempered by a realistic sensitivity to individual difference:

> To individualize standards for the day's work; requiring not so rigidly that each shall accomplish the same task, as that each shall exercise his or her capacity to its full measure in the given task. In other words, to require the best the child can do and to demand no more. (as cited in Sarason & Doris, 1979, p. 264)

Sarason and Doris noted that Barr's words had little influence on the ethos of schools, which continued to view public education for exceptional learners as a brief, youthful stop en route to adult life in an institution. The need for articulation between special and general educators was nice but not necessary. Was it the organizational design of separate systems that inhibited this communication? Or was it—and is it still—the lack of consensus about the purpose of schooling and why we pursue the education of exceptional learners in particular?

The concept of the least restrictive environment, the legal term that spawned the educational strategy of mainstreaming, weaves together all elements of educational place and practice and requires that the purposes of schooling be more finely tuned. Sarason and Doris (1979) contended that "mainstreaming puts back on the discussion table the question of.... What are schools for? How shall we judge them?" (p. 394). In their view, "schooling has two coequal goals: productive learning and mutuality in living" (p. 407).

Often a clamor is made in school reform for change from one practice to another, from an either to an or, from separate to inclusive settings, from a continuum of placements to a constellation of services. Before changes of this nature can be managed, however, "there are still major dilemmas because of multiple and competing purposes of schooling, but it is precisely within this morass that educational reform must find its way" (Fullan, 1991, p. 15). Cousins (1974) remarked on the leader's need "to brood creatively about purpose" (p. 4) without being overwhelmed by discontinuity and "unremitting arbitration"— two pitfalls familiar to any educational administrator coping with issues of student placement. Sarason and Doris (1979) noted that too often when the purposes of mainstreaming have been pondered, discussions have too quickly become "mired in the controversies centering around law, procedures, administration, and funding" (p. 392).

As our conceptual, historical, and empirical examination of the LRE has attempted to portray, the issues at the heart of instructional settings for exceptional learners exceed the limits of law and reach back into the collective psyche that struggles with the notion of difference and how to fairly provide, at once, nurturance and independence. Embedded in the concept of LRE is the elemental struggle of aligning personal interests and public concerns. Howe's (1996) notion of social justice as the ethical center of social institutions helps to conceive of educational options that do not negatively discriminate with regard to democratic character and productive learning but rather respond flexibly to students whose needs cannot be met in a conventional manner or for whom the purpose of schooling is no less significant, but qualitatively different.

A full educational opportunity—an appropriate public education that is firmly fixed on productive learning for each student, that acknowledges the dynamic reciprocity between student and setting, and that marshals its resources under the guiding principle of social justice—has much to offer America's youth. If, and when, these benefits can be assured for all, then the dynamic mechanism inherent in the concept of LRE and implemented through its continuum can be set aside for a dynamic reciprocity that rests with confidence upon the primary value of social institutions—social justice.

Appendix
Notable LRE Cases: 1980s

Case	Age	Disability	LRE	Rationale
Roncker v. Walter, 700 F.2d 1058 (6th Cir. 1983).	9-year-old male	Moderate mental retardation	The 6th Circuit Court refused to intervene. Instead of determining the LRE for Neill, the Federal Court developed a feasibility test for the district to use to determine if its proposal to move Neill from a separate class in a public school to a county program where he would have no interaction with nondisabled children violated the LRE requirements.	The Court cited lack of significant progress for Neill during the previous 18 months. The Court acknowledged that a learner's need for an appropriate education might conflict with preferences for integration and that factors could be considered in determining whether education in the regular setting could be provided satisfactorily.
Mark A. ex rel. Aleah A. v. Grantwood Area Educational Agency, EHLR 557:412 (8th Cir. 1986).	Preschool male	Multiple disabilities	The 8th Circuit Court held that the LRE was a public school self-contained program.	The Court found that it was not necessary for the district to provide a private, integrated preschool as it was not correct that the mainstreaming provision could only be satisfied by providing instruction in the presence of nondisabled students. Students without

Case	Age	Disability	LRE	Rationale
				disabilities would be in the public school, if not in the immediate class.
Wilson v. Marana Unified School District No. 6, 735 F.2d 1176 (9th Cir. 1984).	2nd grade female	Physical disability: cerebral palsy	The 9th Circuit Court found that the LRE for Jessica was a school in a neighboring district with a teacher trained in educating students with physical disabilities.	The Court sympathized with the Wilsons' position favoring the continuation of her program at the local school with a teacher certi- fied in learning disabilities but also understood the district's desire to address Jessica's lack of progress as effectively as possible. The Court expressed judicial restraint in refraining to substitute its own notions of educational policy for those of the school dis- trict. The Court held that, although the mainstreaming requirement is important, "it must be balanced with the primary objective of providing an appropriate educa- tion, and accordingly, removal of a child from the regular education environment may be necessitated by the nature or severity of the disability" (Pitasky, 1996, p. 5).

| *Lachman v. Illinois State Board of Education*, 852 F.2d 290 (7th Cir. 1988). | 7-year-old male | Hearing impairment | Although Benjamin's parents sought full-time cued speech instruction in a regular neighborhood classroom, the 7th Circuit Court determined the LRE for Benjamin was placement in a self-contained class in a regional program where he would be instructed along with other hearing-impaired children using a total communication approach. In this case, the Court determined that the issue of LRE was embedded in the context of what was deemed to be appropriate methodology—cued speech—by Benjamin's parents. Consequently, the Lachmans had the burden of challenging the district's recommendation for instruction in total communication, which was provided at the regional center. | The district was not required to establish such customized instruction. The Court held that "we must establish the nature of the main-streaming obligation created by section 1412(5)(B) and clarify the relationship of that statutory language to the general section 1412(1) requirement that handicapped children be provided with a free appropriate public education. The degree to which a challenged IEP satisfies the mainstreaming goal of EAHCA simply cannot be evaluated in the abstract. Rather, that laudable policy objective must be weighed in tandem with the Act's principal goal of ensuring that the public schools provide handicapped children with a free appropriate education. The Court concluded that "the mainstreaming preference of the IDEA is not unqualified and that the educational program for a particular child must be one that can be effectively implemented in a regular classroom before the Act's preference for a regular education can be accomplished" (Pitasky, 1996, p. 5). |

Case	Age	Disability	LRE	Rationale
DeVries v. Fairfax County School Board, **882 F.2d 876 (4th Cir. 1989).**	17-year-old male	Autism	The LRE for Michael was a vocational center 13 miles from his home. It was able to provide him with necessary structure and one-to-one instruction.	Based upon his functional performance, which is richly described in this case, the Court found that if Michael were to attend his home school of 2,300 mostly nondisabled students, he would in effect be monitoring classes rather than participating in a program geared to his future. The Court concluded that mainstreaming was not appropriate for Michael, nor for every child, and must be contingent upon individual appropriateness.
Daniel R. R. v. State Board of Education, **874 F.2d 1036 (5th Cir. 1989).**	6-year-old male	Mental retardation: Down Syndrome	The Court of Appeals for the 5th Circuit upheld the district's action of removing Daniel from a general education preschool class and placing him in a special education class for a substantial portion of the day becuase the school district could show meaningful affirmative attempts to make his integration successful (Champagne, 1992). Essentially, the Court said that "when the provisions of FAPE and mainstreaming are in	The Court instructed that academic achievement was not the sole purpose of mainstreaming and access to regular education could not be denied just because the progress of the student with a disability will not equal that of students in regular education (Pitasky, 1996). However, the Court found it unnecessary for schools to drastically redesign the regular education program for an individual child. In this case,

the Court determined that the teachers, during the 3-month trial period, spent an inordinate amount of time attending to Daniel's needs at the expense of other children in the class and that his curriculum had to be totally modified to allow him meaningful participation

conflict, the mainstreaming mandate becomes secondary to the appropriate education mandate" (Yell, 1995b, p.393).

Notable LRE Cases: Early 1990s

Case	Age	Disability	LRE	Rationale
Greer v. Rome City School District, 950 F.2d 688 (11th Cir. 1991).	Elementary student, female	Mental retardation: Down Syndrome	Because insufficient information was provided by the district on Christy Greer's IEP, the 11th Circuit Court was unable to determine if the LRE for Christy was placement in a regular class in the neighborhood school or the district's proposed placement at another school in a self-contained class with mainstreaming in non-academic areas.	Relying on the test established in the case of Daniel R. R., the Court found that the district failed to consider the critical inquiry demanded of the test's first prong: It had failed to consider whether Christy could progress in the regular classroom if provided with the appropriate aids and services. The minutes from IEP meetings indicated that minimum consideration had been given to other options for her and revealed

Case	Age	Disability	LRE	Rationale
				damning evidence that Christy's IEP had been written without parental input and that placement had been decided before due consideration of her needs. The district was ordered to reconsider its recommendation (Yell, 1995b).
Amann v. Stow School System, 982 F.2d 644 (1st Cir. 1992).	14-year-old male	Learning disability	The 1st Circuit Court determined that for this student, both FAPE and LRE could be provided in a public setting that afforded interaction with non-disabled peers.	This placement obviated the need for the state to provide a private program maximizing the student's academic benefit. The Court held that federal law does not require a maximizing view of the IDEA, but one that provides the lower standard of a minimum floor of opportunity (Pitasky, 1996).
Teague Independent School District v. Todd L., 999 F.2d 127 (5th Cir. 1993).	17-year-old male	Multiple disabilities: a variety of behavioral, learning, and speech disorders.	The 5th Circuit Court determined that a public school placement rather than a residential psychiatric institution was considered the LRE for this high school student with multiple disabilities.	Despite the student's low frustration tolerance and outbursts in reaction to stress, the Court held that placement in a special education class at the public high school allowed him the chance to interact with nondisabled peers and to participate more fully in his community.

Case			
Oberti v. Board of Education of the Borough of Clementon School District, 995 F.2d 1204 (3rd Cir. 1993).	8-year-old male	Mental retardation: Down Syndrome	The 3rd Circuit Court determined that the LRE for Rafael was the regular classroom, following the school district's failure to provide him with appropriate aids and services in a part-time regular kindergarten. The Court held that Rafael's IEP could be implemented within the regular class but that the district had not made an adequate attempt to support him there (Yell, 1995b). The Court placed the burden of proof on the school district for the following year and stressed, in doing so, that it was not embracing the full-inclusion concept.	Once again, the Daniel R. R. test was used. The Court determined that despite Rafael's serious and aggressive behavior problems directed toward his teachers and peers, no plan to manage his behavior was incorporated into his IEP and no consultation was provided to his regular educator. His afternoons in a special class were free from such behavioral outbursts. Based on the district's failure to support his integrated education, the Court determined that it had not been established that Rafael could not succeed in a regular class. Significantly, the Court held that more than academic progress must be used to justify a special placement, stating that parallel, not identical, instruction might be required.
Sacramento City Unified School District v. Rachel H., 14 F.3d 1398 (9th Cir. 1994).	11-year-old female	Moderate mental retardation	The 9th Circuit Court established a four-pronged test to determine that the LRE for Rachel Holland was the regular classroom for the full day with appropriate aids and services, rather than the district's proposed placement in special	The Court held that "mainstreaming is the starting point . . . placement in other than a regular class is a fall-back choice made only after it is determined that placement in regular classes will be unsuccessful." In holding for the

209

Case	Age	Disability	LRE	Rationale
			special classes for academic subjects with mainstreaming for art, music, lunch and recess. Differing from the other frameworks used in *Roncker* or *Daniel R. R.*, this test did not require balancing the benefits of special or regular class instruction but considered only the benefit of regular education for Rachel with appropriate support, the nonacademic benefits of the regular class, her effect on other students within that class, and the financial costs of her inclusion.	Hollands in this instance, the Court "by emphasizing a test for (as opposed to an absolute right to) inclusion . . . implicitly sanctioned inclusion and removal" (Siegel, 1994, p.48). The Court instructed that all future appropriate placements for Rachel should be similarly determined by this four-pronged framework.

Notable LRE Cases: Mid-1990s

Case	Age	Disability	LRE	Rationale
McWhirt by McWhirt v. Williamson County Schools, 23 IDELR 509 (6th Cir. 1994).	Fourth-grade female	Severe multiple disabilities affecting her verbal skills, ambulation, health, and social / emotional development.	Th 6th Circuit Court determined the LRE was a separate class with mainstreaming opportunities.	After all of the school personnel testified that involved resource room support had not met either her physical or her educational needs, the Court held that the regular classroom was incapable of meeting her needs.

Case	Student	Impairment	Court Determination	Holding
Carlisle Area School District v. Scott P., 23 IDELR 293 (3rd Cir. 1995).	20-year-old high school student, male	Visual impairment: brain injuries and blindness sustained in an accident	The 3rd Circuit Court determined that placement in a physical support class at a public high school was the LRE.	Although the student's parents sought a residential setting for him, the Court held that the district's placement, with academic, social, and vocational instruction with other students who were blind, would provide him with educational benefit in a less restrictive setting.
Poolaw v. Bishop, 23 IDELR 406 (9th Cir. 1995).	13-year-old male	Hearing impairment: profoundly deaf with communication skills described as primitive.	The 9th Circuit Court determined that the LRE for Lionel was a state residential school for the deaf.	Lionel, whose parents moved residences frequently, had been previously mainstreamed with appropriate aids and services in several states, yet he could neither read nor write. Based upon his records from multiple schools, the Court held that to receive an academic benefit, Lionel required intensive instruction in American Sign Language, which was only provided in Arizona at the state school. The Court held that Lionel's currently profound academic needs outweighed the social benefits of a regular setting, including peer interaction and the influence of his Native American culture.

Case	Age	Disability	LRE	Rationale
Clyde K. ex re. Ryan D. v. Puyallup School District, 35 F.3d 1396 (9th Cir. 1994).	15-year-old male	Tourette Syndrome and ADHD	The 9th Circuit Court determined that placement in an off-campus self-contained program was the LRE for Ryan.	Ryan was failing in his mainstreamed setting and disrupting the environment with taunts and profanity directed at students and teachers. The Court, employing the *Holland* test, deter-mined that Ryan derived no academic benefit from his regular class placement and was, in fact, regressing. In addition, his non-academic benefits were minimal. The cost of a personal aide was irrelevant in determining whether Ryan would be included in a regular class because the Court determined that this service would not be of benefit to him. Most important to the Court were the overwhelmingly negative effects of what it termed Ryan's "dangerously agressive" behavior and the reality that his explicit taunts could initiate a Title IX sexual harassment charge.

Harmann by Hartmann v. Loudoun County Board of Education, **26 IDELR 167, 96-2809 (4th Cir. 1997).**	11-year-old male	Autism	The 4th Circuit Court determined that partial mainstreaming met the LRE requirement for Mark, reversing a district court's determination that the LRE for him was the regular classroom.	In its reversal, the circuit court found that the district court did not give "due weight" to the previous administrative hearings failing to consider the school district's discretion when determining appropriate programming for one of its students. The circuit court held that: (1) mainstreaming is a preference not a mandate; (2) overwhelming evidence was ignored that Mark made minimal if any progress in his inclusive placement; (3) the inclusive accommodations of the second district need not be replicated because they approached a potential maximizing standard exceeding the *Rowley* educational benefit standard; (4) the district court failed to consider the disruptive effects of Mark's behavior on the regular classroom; (5) the Loudoun County school district IEP was appropriate because it provided Mark with both educational benefit and opportunities for mainstreaming.

References

Abeson, A., Burgdorf, R. L., Casey, P. J., Kunz, J. W., & McNeil, W. (1975). Access to opportunity. In N. Hobbs (Ed.), *Issues in the classification of children* (Vol. 2, pp. 270–292). San Francisco: Jossey-Bass.

Alexander, P. A., Murphy, P. K., & Woods, B. S. (1996). Of squalls and fathoms: Navigating the seas of educational innovation. *Educational Researcher, 25*(3), 31–39.

Allan, J. (1996). Foucault and special educational needs: A "box of tools" for analyzing children's experiences of mainstreaming. *Disability & Society, 11,* 219–233.

Amann v. Stow School System, 982 F.2d 644 (1st Cir. 1992).

Anderson-Inman, L. (1981). Transenvironmental programming: Promoting success in the regular class by maximizing the effect of resource room assistance. *Journal of Special Education Technology, 4,* 3–12.

Aristotle. (1976). *The Ethics of Aristotle* (J.A.K. Thomson, Trans). New York: Penguin.

Arnold, J. B., & Dodge, H. W. (1994, October). Room for all. *The American School Board Journal,* 22–26.

Bailey, D. B. (1989). Issues and directions in preparing professionals to work with young handicapped children and their families. In J. J. Gallagher, P. L. Trohanis, & R. M. Clifford (Eds.), *Policy implementation and PL 99-457.* Baltimore: Paul H. Brookes.

Bancroft, R. (1976). Special education: Legal aspects. In P. A. O'Donnell & R. H. Bradfield (Eds.), *Mainstreaming: Controversy and consensus* (pp. 11–21). San Rafael: CA: Academic Therapy.

Barth, R. S. (1993). Reflections on a conversation. *Journal of Personnel Evaluation in Education, 7*(3), 212–221.

Bartlett, L. D. (1993). Mainstreaming: On the road to clarification. *Education Law Reporter, 76,* 17–25.

Bateman, B. (1992). Learning disabilities: The changing landscape. *Journal of Learning Disabilities, 25,* 29–36.

Bateman, B. (1994). Who, how, and where: Special education's issues in perpetuity. *The Journal of Special Education, 27,* 509–520.

Bateman, B. (1996). *Better IEPs.* Longmont, CO: Sopris West.

Bateman, B., & Chard, D. J. (1995). Legal demands and constraints on placement decisions. In J. M. Kauffman, J. W. Lloyd, D. P. Hallahan, & T. A. Astuto (Eds.), *Issues in educational placement: Students with emotional and behavioral disorders* (pp. 285–316). Hillsdale, NJ: Lawrence Erlbaum Associates.

Bell, D. A. (1980). Brown v. Board of Education and the interest–convergence dilemma. *Harvard Law Review, 93,* 518–533.

Bellah, F. N., Madsen, R., Sullivan,W. M., Swidler, A., & Tipton, S. M. (1985). *Habits of the heart: Individualism and commitment in American life.* New York: Harper & Row.

Bigge, J. L. (1991). *Teaching individuals with physical and multiple disabilities.* Columbus, OH: Merrill.

Biklen, D. (1985). *Achieving the complete school.* New York: Teachers College Press.

Billingsley, B., Peterson, D., Bodkins, D., & Hendricks, M. (1993). *Program leadership for serving students with disabilities.* Project report, Virginia Polytechnic and State University, Blacksburg, VA.

Blatt, B. (1987). *The conquest of mental retardation.* Austin, TX: Pro-Ed.

Borthwick-Duffy, S. A., Palmer, D. S., & Lane, K. L. (1996). One size doesn't fit all: Full inclusion and individual differences. *Journal of Behavioral Education, 6,* 311–329.

Bos, C. S., & Vaughn, S. (1994). *Strategies for teaching students with learning and behavior problems.* Boston: Allyn & Bacon.

Brigham, F. J., & Kauffman, J. M. (in press). Creating supportive environments for students with emotional or behavioral disorders. *Effective School Practices.*

Bronfenbrenner, U. (1979). *The ecology of human development: Experiments by nature and design.* Cambridge, MA: Harvard University Press.

Brown v. the Board of Education, 347 U. S. 483 (1954).

Bruininks, R., Thurlow, M. L., & Ysseldyke, J. E. (1992). Assessing the right outcomes: Prospects for improving education for youth with disabilities. *Education and Training in Mental Retardation, 27,* 93–100.

Bureau of Education for the Handicapped. (1976, August 20). *First consolidated draft of proposed regulations under part B of the Education of the Handicapped Act as amended by Public Law 94-142.* Washington, DC: U. S. Office of Education.

Burgdorf, R. L., Jr. (1980). *The legal rights of handicapped persons: Cases, materials, and text.* Baltimore, MD: Paul H. Brookes.

Butler, R., & Marinov-Glassman, D. (1994). The effects of educational placement and grade level on the self-perceptions of low achievers and students with learning disabilities. *Journal of Learning Disabilities, 27,* 325–334.

Cannon, G. S., Idol, L., & West, J. F. (1992). Educating students with mild handicaps in general classrooms: Essential teaching practices for general and special educators. *Journal of Learning Disabilities, 25,* 300–317.

Carlberg, C., & Kavale, K. (1980). The efficacy of special versus regular class placement for exceptional children: A meta-analysis. *Journal of Special Education, 14,* 295–309.

Carlisle Area School District v. Scott P., 23 IDELR 293 (3rd Cir. 1995).

Carnegie Foundation. (1995). *Draft: Report of the Carnegie Task Force on learning in the primary grades.* New York: Author.

Carnine, D. W. (1994a). *Becoming a better consumer of educational research.* Eugene, OR: National Center to Improve the Tools of Educators.

Carnine, D. W. (1994b). *Smart schools: Beyond innovation to educational reform or looking for reform in all the wrong places.* Eugene, OR: National Center to Improve the Tools of Educators.

Centra, N. A. (1990). *A qualitative study of high school students in a resource program.* Unpublished doctoral dissertation, Syracuse University, Syracuse, NY.

Champagne, J. (1992). *LRE: Decisions in sequence.* Symposium conducted at the Annual conference of the National Association of Private Schools for Exceptional children, Washington, DC.

Clyde K. ex re. Ryan D. v. Puyallup School District, 35 F. 3d 1396 (9th Cir. 1994).

Cohen, M. (1993). The politics of special ed. *The Special Educator, 8,* 266.

Coleman, J. (1968). The concept of equality of educational opportunity. *Harvard Educational Review, 38,* 17.

Conn, P. (1996). *Pearl S. Buck: A cultural biography.* New York: Cambridge University Press.

Cook, L. H., & Boe, E. E. (1995). Who is teaching students with disabilities? *Teaching Exceptional Children, 20*(1), 70–72.

Council for Exceptional Children. (1977). *Mainstreaming: 1977 topical bibliography.* Reston, VA: Exceptional Child Education Resources Topical Bibliography Series, No. 710. (ERIC Document Reproduction Service No. ED146739 - EC102860)

Cousins, N. (1974, November 16). Thinking through leadership. *Saturday Review World, 4.*

Crockett, J. B., & Kauffman, J. M. (1998). Classrooms for students with learning disabilities: Realities, dilemmas, and recommendations for service delivery. In B. Y. L. Wong (Ed.), *Learning about learning disabilities* (2nd ed., pp. 489–525). San Diego, CA: Academic Press.

Cruickshank, W. M. (1967). Current educational practices with exceptional children. In W. M. Cruickshank & G. O. Johnson (Eds.), *Education of exceptional children and youth* (2nd ed., pp. 45–98). Englewood Cliffs, NJ: Prentice-Hall.

Cruickshank, W. M. (1977). Guest editorial. *Journal of Learning Disabilities, 10*, 193–194.

Cruickshank, W. M., Morse, W. C., & Grant, J. O. (1990). *The Individual Education Planning committee: A step in the history of special education.* Ann Arbor, MI: University of Michigan Press.

Daniel R. R. v. State Board of Education, 874 F.2d 1036 (5th Cir. 1989).

Danielson, L. C., & Bellamy, G. T. (1989). State variation in placement of children with handicaps in segregated environments. *Exceptional Children, 55*, 448–455.

Deno, E. (1970). Special education as developmental capital. *Exceptional Children, 37*, 229–237.

DeVries v. Fairfax County School Board, 882 F.2d 876 (4th Cir. 1989).

D. F. v. Western School Corporation, 23 IDELR 1121 (S.D. Ind. 1996).

Dionne, E. J., Jr. (1997, January 19). Paul Wellstone: Radical realist. *The Washington Post Magazine,* 8–13, 22–26.

Dorn, S., Fuchs, D., & Fuchs, L. (1996). A historical perspective on special education reform. *Theory into Practice, 35*(1), 12–19.

Dunlap, G., & Childs, K. E. (1996). Intervention research in emotional and behavioral disorders: An analysis of studies from 1980–1993. *Behavioral Disorders, 21*, 125–136.

Dunn, L. M. (1968). Special education for the mildly retarded: Is much of it justifiable? *Exceptional Children, 35*, 5–22.

Dupre, A. P. (1998). Disability, deference, and the integrity of the academic enterprise. *Georgia Law Review, 32*, 393-473.

Durden, W. G. (1995, October 4). Where is the middle ground? *Education Week,* 48–38.

Edson, C. H. (1986). Our past and present: Historical inquiry in education. *Journal of Thought (Special Topic Edition: Qualitative Research) 21*(3) 13–27.

Education and training of the handicapped: Hearings before the ad hoc sub-committee on the handicapped. 89th Cong., 2d Sess. 2 (1966).

Education for All Handicapped Children Act of 1975 (Pub. L. No. 94-142, §§ 1400–1461.

Ellet, L. (1993). Instructional practices in mainstreamed secondary classrooms. *Jounal of Learning Disabilities, 26*, 57–64.

English, F. W. (1997, March). The problem with PBL (problem based learning). *Teaching in Educational Administration, 4*(1), 1–2.

Epstein, M. H., Quinn, K. P., & Cumblad, C. (1994). A scale to assess the restrictiveness of educational settings. *Journal of Child and Family Studies, 3*(1), 107–119.

Ft. Zumwalt School District v. Missouri State Board of Education, 24 IDELR 222 (E.D. Mo. 1996).

Ft. Zumwalt School District v. Clynes, 26 IDELR 172 (8th Cir. 1997).

Fuchs, D., & Fuchs, L. (1991). Framing the REI debate: Abolitionists versus conservationists. In J. W. Lloyd, N. N. Singh, & A. C. Repp (Eds.), *The Regular Education Initiative: Alternative perspectives on concepts, issues, and models* (pp. 242–255). Sycamore, IL: Sycamore Press.

Fuchs, D., & Fuchs, L. S. (1994). Inclusive schools movement and the radicalization of special education reform. *Exceptional Children, 60*, 294–309.

Fuchs, D., & Fuchs, L. S. (1995a). Special education can work. In J. M. Kauffman, J. W. Lloyd, D. P. Hallahan, & T. A. Astuto (Eds.), *Issues in educational placement: Students with emotional and behavioral disorders* (pp. 363–377). Hillsdale, NJ: Lawrence Erlbaum Associates.

Fuchs, D., & Fuchs, L. S. (1995b). What's "special" about special education? *Phi Delta Kappan, 76*, 522–530.

Fuchs, D., Fuchs, L. S., & Fernstrom, P. (1993). A conservative approach to special education reform: Mainstreaming through transenvironmental programming and curriculum-based measurement. *American Educational Research Journal, 30*(1), 149–177.

Fuchs, D., Fuchs, L. S., & Fernstrom, P., & Hohn, M. (1991). Toward a responsible reintegration of behaviorally disordered students. *Behavioral Disorders, 16*, 133–147.

Fuchs, L. S. , Fuchs, D., & Hamlett, C. L. (1989). Effects of alternative goal structures within curriculum-based measurement. *Exceptional Children, 55*, 429–438.

Fuchs, L. S. , Fuchs, D., Hamlett, C. L., Phillips, N. B., & Bentz, J. (1994). Classwide curriculum-based measurement: Helping general educators meet the challenge of student diversity. *Exceptional Children, 60,* 518–537.

Fuchs, D., Roberts, P. H., Fuchs, L. S., & Bowers, J. (1996). Reintegrating students with learning disabilities into the mainstream: A two-year study. *Learning Disabilities Research and Practice, 11,* 214–229.

Fullan, M. G. (1991) *The new meaning of educational change.* New York: Teachers College Press.

Gajria, M., Salend, S. J., & Hemrick, M. A. (1994). Teacher acceptability of testing modifications for mainstreamed students. *Learning Disabilities Research and Practice, 9,* 236–243.

Gallagher, J. J. (1984). The evolution of special education concepts. In B. Blatt & R. J. Morris (Eds.), *Perspectives in special education: Personal orientations* (pp. 101–124). Glenview, IL: Scott, Foresman.

Gallagher, J. J. (1990). New patterns in special education. *Educational Researcher, 19*(5), 34–36.

Gallagher, J. J. (1994). The pull of societal forces on special education. *The Journal of Special Education, 27,* 521–530.

Gardner, H. (1995). *Leading minds: An anatomy of leadership.* New York: HarperCollins.

Garnett, K. (1996). *Thinking about inclusion and learning disabilities: A teacher's guide.* Reston, VA: Council for Exceptional Children.

Gartner, A., & Lipsky, D. K. (1987). Beyond special education: Toward a quality system for all students. *Harvard Educational Review, 57,* 367–395.

Gartner, A., & Lipsky, D. K . (1989). *The yoke of special education: How to break it.* Rochester, NY: National Center on Education and Economy.

Gartner, A., & Lipsky, D. K. (1997). *Inclusion and school reform: Transforming America's classrooms.* Baltimore, MD: Paul H. Brookes.

Gerber, M. M. (1996). Reforming special education: "beyond inclusion." In C. Christensen & F. Rizvi (Eds.), *Disability and the dilemmas of education and justice* (pp. 156–174). Philadelphia: Open Unversity Press.

Gerry, M. H., & Benton, J. M. (1986). Section 504: The larger umbrella. In M. Ballard, D. A. Ramirez, & F. J. Weintraub (Eds.), *Special education in America: Its legal and governmental foundations.* Reston, VA: Council for Exceptional Children.

Gilhool, T. K. (1976). Education: An inalienable right. In F. J. Weintraub, A. Abeson, J. Ballard, & M. LaVor (Eds.), *Public policy and the education of exceptional children* (pp. 14–21). Reston, VA: Council for Exceptional Children.

Gorn, S. (1996). *What's hot, what's not: Trends in special education litigation.* Horsham, PA: LRP Publications.

Gottlieb, J., Alter, M., & Gottlieb, B. W. (1991). Mainstreaming academically handicapped children in urban schools. In J. W. Lloyd, N. N. Singh, & A. C. Repp (Eds.), *The regular education initiative: alternative perspectives on concepts, issues, and models* (pp. 95–112). Sycamore, IL: Sycamore Press.

Gottlieb, J., Alter, M., & Gottlieb, B. W., & Wishner, J. (1994). Special education in urban America: It's not justifiable for many. *Journal of Special Education, 27,* 453–465.

Greenwood, C.R. (1996). Research on the practices and behavior of effective teachers at the Juniper Gardens Children's Project: Implications for the education of diverse learners. In D. Speece & B. Keogh (Eds.). *Research on classroom ecologies: Implications for inclusion of children with learning disabilities* (pp. 39-67). Mahwah, NJ: Lawrence Erlbaum Associates.

Greer v. Rome City School District, 950 F.2d 688 (11th Cir. 1991).

Gresham, F. M., & MacMillan, D. R. (1997a). Autistic recovery? An analysis and critique of the empirical evidence on the Early Intervention Project. *Behavioral Disorders, 22,* 185–201.

Gresham, F. M., & MacMillan, D. R. (1997b). Denial and defensiveness in the place of fact and reason: Rejoinder to Smith and Lovaas. *Behavioral Disorders, 22,* 219–223.

Gross, J., & Vance, V. (1975). Mainstream educator training in a cooperative joint agreement and intermediate unit district. In R. Johnson, R. Weatherman, & A. Rehmann (Eds.), *Leadership Series in Special Education 103* (pp. 106–107). Minneapolis, MN: University of Minnesota.

Guralnick, M. J. (1982). Mainstreaming young handicapped children: A public policy and ecological systems analysis. In B. Spodek (Ed.), *Handbook of research in early childhood education* (pp. 456–500). New York: The Free Press.

Hallahan, D. P., & Cruickshank, W. M. (1973). *Psycho-educational foundations of learning disabilities.* Englewood Cliffs, NJ: Prentice-Hall.

Hallahan, D. P., & Kauffman, J. M. (Eds.). (1995). *The illusion of full inclusion: A comprehensive critique of a current special education bandwagon.* Austin, TX: Pro-ed.

Hallahan, D. P., & Kauffman, J. M. (1997). *Exceptional learners: Introduction to special education* (7th ed.). Boston: Allyn & Bacon.

Hallahan, D. P., Kauffman, J. M., & Lloyd, J. W. (1996). *Introduction to learning disabilities.* Boston: Allyn & Bacon.

Halpern S. C. (1995). *On the limits of the law: The ironic legacy of Title VI of the 1964 Civil Rights Act.* Baltimore: Johns Hopkins University Press.

Hamilton, D. (1989). *Toward a theory of schooling.* London: Falmer.

Harkin, T. (1993, September). Future goals: Application of the Goals 2000: Education America Act to individuals with disabilities. *Exceptional Parent,* 25–27.

Hartmann by Hartmann by Loudoun County Board of Education, 24 IDELR 1171 (E.D. Va. 1996); 26 IDELR 167, 96-2809 (4th Cir. 1997).

Hays, T. S. (1993). An historical content analysis of publications in gifted education journals. *Roeper Review, 16*(1), 41–43.

Hendrick Hudson District Board of Education v. Rowley, 458 U. S. 176, 102 S.Ct. 3034 (1982).

Heron, T. E., & Skinner, M. E. (1981). Criteria for defining the regular classroom as the least restrictive environment for LD students. *Learning Disabilities Quarterly, 4,* 115–121.

Heumann, J. (1993, November 2) Oberti decision is core of the ED's inclusion position. *The Special Educator, 8,* 8.

Hirth, M. A., & Valesky, T. C. (1990). Survey of universities: Special education knowledge requirements in school administrator preparation programs. *Planning and Changing, 21*(3), 165–172.

Holland (1994). See *Sacramento City Unified School District v. Rachel H.*

Houck, C. K., & Rogers, C. J. (1994). The special/general education integration intitiative for students with specific learning disabilities: A "snapshot" of program change. *Journal of Learning Disabilities, 27,* 435–453.

Howe, K. R. (1996). Educational ethics, social justice and children with disabilities. In C. Christensen & F. Rizvi (Eds.), *Disability and the dilemmas of education and justice* (pp. 46–62). Philidelphia: Open Unversity Press.

Hudson by Hudson v. Bloomfield Hills Public Schools, 23 IDELR 613 (E.D. Mich. 1995); 25 IDELR 607 (6th Cir. 1997).

Huefner, D. S. (1994). The mainstreaming cases: Tensions and trends for school administrators. *Educational Administration Quarterly, 30*(1), 27–55.

Hungerford, R. H. (1950). On locusts. *American Journal of Mental Deficiency, 54,* 415–418.

Hurst, A. (1984). Adolescence and physical impairment: An interactionist view. In L. Barton, & S. Tomlinson (Eds.), *Special education and social interests* (pp. 192–227). New York: Nicholas.

Individuals with Disabilities Education Act of 1990, 20 U.S.C. § 1401 *et seq.*, Individuals with Disabilities Act Amendments of 1997, 105th Congress.

Jacobson, L. (1997, January 29). PTA issues parent-involvement standards for schools. *Education Week, 16(18),* 8.

Jacobson, J. W., Mulick, J. A., & Schwartz, A. A. (1995). A history of facilitated communication: Science, pseudoscience, and antiscience. *American Psychologist, 50,* 750–765.

Jenkins, J. R., Jewell, M., Leicester, N., O'Connor, R. E., Jenkins, L. M., & Troutner, N. M. (1994). Accommodations for individual differences without classroom ability groups: An experiment in school restructuring. *Exceptional Children, 60,* 344–358.

Johnson, L. J., & Bauer, A. M. (1992). *Meeting the needs of special students: Legal, ethical, and practical ramifications.* Newbury Park, CA: Corwin.

Johnson, L. J., & Pugach, M. C. (1990). Classroom teachers' views of intervention strategies for learning and behavior problems: Which are reasonable and how frequently are they used? *The Journal of Special Education, 24,* 69–84.

Jones, R. A. (1995). *The child-school interface.* London: Cassell.

Kari H. v. Franklin Special School District, 23 IDELR 538 (M.D. Tenn. 1995); 26 IDELR 569 (6th Cir. 1997).

Katsiyannis, A., Conderman, G., & Franks, D. J. (1995). State practices on inclusion: A national review. *Remedial and Special Education, 16,* 279–287.

Kauffman, J. M. (1981). Historical trends and contemporary issues in special education in the United States. In J. M. Kauffman & D. P. Hallahan (Eds.), *The handbook of special education* (pp. 3–23). Englewood Cliffs, NJ: Prentice-Hall.

Kauffman, J. M. (1989). The regular education initiative as Reagan-Bush educational policy: A trickle-down theory of education of the hard-to-teach. *The Journal of Special Education, 23,* 256–278.

Kauffman, J. M. (1991). Purposeful ambiguity: Its value in defining emotional or behavioral disorders. In R. B. Rutherford, S. A. DiGangi, & S. R. Mathuyr (Eds.), *Monograph in Severe Behavioral Disorders of Children and Youth* (pp. 1–7). Tempe, AZ: Arizona State University, Teacher Educators for Children with Behavior Disorders, and Council for Children with Behavioral Disorders.

Kauffman, J. M. (1992). Foreword. In K. R. Howe & O. B. Miramontes, *The ethics of special education* (pp. xi–xvii). New York: Teachers College Press.

Kauffman, J. M. (1993). How we might achieve the radical reform of special education. *Exceptional Children, 60,* 6–16.

Kauffman, J. M. (1994). Places of change: Special education's power and identity in an era of educational reform. *Journal of Learning Disabilities, 27,* 610–618.

Kauffman, J. M. (1995). Why we must celebrate a diversity of restrictive environments. *Learning Disabilities Research and Practice, 10,* 225–232.

Kauffman, J. M. (1997a). Caricature, science, and exceptionality. *Remedial and Special Education, 18,* 130–132.

Kauffman, J. M. (1997b). *Characteristics of emotional and behavioral disorders of children and youth* (6th ed.). Englewood Cliffs, NJ: Prentice-Hall.

Kauffman, J. M., & Hallahan, D. P. (1993). Toward a comprehensive delivery system for special education. In J. I. Goodlad & T. C. Lovitt (Eds.), *Integrating general and special education* (pp. 73–102). Columbus, OH: Merrill.

Kauffman, J. M., & Lloyd, J. W. (1995). A sense of place: The importance of placement issues in contemporary special education. In J. M. Kauffman, J. W. Lloyd, D. P.Hallahan, & T. A. Astuto (Eds.), *Issues in educational placement: Students with emotional and behavioral disorders* (pp. 3–19). Hillsdale, NJ: Lawrence Erlbaum Associates.

Kauffman, J. M., & Smucker, K. (1995). The legacies of placement. In J. M. Kauffman, J. W. Lloyd, D. P.Hallahan, & T. A. Astuto (Eds.), *Issues in educational placement: Students with emotional and behavioral disorders* (pp. 21–44). Hillsdale, NJ: Lawrence Erlbaum Associates.

Kauffman, J. M., & Trent, S. C. (1991). Issues in service delivery for students with learning disabilities. In B. Y. L. Wong (Ed.), *Learning about learning disabilties* (pp. 465–481). San Diego, CA: Academic Press.

Kaufman, M. J., Gottlieb, J., Agard, J. A., & Kukic, M. (1975). Mainstreaming: Toward an explication of the construct. In C. J. Meisel (Ed.), *Mainstreaming handicapped children: Outcomes, controversies, and new directions* (pp. 1–9). Hillsdale, NJ: Lawrence Erlbaum Associates.

Kavale, K. A., Fuchs, D., & Scruggs, T. E. (1994). Setting the record straight on learning disability and low achievement: Implications for policymaking. *Disabilities Research & Practice, 9*, 70–77.

Kearney, C. A., & Durand, V. M. (1992). How prepared are our teachers for mainstreamed classroom settings? A survey of postsecondary schools of education in New York State. *Exceptional Children, 59*, 6–11.

Keogh, B. K. (1988). Improving services for problem learners: Rethinking and restructuring. *Journal of Learning Disabilities, 21*, 19–22.

Keogh, B. K. (1994). What the special education research agenda should look like in the year 2000. *Learning Disabilities Research and Practice, 9*, 62–69.

Keogh, B. K., & Speece, D. L. (1996). Learning disabilities within the context of schooling. In D. Speece & B. K. Keogh (Eds.), *Research on classroom ecologies: Implications for inclusion of children with learning disabilities* (pp. 1–14). Mahwah, NJ: Lawrence Erlbaum Associates.

Kirk, S. A. (1993). Autobiographical remarks. In G. A. Harris & W. D. Kirk (Eds.), *The foundations of special education: Selected papers and speeches of Samuel A. Kirk* (pp. 9–39). Reston, VA: Council for Exceptional Children.

Kirk, S. A., & Gallagher, J. J. (1979). *Educating exceptional children* (3rd ed.). Boston, MA: Houghton Mifflin.

Kirk, S. A., Gallagher, J. J., & Anastasiow, N. J. (1993). *Educating exceptional children* (7th ed.). Boston, MA: Houghton Mifflin.

Kirk, S.A. (1941). Editorial. *Exceptional Children, 8*, 35.

Kirp, D. J. (1995). Changing conceptions of educational equity. In D. Ravitch & M. S. Vinovskis (Eds.), *Learning from the past: What history teaches us about school reform* (pp. 97–112). Baltimore, MD: Johns Hopkins University Press.

Korinek, L., McLaughlin, V., & Walther–Thomas, C. S. (1995). Least restrictive environment and collaboration: A bridge over troubled water. *Preventing School Failure, 39(*3), 6–12.

Kotler, M. A. (1994). The Individuals with Disabilities Education Act: A parent's perspective and proposal for change. *University of Michigan Journal of Law Reform, 27*, 331–397.

Kritsonis, M. A. (1992–1993). A study of elementary school principals' knowledge about special education and special education teachers' perceptions of their principals' knowledge. *National Forum of Applied Educational Research Journal, 5*(2), 62–68.

Lachman ex rel. Lachman v. Illinois State Board of Education, 852 F.2d 290 (7th Cir. 1988).

Lake v. Cameron, 124 U S. App. D. C. 364 F. 2d (1966).

Lange, C., & Ysseldyke, J. E. (1994). How school choice affects students with special needs. *Educational Leadership, 52*(3), 84–85.

Larry P. v. Riles, 343 F. Supp. 1306 (N.D. Cal. 1972) (preliminary injunction). Aff'd 502 F. 2d 963 (9th cir. 1974); 495 F. Supp. 926 (N.D. Cal. 1979) (decision on merits). Order modifying judgment, C-71-2270 RFP, Sept. 25, 1986.

Lazerson, M. (1973). Revisionism and American educational history. *Harvard Educational Review, 43*, 269–283.

Lazerson, M. (1983). The origins of special education. In J. G. Chambers & W. T. Hartman (Eds.), *Special education policies: Their history, implementation, and finance*. Philidelphia, PA: Temple University Press.

Letter to Anonymous, 22 IDELR 738, OSEP, 1995.

Letter to Anonymous, 24 IDELR 962, OSEP, 1996.

Lieberman, L. M. (1996). Preserving special education...for those who need it. In W. Stainback & S. Stainback (Eds.), *Controversial issues confronting special education* (pp. 16–27). Needham Heights, MA: Allyn & Bacon.

Lipsky, D. K. (1994). National survey gives insight into inclusive movement. *Inclusive Education Programs, 1*(3), 4–7.

Lloyd, J. W., & Gambatese, C. (1990). Reforming the relationship between regular and special education: Background and issues. In J. W. Lloyd, N. N. Singh, & A. C. Repp (Eds.), *The*

Regular Education Initiative: Alternative perspectives on concepts, issues, and models (pp. 3–13). Sycamore, IL: Sycamore Press.

Lochner v. New York, 198 U. S. 48, 69 (1908).

Low, J. (1996). Negotiating identities, negotiating environments: An interpretation of the experiences of students with disabilities. *Disability & Society, 11*, 235–248.

MacMillan, D. L., Gresham, F. M., & Forness, S. R. (1996). Full inclusion: An empirical perspective. *Behavioral Disorders, 21*, 145–159.

MacMillan, D. L., & Hendrick, I. G. (1993). Evolution and legacies. In J. I. Goodlad, & T. C. Lovitt (Eds.), *Integrating general and special education* (pp. 23–48). Columbus, OH: Merrill.

MacMillan, D. L., & Semmel, M. I. (1977). Evaluation of mainstreaming programs. *Focus on Exceptional Children, 9*, 1–14.

McWhirt by McWhirt v. Williamson County Schools, 23 IDELR 509 (6th Cir. 1994).

Maloney, M., & Shenker, B. (1995). *The continuing evolution of special education law: 1978 to 1995*. IDELR Special Report No. 12. Horsham, PA: LRP Publications.

Margolis, H., & Tewel, K. (1990). Understanding least restrictive environment: A key to avoiding parent-school conflict. *The Urban Review, 22*, 283–298.

Mark A. ex rel. Alleah A. v. Grantwood Area Educational Agency, EHLR 557:412 (8th Cir. 1986).

Marston, D. (1987–1988). The effectiveness of special education: A time series analysis of reading performance in regular and special education settings. *The Journal of Special Education, 21*(4), 13–26.

Martin, E. W. (1995a). Case studies on inclusion: Worst fears realized. *The Journal of Special Education, 29*(2), 192–199.

Martin, E. W. (1995b). Funding dedicated to serving special education students essential. *CEC Today, 2*(6), 14.

Martin, R. (1991). *Extraordinary children, ordinary lives: Stories behind special education case law*. Champaign, IL: Research Press.

Mather, N., & Roberts, R. (1994). Learning disabilities: A field in danger of extinction? *Learning Disabilities & Practice, 9*(1), 49–58.

McWhirt by *McWhirt v. Williamson County Schools*, 23 IDELR 509 (6th Cir. 1994).

Meadows, N. B., Neel, R. S., Scott, C. M., & Parker, G. (1994). Academic performance, social competence, and mainstreamed students with serious behavioral disorders. *Behavioral Disorders, 19*, 170–180.

Meredith, B., & Underwood, J. (1995). Irreconcilable differences? Defining the rising conflict between regular and special education. *Journal of Law and Education, 24*(2), 195–226.

Meyers, J., Truscott, S., Borelli, C., Gelzheiser, L., & Meyers B. (1997, March). *Is special education forgotten in educational reform?* Paper presented at the annual meeting of the American Educational Research Association, Chicago, IL.

Mills v. Board of Education of the District of Columbia, 348 F.Supp. 866 (1972).

Mordick, EHLR 211:160, OSEP, 1979.

Morse, W. C. (1984). Personal perspective. In B. Blatt & R. J. Morris (Eds.), *Perspectives in special education: Personal orientations* (pp. 101–124). Glenview, IL: Scott, Foresman.

Morsink, C. V., & Lenk, L. L. (1992). The delivery of special education programs and services. *Remedial and Special Education, 13*(6), 33–43.

M. R. v Lincolnwood Board of Education, District 74, 20 IDELR 1323 (N.D. Ill. 1994).

National Association of State Boards of Education. (1992). *Winners all: A call for inclusive schools*. Alexandria, VA: Author.

National Center for Law and the Handicapped. (1976, December 16). *Comments on the third draft consolidated concept paper under Part B of the Education of the Handicapped Act as amended by P.L. 94-142, October 18, 1976*. South Bend, IN: Author.

National Diffusion Network. (1980, Winter). *Educational programs that work: Special education*. Washington, DC: United States Office of Education.

New York State Education Department/The University of the State of New York. (1993). *Draft policy statement on least restrictive environment.* Albany, NY: Author.

New York State Education Department/The University of the State of New York. (1994). *Least restrictive environment implementation policy paper.* Albany, NY: Author.

New York State Regents Commission on Disability. (1993). *Committee for Elementary, Middle, and Secondary Education Report.* Albany, NY: Author.

Nietupski, J. A. (1995). The evolution of the LRE concept for students with severe disabilities. *Preventing School Failure, 39*(3), 40–46.

Oberti v. Board of Education of the Borough of Clementon School District, 995 F.2d 1204 (3rd Cir 1993).

Odom, S. L., Peck, C. A., Hanson, M., Beckman, P. J., Kaiser, A. P., Lieber, J., Brown, W. H., Horn, E. M., & Schwartz, I. S. (1996). Inclusion at the preschool level: An ecological systems analysis. *Social Policy Report: Society for Research in Child Development, X(*2&3), 18–30.

Osborne, A. G. (1990). When has a school district met its obligation to mainstream handicapped students under the EHA? *Education Law Reporter, 58,* 445–455.

Osborne, A. G. (1992a). The IDEA's least restrictive environment mandate: Implications for public policy. *Education Law Reporter, 71,* 369–380.

Osborne, A. G. (1992b). Legal standards for an appropriate education in the post-*Rowley* era. *Exceptional Children, 58,* 488–494.

Osborne, A. G., & DiMattia, P. (1994). The IDEA's least restrictive environment mandate: Legal implications. *Exceptional Children , 60*(1), 6–14.

Osborne, A. G., DiMattia, P., & Curran, F. X. (1993). *Effective management of special education programs: A handbook for school administrators.* New York: Teachers College Press.

Osgood, R. (1997, March). *Becoming a special educator: Specialized professional training for teachers of children with disabilities in Boston, 1870-1930.* Paper presented at the annual meeting of the American Educational Research Association, Chicago, IL.

Osin, L., & Lesgold, A. (1996). A proposal for the reengineering of the educational system. *Review of Educational Research, 66,* 621–656.

Padeliadu, S., & Zigmond, N. (1996). Perspectives on students with learning disabilities on special education placement. *Learning Disabilities Research and Practice, 11(*1), 15–23.

Pennsylvania Association for Retarded Children (PARC) v. Commonwealth of Pennsylvania, 334 F.Supp. 1257 (E.D. Pa., 1971).

Pitasky, V. M. (1996). *The current legal status of inclusion.* Horsham, PA: LRP Publications.

Poolaw v. Bishop, 23 IDELR 406 (9th Cir. 1995).

Potts, P. (1995). What's the use of history? Understanding educational provision for disabled students and those who experience difficulties in learning. *British Journal of Educational Studies, XXXXIII*(4), 398–411.

Pugach, M. C., & Warger, C. L. (1993). Curriculum considerations. In J. I. Goodlad & T. C. Lovitt (Eds.), *Integrating general and special education* (pp. 125–148). Columbus, OH: Merrill.

Ramirez v. Brown, 9G. 3d 199, 104 Ca. R. 137, 507 P.2d 1345, 1353 (1973).

Ravitch, D. (1981). Forgetting the questions: The problem of educational reform. *American Scholar, 50*(3), 329–340.

Rehabilitation Act of 1973, 29 U.S.C. 794 § 504 *et seq.*

Reynolds, M. (1962). A framework for considering some issues in special education. *Exceptional Children, 28,* 367–370.

Reynolds, M. (1976). Mainstreaming: Historical perspectives. In P. A. O'Donnell & R. H. Bradfield (Eds.), *Mainstreaming: Controversy and consensus* (pp. 39–51). San Rafael, CA: Academic Therapy.

Reynolds, M. (1989). An historical perspective: The delivery of special education to mildly disabled and at-risk students. *Remedial and Special Education, 10,* 7–11.

Reynolds, M. (1991, December). Progressive inclusion. *Quality Outcomes Driven Education,* 11–14.

Richards, EHLR 211:433, OSEP, 1987.

Richardson, J. G. (1980). Historical change in school classification. *Educational Research Quarterly*, *5*(3), 50–62.

Richardson, J. G. (1994). Common, delinquent, and special: On the formalization of common schooling in the American states. *American Educational Research Journal*, *31*, 695–723.

Rieth, H. J., & Polsgrove, L. (1994). Curriculum and instructional issues in teaching secondary students with learning disabilities. *Learning Disabilities Research and Practice*, *9*, 118–126.

Riley, R. (1993). Statement by U. S. Secretary of Education R. W. Riley, re: the inclusion of special needs students in regular classrooms. *U. S. Department of Education News*.

Roberts, R., & Mather, N. (1995). The return of students with learning disabilities to regular classrooms: A sellout? *Learning Disabilities Research and Practice*, *10*, 46–58.

Roncker v. Walter, 700 F.2d. 1058 (6th Cir. 1983).

Rothman, D. J. (1971). *The discovery of the asylum: Social order and disorder in the new republic*. Boston, MA: Little, Brown.

Rowley (1982). See *Hendrick Hudson District Board of Education v. Rowley*.

Rude, H. A., & Anderson, R. E. (1992). Administrator effectiveness in support of inclusive schools. *CASE in POINT, VII*(1), 31–37.

Sachais, EHLR 211:405, OSERS, 1986.

Sacramento City Unified School District v. Rachel H., 14 F. 3d 1398 (9th Cir. 1994).

Sage, D. D., & Burello, L. C. (1994). *Leadership in educational reform: An administrator's guide to changes in special education*. Baltimore, MD: Paul H. Brookes.

Salem, J. M., & Fell, B. P. (1988). The impact of PL 94-142 on residential schools for the deaf: A follow-up to the 1977 survey. *American Annals of the Deaf, 133*, 68–75.

Salisbury, C. L., & Smith, B. J. (1991). The least restrictive environment: Understanding the options. *Principal, 71*, 24–25, 27.

Sands, D. J., Adams, L., & Stout, D. M. (1995). What is the nature and use of curriculum in special education? *Exceptional Children, 62*, 68–83.

Sarason, S. B. (1996). *Barometers of change: Individual, educational, and social transformation*. San Francisco, CA: Jossey-Bass.

Sarason, S. B., & Doris, J. (1979). *Educational handicap, public policy, and social history*. New York: Free Press.

Sawyer, R. J., McLaughlin, M. J., & Winglee, M. (1994). Is integration of students with disabilities happening? *Remedial and Special Education, 13*(4), 204–215.

Scanlon, D., Deschler, D. D., & Schumaker, J. B. (1996). Can a strategy be taught and learned in secondary inclusive classrooms? *Learning Disabilities and Practice, 1*, 41–57.

Schrag, J. (1994). *Organizational, instructional, and curricular strategies to support the implementation of unified, coordinated, and inclusive schools*. Reston, VA: Council for Exceptional Children.

Schumaker, J. B., & Deshler, D. D. (1988). Implementing the regular education initiative in secondary schools: A different ball game. *Journal of Learning Disabilities, 21*, 36–42.

Schumm, J. S., & Vaughn, S. (1991). Making adaptations for mainstreamed students: Regular classroom teachers' perspectives. *Remedial and Special Education, 12*(4), 18–27.

Schumm, J. S., & Vaughn, S. (1992). Planning for mainstreamed special education students. *Exceptionality, 3*, 81–90.

Schumm, J. S., Vaughn, S., Haager, D., McDowell, J., Rothlein, L., & Saumell, L. (1995). General education teacher planning: What can students with learning disabilities expect? *Exceptional Children, 61*, 335–352.

Scruggs, T. E., & Mastropieri, M. A. (1995). What makes special education special? Evaluating inclusion programs with the PASS variables. *Journal of Special Education, 29*, 224–233.

Scruggs, T. E., & Mastropieri, M. A. (1996). Teacher perceptions of mainstreaming/inclusion, 1958-1995: A research synthesis. *Exceptional Children, 63*, 59-74.

Semmel, M. I., Gerber, M. M., & MacMillan, D. L. (1994). A legacy of policy analysis research in special education. *The Journal of Special Education, 27,* 481–495.

Semmel, M. I., Gottlieb, J., & Robinson, N. M. (1979). Mainstreaming: Perspectives on educating handicapped children in the public schools. In D. Berliner (Ed.), *Review of research in education* (pp. 223–279). Washington, DC: American Educational Research Association.

Shanker, A. (1994, February 6). Inclusion and ideology. *The New York Times,* p. E 7.

Shapiro, J. P. (1993). *No pity: People with disabilities forging a new civil rights movement.* New York: Random House.

Shelton v. Tucker, 364 U. S. 479, 483 (1960).

Siegel, L. M. (1994). *Least restrictive environment: The paradox of inclusion.* Horsham, PA: LRP Publications.

Silver, K. (1993, September 29). *Testimony of Karen E. Silver before the New York State Education Department Public Hearing on Least Restrictive Environment.*

Skrtic, T. M. (1991). The special education paradox: Equity as the way to excellence. *Harvard Educational Review, 61*(2), 148–182.

Smith v. Sampson, 349 F.Supp. 268, 271 (D.N.H. 1972).

Smith, T., & Lovaas, O. I. (1997). The UCLA Young Autism Project: A reply to Gresham and MacMillan. *Behavioral Disorders, 22,* 202–218.

Snell, M. E. (1991). Schools are for all kids: The importance of integration for students with severe disabilities and their peers. In J. W. Lloyd, N. N. Singh, & A. C. Repp (Eds.), *The Regular Education Initiative: Alternative perspectives on concepts, issues, and models* (pp. 133–148). Sycamore, IL: Sycamore Press.

Society: The story rug is now full. (1995, April 3). *Newsweek,* p. 58.

Special educators worldwide work for common goal. (1995, August). *CEC Today, 2*(2) , 10.

St. Louis Developmental Disability Treatment Center Parents Association v. Mallory, 767 F. 2d 518 (8th Cir. 1984).

Stainback, W., & Stainback, S. (1988). Letter to the editor. *Journal of Learning Disabilities, 21,* 452–453.

Stockard, J., & Mayberry, M. (1992). *Effective educational environments.* Newbury Park, CA: Corwin.

Student v. Somerset County Board of Education, 24 IDELR 743 (D. Md. 1996).

Sunstein, C. R. (1996). *Legal reasoning and political conflict.* New York: Oxford University Press.

Tate, W. F. (1997). Critical race theory and education: History, theory, and implications. In M. W. Apple (Ed.), *Review of research in education* (pp. 195–247). Washington, DC: American Educational Research Association.

Taylor, S. (1988). Caught in the continuum: A critical analysis of the principle of the least restrictive environment. *Journal of the Association for Persons with Severe Handicaps (JASH), 13,* 41–53.

Taylor, S., Biklen, D., Lehr, S., & Searle, S. (1987). *Purposeful integration... Inherently equal.* Syracuse, NY: Syracuse University Center on Human Policy.

Teague Independent School District v. Todd L., 999 F.2d 127 (5th Cir. 1993).

Toomer v. Witsell, 334 U. S. 385 (1948).

Tucker, J. A. (1989). Less required energy: A response to Danielson and Bellamy. *Exceptional Children, 55,* 456–458.

Turnbull, H. R. (Ed.). (1981). *The least restrictive alternative: Principles and practices.* Washington, DC: American Association on Mental Retardation.

Turnbull, H. R. (1990). *Free appropriate public education: The law and children with disabilities.* Denver, CO: Love.

Turnbull, H.R., Rainbolt, K., & Buchele-Ash, A. (1997). *Individuals with Disabilities Education Act: Digest and significance of 1997 Amendments.* Beach Center on Families and Disability. University of Kansas.

Tweedie, J. (1983). The politics of legalization in special education reform. In J. G. Chambers & W. T. Hartman (Eds.), *Special education policies: Their history, implementation and finance.* Philadelphia, PA: Temple University Press.

Underwood, J., & Mead, J. F. (1995). *Legal aspects of special education and pupil services.* Boston: Allyn & Bacon.

Urban, W., & Wagoner, J. L., Jr. (1996). *American education: A history.* New York: McGraw-Hill.

U. S. Congress House of Representatives, Committee on Education and Labor. (1975, June 26). 94th Congress, 1st Session. House Report No. 94-332, pp. 132-133. In U. S. Senate, Committee on Labor and Public Welfare, Subcommittee on the Handicapped. (1976). *Education of the Handicapped Act as amended through December 31, 1975.* (Report No. 72-611). Washington, DC: U. S. Government Printing Office.

U. S. Department of Education. (1980). *To assure the free appropriate public education of all handicapped children.* Second Annual Report to Congress. Education of the Handicapped Act. Washington, DC: Author.

U. S. Department of Education. (1996). *Eighteenth annual report to congress on the implementation of the Individuals with Disabilities Education Act.* Washington, DC: Office of Special Education Programs, U. S. Government Printing Office.

U. S. Department of Education (1997a). *The Individuals with Disabilities Education Act amendments curriculum.* Washington, DC: Author.

U. S. Department of Education. (1997b). *Nineteenth annual report to congress on the implementation of the Individuals with Disabilities Education Act.* Washington, DC: Office of Special Education Programs, U. S. Government Printing Office.

U.S. Senate, Committee on Labor and Human Resources. (1997). *Report [to accompany S. 717].* Washington, DC: Government Printing Office.

Vander Malle v. Ambach, EHLR 559:164 (S.D.N.Y., 1987).

Vaughn, S., & Schumm, J. S. (1996). Classroom ecologies: Classroom interactions and implications for inclusion of students with learning disabilities. In D. Speece & B. K. Keogh (Eds.), *Research on classroom ecologies: Implications for inclusion of children with learning disabilities* (pp. 107–124). Mahwah, NJ: Lawrence Erlbaum Associates.

Verstegen, D. A. (1996). Integrating services and resources for children under the Individuals with Disabilities Education Act (IDEA): Federal perspectives and issues. *Journal of Education Finance, 21,* 477–505.

Verstegen, D. A., & Martin, P. (1995, March). *A summary of position statements on the inclusion of special education students into the general classroom and excerpts on funding from fifteen national associations.* Paper presented at the American Education Finance Association Annual Conference, Savannah, GA.

Villa, R. A., & Thousand, J. S. (1995). *Creating an inclusive school.* Alexandria, VA: Association for Supervision and Curriculum Development.

Visco v. School District of Pittsburgh, 684 F.Supp. 1310, 1315-16 (W.D. Pa. 1988).

Wagner, M. (April, 1990). *The school programs and school performance of secondary students classified as learning disabled: Findings from the national longitudinal transition study of special education students.* Paper presented at the meetings of Division G., American Educational Research Association, Boston, MA.

Walker, H. M., & Bullis, M. (1991). Behavior disorders and the social context of regular class integration: A conceptual dilemma? In J. W. Lloyd, N. N. Singh, & A. C. Repp (Eds.), *The regular education initiative: Alternative perspectives on concepts, issues, and models* (pp. 75–93). Sycamore, IL: Sycamore Press.

Walker, H. M., Colvin, G., & Ramsey, E. (1995). *Antisocial behavior is school: Strategies and best practices.* Monterey, CA: Brooks/Cole.

Walker, L. J. (1987). Procedural rights in the wrong system: Special education is not enough. In A. Gartner & T. Joe (Eds.), *Images of the disabled, disabled images* (pp. 97–115). New York: Praeger.

Weiner, R. (1985). *PL 94-142: Impact on the schools.* Arlington, VA: Capitol Publications.

Weintraub, F. J. (1976). Politics: The name of the game. In F. J. Weintraub, A. Abeson, J. Ballard, & M. LaVor (Eds.), *Public policy and the education of exceptional children* (pp. 14–21). Reston, VA: Council for Exceptional Children.

Weintraub, F. J., Abeson, A., & Braddock, D. (1971). *State law and education of handicapped children: Issues and recommendations.* Arlington, VA: Council for Exceptional Children.

Weintraub, F. J., & Abeson, A. (1972). Appropriate education for all handicapped children: A growing issue. *Syracuse Law Review, 23,* 1056.

Weintraub, F. J., & Ballard, J. (1986). Introduction: Bridging the decades. In M. Ballard, B. A. Ramirez, & F. J. Weintraub (Eds.), *Special education in America: Its legal and governmental foundations.* Reston, VA: Council for Exceptional Children.

Weber, M. C. (1992). *Special education law and litigation treatise.* Horsham, PA: LRP Publications.

Will, M. (1986a). *Clarifying the standards: Placement in a least restrictive environment.* Washington, DC: U. S. Department of Education.

Will, M. (1986b). *Educating students with learning problems: A shared responsibility.* Washington, DC: U. S. Department of Education.

Willis, S. (1994, October). Making schools more inclusive. *ASCD Curriculum Update,* 1–8.

Wilson v. Marana Unified School District No. 6, 735 F.2d 1176 (9th Cir. 1984).

Winschel, J. F. (1980). Mainstreaming: A still audible dissent. In J. W. Schifani, R. M. Anderson, & S .J. Odle (Eds.), *Implementing learning in the least restrictive environment: Handicapped children in the mainstream* (p. 492). Baltimore, MD: University Park Press.

Winzer, M. A. (1993). *The history of special education: From isolation to integration.* Washington, DC: Gallaudet University Press.

Wolfensberger, W. (1972). *Normalization.* Toronto: National Institute on Mental Retardation.

Wolfensberger, W. (1983). Social role valorization: A proposed new term for the principle of normalization. *Mental Retardation, 21,* 224.

Wyatt v. Stickney, 344 F.Supp. 387 (M.D. Ala., 1972).

Yell, M. L. (1990). The use of corporal punishment, suspension, expulsion, and time out with behaviorally disordered students in public schools: Legal considerations. *Behavioral Disorders, 15,* 100–109.

Yell, M. L. (1995a). *Clyde K. and Sheila K. v. Puyallup School District*: The courts, inclusion, and students with behavioral disorders. *Behavioral Disorders, 20,* 179–189.

Yell, M. L. (1995b). Least restrictive environment, inclusion, and students with disabilities: A legal analysis. *The Journal of Special Education, 28,* 389–404.

Yell, M. L. (1998). *The law and special education.* Englewood Cliffs, NJ: Prentice-Hall.

Yoshida, R. (1986). Setting goals for mainstream programs. In C. J. Meisel (Ed.), *Mainstreaming handicapped children: Outcomes, controversies, and new directions* (pp. 11–19). Hillsdale, NJ: Lawrence Erlbaum Associates.

Zettel, J. J., & Ballard, J. (1986). The education for all handicapped children act of 1975 (P.L. 94–142): Its history, origins, and concepts. In J. Ballard, B. A. Ramirez, & F. J. Weintraub (Eds.), *Special education in America: Its legal and governmental foundations* (pp. 11–22). Reston, VA: Council for Exceptional Children.

Zigler, E. (1996). Forward. In D.Speece & B. K. Keogh (Eds.), *Research on classroom ecologies: Implications for inclusion of children with learning disabilities* (pp. ix–x). Mahwah, NJ: Lawrence Erlbaum Associates.

Zigler, E., & Hall, N. (1986). Mainstreaming and the philosophy of normalization. In C. J. Meisel (Ed.), *Mainstreaming handicapped children: Outcomes, controversies, and new directions* (pp. 1–9). Hillsdale, NJ: Lawrence Erlbaum Associates.

Zigler, E., Hodapp, R. M., & Edison, M. R. (1990). From theory to practice in the care and education of mentally retarded individuals. *American Journal on Mental Retardation, 95,* 1–12.

Zigmond, N. (1995). An exploration of the meaning and practice of special education in the context of full inclusion of students with learning disabilities. *The Journal of Special Education, 29,* 109–115.

Zirkel, P. (1996). Inclusion: Return of the pendulum? *The Special Educator, 12*(9), 1, 5.

Author Index

A

Abeson, A., 39, 55, 214, 217, 226
Adams, L., 147, 223
Agard, J. A., 27, 219
Alexander, P. A., 8, 214
Allan, J., 38, 39, 47, 214
Alter, M., 4, 29, 217
Anastasiow, N. J., 6, 22, 128, 129, 177, 179, 220
Anderson, R. E., 24, 223
Anderson, R. M., 226
Anderson-Inman, L., 139, 214
Aristotle, 68, 214
Arnold, J. B., 120, 214

B

Bailey, D. B., 12, 214
Ballard, J., 54, 56, 86, 218, 226
Balsdon, B., 11, 181
Bancroft, R., 84, 85, 214
Barth, R. S., 65, 214
Bartlett, L. D., 117, 214
Bateman, B., 1, 3, 5, 17, 18, 29, 74, 82, 95, 97, 98, 100, 101, 102, 115, 116, 118, 129, 148, 214
Bauer, A. M., 21, 219
Beckman, P. J., 222
Bell, D. A., 192, 214
Bellah, F. N., 336, 214
Bellamy, G. T., 15, 16, 216, 224
Benton, J. M., 52, 53, 217
Bentz, J., 143, 217
Bigge, J. L., 171, 214
Biklen, D., 28, 134, 135, 162, 214, 224
Billingsley, B., 21, 214
Blatt, B., 43, 57, 215, 217, 221
Bodkins, D., 21, 214
Boe, E. E., 142, 215
Borelli, C., 31, 221
Borthwick-Duffy, S. A., 178, 214
Bos, C. S., 143, 146, 214
Bowers, J., 138, 217
Bradfield, R. H., 214, 222

Brigham, F. J., 147, 215
Bronfenbrenner, U., 66, 126, 195, 215
Brown, W. H., 222
Bruininks, R., 148, 165, 215
Buchele-Ash, A., 79, 224
Bullis, M., 30, 225
Burello, L. C., 95, 223
Burgdorf, Jr., R. L., 34, 57, 83, 86, 87, 98, 114, 134, 214, 215
Butler, R., 30, 215

C

Cannon, G. S., 24, 215
Carlberg, C., 149, 215
Carnine, D. W., 23, 150, 159, 215
Casey, P. J., 39, 214
Cattell-Gordon, D., 11, 180-181
Centra, N. A., 26, 215
Champagne, J., 97, 98, 104, 120, 215
Chard, D., 18, 74, 82, 95, 100, 101, 115, 116, 214
Childs, K. E., 151, 216
Cohen, M., 23, 24, 25, 26, 215
Coleman, J., 52, 215
Colvin, G., 147, 225
Conderman, G., 74, 219
Conn, P., 174, 215
Cook, L. H., 142, 215
Cousins, N., 201, 215
Crockett, J. B., 1, 2, 6, 10, 11, 12, 34, 81, 123, 124, 159, 161, 215
Cruickshank, W. M., 36, 40, 41, 126, 151, 215, 216, 218
Cumblad, C., 139, 216
Curran, F. X., 26, 222

D

Danielson, L. C., 15, 16, 216, 224
Deno, E., 55, 137, 140, 164, 214
Deshler, D. D., 30, 223
DiMattia, P., 4, 26, 134, 222
Dionne, Jr., E. J., 12. 216
Dodge, H. W., 120, 214

Doris, J., 125, 200, 201, 223
Dorn, S., 62, 216
Dunlap, G., 151, 216
Dunn, L. M., 35, 129, 216
Durand, V. M., 24, 220
Durden, W. G., 194, 195, 196, 216

E

Edison, M. R., 175, 226
Edson, C. H., 7, 216
Ellet, L., 143, 144, 216
English, F. W., 10, 216
Epstein, M. H., 139, 140, 216

F

Fell, B. P., 133, 223
Fernstrom, P., 19, 139, 216
Forness, S. R., 28, 221
Franks, D. J., 74, 219
Fuchs, D., 11, 19, 20, 22, 24, 25, 31, 62,
    138, 139, 141, 143, 144, 147, 149, 151,
    159, 165-169, 216, 217, 220
Fuchs, L. S., 19, 20, 22, 24, 25, 31, 62,
    138, 139, 143, 144, 147, 149, 151, 216,
    217
Fullan, M. G., 201, 217

G

Gajria, M., 144, 217
Gallagher, J. J., 10, 22, 38, 48, 49, 50, 57,
    58, 59, 60, 67, 84, 125, 126, 129, 131,
    132, 177, 178, 188, 193, 214, 217, 220
Gambatese, C., 31, 220
Gardner, H., 10, 217
Garnett, K., 13, 217
Gartner, A., 1, 19, 20, 21, 26, 135, 162,
    218, 225
Gelsheiser, L., 31, 221
Gerber, M. M., 87, 123, 129, 217, 224
Gerry, M. H., 52, 53, 217
Gilhool, T. K., 35, 48, 57, 58, 80, 84, 85,
    89, 90, 91, 92, 94, 116, 217
Gorn, S., 100, 217
Gottlieb, B. W., 4, 27, 29, 217
Gottlieb, J., 4, 27, 29, 91, 136, 138, 143,
    146, 149, 165, 217, 219, 224
Grant, J. O., 40, 216
Greenwood, C. R., 139, 165, 217
Gresham, F. M., 28, 180, 217, 221, 224

Gross, J., 133, 218
Guralnick, M. J., 66, 218

H

Haager, D., 223
Hall, N., 38, 61, 66, 226
Hallahan, D. P., 1, 6, 22, 23, 61, 141, 149,
    151, 214, 216, 218, 219
Halpern, S. C., 63, 64, 68, 70, 190, 191,
    192, 193, 218
Hamilton, D., 128, 218
Hamlett, C. L., 143, 147, 216, 217
Hanson, M., 221
Harkin, T., 21, 218
Hays, T. S., 151, 218
Hemrick, M. A, 144, 217
Hendrick, I. G., 43, 221
Hendricks, M., 21, 214
Heron, T. E., 134, 218
Heumann, J., 21, 218
Hirth, M. A., 3, 218
Hohn, M., 139, 216
Horn, E. M., 222
Houck, C. K., 148, 218
Howe, K. R., 195, 196, 197, 198, 199,
    200, 202, 218, 219
Huefner, D.S., 98, 100, 114, 115, 116,
    117, 165, 218
Hurst, A., 26, 27, 218

I-J

Idol, L., 24, 215
Jacobson, J. W., 64, 218
Jacobson, L., 172, 218
Jenkins, J. W., 148, 165, 219
Jenkins, L. M., 219
Jewell, M., 219
Johnson, G. O., 215
Johnson, L. J., 21, 143, 219
Johnson, R., 215
Jones, R. A., 127, 136, 219

K

Kaiser, A. P., 222
Katsiyannis, A., 73, 219
Kauffman, J. M., 1, 4, 6, 9, 12, 20, 22, 23,
    30, 34, 46, 61, 62, 63, 65, 66, 70, 73,
    101, 125, 126, 141, 147, 149, 165, 193,
    214, 215, 216, 218, 219

Kaufman, M. J., 27, 138, 219
Kavale, K. A., 141, 149, 215, 220
Kearney, C. A., 24, 220
Keogh, B. K., 29, 30, 31, 139, 140, 217,
  220, 225, 226
Kirk, S. A., 22, 35, 37, 38, 48, 49, 62, 67,
  176, 179, 220
Kirp, D. J., 51, 195, 196, 220
Korinek, L., 136, 220
Kotler, M. A., 172, 179, 180, 181, 188,
  189, 190, 220
Kritsonis, M. A., 12, 220
Kukic, M., 27, 219
Kunz, J. W., 39, 214

L

Lane, K. L., 178, 214
Lange, C., 26, 220
Lazerson, M., 9, 42, 43, 45, 47, 220
Lehr, S., 135, 224
Leicester, N., 219
Lenk, L. L., 4, 136, 144, 221
Lesgold, A., 127, 128, 222
Lieber, J., 222
Lieberman, L. M., 11, 143, 150, 159, 163,
  220
Lipsky, D. K., 1, 4, 11, 19, 20, 21, 24, 26,
  135, 159, 162, 217, 220
Lloyd, J. W., 20, 31, 62, 125, 126, 149,
  214, 216, 217, 218, 219, 220, 224, 225
Lovaas, O. I., 180, 217, 224
Low, J., 65, 221

M

MacMillan, D. R., 28, 43, 87, 138, 150,
  151, 180, 217, 221, 224
Madsen, R., 36, 214
Maloney, M., 5, 99, 114, 120, 221
Margolis, H., 173, 221
Marinov-Glassman, D., 30, 215
Marston, D., 149, 221
Martin, E. W., 1, 2, 6, 10, 17, 22, 28, 48,
  49, 52, 53, 74, 75, 76, 77, 78, 81, 90,
  92, 93, 148, 172, 173, 178, 187, 221
Martin, P., 23, 225
Martin, R., 96, 104, 221
Mastropieri, M. A., 12, 26, 142, 223
Mather, N., 30, 143, 145, 146, 221, 223
McDowell, J., 223

McLaughlin, M., 14, 223
McLaughlin, V., 136, 220
McNeil, W., 39, 214
Mead, J. F., 97, 140, 225
Meadows, N. B., 24, 221
Meredith, B., 130, 131, 132, 221
Meyers, B., 31, 221
Meyers, J., 31, 221
Morse, W. C., 39, 40, 216, 221
Morsink, C. V., 4, 136, 144, 221
Mulick, J. A., 64, 218
Murphy, P. K., 8, 214

N

Neel, R. S., 24, 221
Nietupski, J. A, 134, 222

O

Odom, S. L., 66, 149, 150, 222
Osborne, A. G., 4, 26, 89, 95, 96, 98, 99,
  114, 134, 222
Osgood, R., 43, 44, 45, 222
Osin, L., 127, 128, 222

P-Q

Padeliadu, S., 26, 222
Palmer, D. S., 178, 214
Parker, G., 24, 221
Peck, C. A., 222
Peterson, D., 21, 214
Phillips, N. B., 143, 217
Pitasky, V. M., 17, 27, 74, 103, 104, 105,
  106, 108, 109, 112, 118, 119, 222
Polsgrove, L., 142. 147, 223
Potts, P., 10, 222
Pugach, M. C., 143, 145, 147, 219, 222
Quinn, K. P., 139, 216

R

Rainbolt, K., 79, 224
Ramsey, E., 147, 225
Ravitch, D., 8, 220, 222
Reynolds, M., 11, 38, 55, 62, 66, 137,
  140, 159-161, 165, 175, 177, 222
Richardson, J. G., 38, 151, 223
Rieth, H. J., 142, 147, 223
Riley, R., 119, 172, 223

Roberts, P. H., 138, 217
Roberts, R., 30, 143, 145, 146, 221, 223
Robinson, N. M., 138, 224
Rogers, C. J., 148, 218
Rothlein, L., 223
Rude, H. A., 223

S

Sage, D. D., 12, 95, 223
Salem, J. M., 133, 223
Salend, S. J., 144, 217
Salisbury, C. L., 28, 134, 223
Sands, D. J., 147, 223
Sarason, S. B., 37, 67, 125, 200, 201, 223
Saumell, L., 223
Sawyer, R. J., 14, 16, 223
Scanlon, D., 146, 223
Schrag, J., 147, 223
Schumaker, J. B., 30, 143, 223
Schumm, J. S., 24, 139, 143, 144, 145,
    146, 223, 225
Schwartz, A. A., 64, 218
Schwartz, I. S., 222
Scott, C. M., 24, 221
Scruggs, T. E., 12, 26, 141, 142, 220, 223
Searle, S., 135, 224
Semmel, M. I., 87, 129, 130, 138, 221,
    224
Shanker, A., 20, 224
Shapiro, J. P., 40, 41, 224
Shenker, B., 5, 99, 120, 221
Siegel, L. M., 5, 68, 86, 94, 95, 108, 224
Silver, K., 11, 183-187
Silver, R., 183
Skinner, M. E., 134, 218
Skrtic, T. M., 28, 224
Smith, B. J., 28, 134, 223
Smith, T., 180, 217, 224
Smucker, K., 39, 219
Snell, M. E., 21, 224
Speece, D. L., 139, 140, 217, 220, 225,
    226
Stainback, S., 1, 20, 162, 220, 224
Stainback, W., 1, 20, 162, 220, 224
Stedman, D., 10, 35, 48, 51, 57-59, 174,
    177, 193
Stout, D. M., 223
Sullivan, W. M., 36, 214
Sunstein, C. R., 33, 69, 70, 71, 72, 73, 98,
    122, 196, 224
Swidler, A., 36, 214

T

Tate, W. F., 69, 192, 193, 224
Taylor, S., 135, 136, 162, 224
Tewel, K., 173, 221
Thousand, J. S., 4, 162, 225
Thurlow, M. L., 148, 215
Tipton, S. M., 36, 214
Trent, S. C., 12, 219
Troutner, N. M., 219
Truscott, S., 31, 221
Tucker, J. A., 132, 224
Turnbull, H. R., 51, 54, 60, 79, 82, 83, 85,
    86, 88, 89, 91, 93, 94, 97, 103, 121,
    132, 224
Tweedie, J., 172, 225

U-V

Underwood, J., 97, 130, 131, 132, 140,
    221, 225
Urban, W., 191, 225
Valesky, T. C., 3, 218
Vance, V., 133, 218
Vaughn, S., 24, 139, 143, 144, 145, 146,
    214, 223, 225
Verstegen, D. A., 16, 17, 23, 24, 225
Villa, R., 4, 162, 225

W

Wagner, M., 22, 225
Wagoner, Jr., J. L., 191, 225
Walker, H. M., 30, 147, 225
Walker, L. J., 61, 74, 225
Walther-Thomas, C. S., 136, 220
Warger, C. L., 145, 147, 222
Weber, M. C., 90, 91, 94, 116, 226
Weiner, R., 74, 226
Weintraub, F. J., 10, 48, 50, 54, 55, 57,
    74, 76, 85, 89, 94, 125, 137, 171, 193,
    217, 226
West, J. F., 24, 215
Will, M., 4, 116, 226
Willis, S., 24, 25, 226
Winglee, M., 14, 223
Winschel, J. F., 151, 226
Winzer, M. A., 7, 44, 45, 47, 174, 175,
    226
Wishner, J., 29, 217
Wolfensberger, W., 60, 62, 226
Woods, B. S., 8, 214

Y-Z

Yell, M. L., 17, 25, 75, 78, 102, 104, 107,
    110, 115, 116, 117, 118, 226
Yoshida, R., 137, 138, 226

Ysseldyke, J. E., 26, 148, 165, 215, 220
Zettel, J. J., 56, 86, 227
Zigler, E., 38, 61, 66, 139, 175, 226
Zigmond, N., 26, 145, 165, 167, 222, 227
Zirkel, P., 102, 106, 227

Subject Index

A

accommodations, 17, 88, 110, 117, 143, 144

administrative issues, 3, 4, 12, 14, 22, 24, 27, 31, 37, 62, 81, 91, 94, 98, 101, 115, 120, 130, 133, 138, 143, 146, 158, 159, 161, 170, 192, 194, 195, 197, 201

Amann v.Stow School System, 982 F.2d 644 (1st Cir. 1992), 108

analytic frameworks to determine LRE, 107, 114-118, 120-121

assessment of students, 46, 61, 77, 80, 118, 129, 136, 138-139, 146, 148, 154, 165, 182, 186-187, 194

Autism, 11, 14, 25, 104, 109-110, 141, 163, 179-181

B

Behavior Management Plans, 117, 119, 147

Blind, 25, 41, 56, 111, 150, 160, 164, 183, 193

Brown v.the Board of Education, 347 U.S. 483 (1954), 21, 37, 52, 63, 87-88, 125, 190-192

burden of proof, 96, 99, 107, 118

Bureau of Education for the Handicapped, 22, 49, 70, 74, 84, 90-93, 163, 172-173, 178

C

Carlisle Area School District v.Scott P., 23 IDELR 293 (3d. Cir. 1995), 111

cascade of services (*see also* continuum of alternative placements), 19, 62, 137, 140, 164

case law charts, 203-213

characteristics of students, 29-31, 141-142

characteristics of teachers, 142

Civil Rights, 20, 60-64
roots of LRE, 60-64
social context, 34-67
see also Title VI of the Civil Rights Act (1964).

Clyde K. ex re. Ryan D. v.Puyallup School District, 35 F. 3d 1396 (9th Cir. 1994), 113, 118

Colonial Era, 40

compulsory school attendance, 36-38, 42, 55-56, 67

continuum of alternative placements, 1, 2, 4, 12, 15, 16, 18, 19, 20, 22, 23, 29, 33, 55, 56, 58, 62, 75, 76, 82, 85, 86, 88, 95, 100, 101, 114, 117, 118, 135, 137, 140, 151, 154, 159, 161, 162, 165, 166, 178, 182, 183, 184, 185, 186, 196, 201, 202

costs (financial), 17, 24, 40, 48, 49, 54, 107, 112, 115, 130, 131, 154, 161, 181, 192, 193

Council for Exceptional Children, 10, 50-51, 55, 74, 152, 159

curricular organization and management, 145-147

D

D.F. v.Western School Corporation, 23 IDELR 1121 (S.D. Ind. 1996), 111

Daniel R.R. v.State Board of Education, 874 F.2d 1036 (5th Cir. 1989), 103-104, 107, 114-118

Deaf, 25, 41, 53-54, 56, 92, 105-106, 111, 133, 140, 160-161, 193

deinstitutionalization, 59-61, 92

democracy, 8, 12, 33, 35-36, 69, 73, 122, 128, 194, 198-202

DeVries v.Fairfax County School Board, 882 F.2d 876 (4th Cir. 1989), 104

DeWeerd, J., 11, 178-179, 242

diversity, 13-14
and disability, 29
in inclusive settings, 147-148

E

early childhood special education, 11, 31, 75, 95, 104, 152, 160, 173, 178-179,182

early intervention, 7, 58, 173, 180-181 245

Education for All Handicapped Children Act--1975 (PL 94-142), 20 U.S.C.

Sections 1400-1461, 2, 4, 6, 7, 17-18,
    22, 29, 37, 54, 73-122, 130, 160, 172-
    173, 181, 189, 193
educational benefit (see FAPE)
educational environments, 1-6, 12-17,
    123-169
educational opportunity, 6-7
    equal opportunity, 53, 55, 60, 64, 67,
    86, 91, 96, 191, 197-200
    full opportunity, 10, 34, 77-81, 94,
    121, 188, 193, 200, 202
*Elementary and Secondary Education
    Act*, 14, 51-52, 54
Emotional or Behavioral Disorders, 14,
    30, 56, 92, 100-101, 105, 108, 112-
    113, 120, 127, 140-141, 147, 149,
    151, 163, 165, 193
equity, 4-5, 17
    instructional settings, 190-193
    productive learning, 62-64
    statewide, 186
    see also placement-neutral funding
ethics, 7-9, 11, 16, 21, 23, 36, 51, 61,
    66, 70, 86-87, 93-94, 123, 125, 127,
    131, 170, 188-202
exceptionality, 37-40, 48, 65-66, 129,
    141, 192-193

F

federal legislation, 74-82
free appropriate public education
    (FAPE), 18, 68-122
Ft. Zumwalt School District v.Clynes, 26
    IDELR 172 (8th Cir. 1997), 112
functional exclusion, 86, 88, 120

G

general/regular education
    classroom environments, 141-155
    interface with special education,
    129-132
Greer v.Rome City Sch. Dist., 950 F.2d
    688 (11th Cir. 1991), 106

H

*Hartmann by Hartmann by Loudoun
    County Board of Education*, 26
    IDELR 167, 96-2809 (4th Cir. 1997),
    109, 114
*Hendrick Hudson District Board of
    Education v.Rowley*, 458 U. S. 176,

102 S.Ct. 3034 (1982), 18, 80, 95-97,
    100, 110, 196

I

inclusion, 1-5
    conflicting views, 23
    definition, 28
    teachers' perceptions, 142
incompletely theorized agreements, 69
individual differences, 30, 37, 128-130,
    144, 194
individualized education program, 17-
    18, 75-76, 80, 97-98, 111, 186
individualized instruction, 127-131, 144,
    148
instructional interventions, 143-145
*Individuals with Disabilities Education
    Act*, 20 U.S.C. 1401 et seq, 74-121
instructional interventions, 40, 191
instructional settings, 12-17,
    dynamic systems, 194-195
    equity, 190-193
    social justice, 195-202

K-L

*Kari H. v. Franklin Special School
    District*, 26 IDELR 569 (6th Cir.
    1997), 108-109
*Lachman ex rel. Lachman v. Illinois
    State Board of Education*, 852 F.2d
    290 (7th Cir. 1988), 105
Lake v. Cameron, 124 U S. App. D. C.
    364 F. 2d (1966), 84-85, 88
Learning Disabilities, 14, 26, 29-30, 47,
    54, 105, 108, 112, 139-141, 146, 148-
    149, 151, 163, 165,
Least Restrictive Alternative, 58, 132
    constitutional basis, 82-86,
    dimensions of the LRA policy, 93-95
    LRA as a presumption, 88-89
    rebutting the presumption, 95-98
Least Restrictive Environment, 59
    and contemporary theorists 159-169
    court decisions and federal directives,
    98-120
    definition of LRE, 215
    educational foundations, 132-140
    historical trends, 7, 123, 151-158
    legal foundations, 17-19
    legal reasoning, 73-98
    origins of the term, 58-62, 90-93
    research issues, 148-151

right-to-education, 85-86
social reform, 20-21
student performance, 22-23
Lochner v. New York, 198 U. S. 48, 69
    (1908), 69

M

mainstreaming, 27, 59
as an educational term, 132-139
teachers' perceptions, 142-143
*Mark A. ex rel. Alleah A. v. Grantwood
    Area Educational Agency,* EHLR 557
    412 (8th Cir. ,1986), 104
*McWhirt by McWhirt v. Williamson
    County Schools,* 23 IDELR 509
    (6th Cir. 1994), 111
Mental Retardation, 14, 30, 35, 48-49,
    57-58, 76, 107-109, 141, 149, 174
*Mills v. Board of Education of the
    District of Columbia,* 348 F.Supp.
    866 (1972), 86, 101
Model Statute, 55-56
Multiple Disabilities, 14, 25, 30, 104,
    111
Myth of Mildness, 187

N-O

Nineteenth Century, 40-41
Normalization, 60-62, 91, 133, 200
*Oberti v. Board of Education of the
    Borough of Clementon School
    District,* 995 F.2d 1204 (3rd Cir
    1993), 107, 118
Office of Special Education and Rehabi-
    litation Services, 99, 101, 116
Office of Special Education Programs,
    14-16, 99, 101-102, 116, 119
outcomes for students, 138-139, 148-
    151, 154-158, 187

P

parental advocacy, 6-7, 170-187
*Pennsylvania Association for Retarded
    Children (PARC) v. Commonwealth of
    Pennsylvania,* 334 F.Supp. 1257
    (E.D. Pa., 1971), 56-59, 85-86, 92,
    101, 137, 178
Physical Disabilities, 1-2, 27, 46, 76,
    105, 141, 183
placement decision-making, 94, 97-98,
    117, 180, 184

placement-neutral funding, 79, 81, 121,
    161, 184-185
placement trends, 14-17, 154-156
politics of placement, 12-33
Poolaw V.Bishop, 23 IDELR 406
    (9th Cir. 1995), 111
principles for educational leaders, 168
productive learning, 62-64, 67, 198-202
Progressive Education, 44-45, 128

R

Ramirez v. Brown, 9G. 3d 199, 104
    Ca. R. 137, 507 P.2d 1345, 1353
    (1973), 83
regular education (see general/regular
    education)
regulations (federal), 81-82, 89, 91, 94-
    95, 109, 124
regulations (state), 96, 121
Rehabilitation Act of 1973 (Section 504)
    29 U.S.C. 794 et seq., 17, 52, 54, 73-
    74, 99
related services, 15-17, 19, 28, 62, 75-
    76, 78-79, 81, 95-99, 101, 141
    definition, 173
residential settings, 1, 19, 38, 42, 62,
    100, 105, 108, 111, 136, 140
    definition, 15
resource rooms, 14, 16, 26, 37-38, 95,
    111, 149, 166
    definition, 15
Right-to-Education, 56, 60, 78, 85-88,
    92, 137, 193, 196
Right-to-Treatment, 84-85, 88
Roncker v.Walter, 700 F.2d. 1058
    (6th Cir. 1983), 103, 107, 114,
    116-117

S

*Sacramento City Unified School District
    v.Rachel H.,* 14 F. 3d 1398 (9th Cir.
    1994), 107-108, 113-115, 117-120
school administrators, 3-4, 12, 22-24,
    27, 94, 130, 143, 161, 185, 192, 194-
    195, 197, 201
school reform, 13, 31, 70, 79, 153-155,
    158, 201
separate/special classes, 1, 14-16, 37-38,
    42-46, 62, 78, 90, 95, 101,103, 107-
    108, 111, 113, 119,-120, 124, 138,
    144, 149, 152, 161, 178
    definition, 15

service delivery
    current realities, 13-14
    dilemmas, 27-31
    goals, 132
    research, 149-151
    room for improvement, 148
Shelton v.Tucker, 364 U. S. 479, 483
    (1960), 83
Smith v.Sampson, 349 F.Supp. 268, 271
    (D.N.H. 1972), 83
social justice, 129, 195-202
special education
    conceptual foundations, 6
    definition, 75
    evolution of law, 100-102
    interface with general education,
    129-132
special schools, 1-3, 14, 25, 27, 46-47,
    62, 94-95, 135, 161
*St. Louis Developmental Disability
    Treatment Cente Parents Association
    v.Mallory,* 767 F. 2d 518 (8th Cir.
    1984), 101
stakeholders, 23-27
*Student v. Somerset County Board of
    Education,* 24 IDELR 743 (D.Md.
    1996), 109, 111

T-V

Title VI of the Civil Rights Act (1964),
    52-53, 64, 190-192
total exclusion, 26, 38, 88
Transenvironmental Programming,
    138-139
Twentieth Century, 1, 47, 170, 190
Vander Malle v. Ambach, EHLR 559
    164 (S.D.N.Y., 1987), 105
Visco v. School District of Pittsburgh,
    684 F.Supp. 1310, 1315-16 (W.D.
    Pa. 1988), 106

W

*Wilson v.Marana Unified School
    District No. 6,* 735 F.2d 1176
    (9th Cir. 1984), 105
*Wolf v.Legislature of the State of
    Utah,* Civil No. 182646 (3rd
    Jud. Dist. Ct. Utah, Jan. 8, 1969),
    87, 91
World War II, 46-47, 51, 174
Wyatt v Stickney, 344 F.Supp. 387 (M.D.
    Ala., 1972), 59, 84-85, 88